# A GIRL, A HORSE AND A DOG

# A GIRL, A HORSE AND A DOG

*Belinda Braithwaite*

COLLINS
8 Grafton Street, London W1
1988

William Collins Sons & Co. Ltd
London · Glasgow · Sydney · Auckland
Toronto · Johannesburg

BRITISH LIBRARY CATALOGUING IN PUBLICATION DATA

Braithwaite, Belinda
A girl, a horse and a dog.
1. France – Description and travel
2. Spain – Description and travel
I. Title
914.4'04838      DC29.3

ISBN 0-00-217724-2

First published 1988
Copyright © Belinda Braithwaite 1988

Photoset in Linotron Palatino by
Rowland Phototypesetting Ltd
Bury St Edmunds, Suffolk
Made and printed in Great Britain by
Butler and Tanner Ltd
Frome and London

For Michael

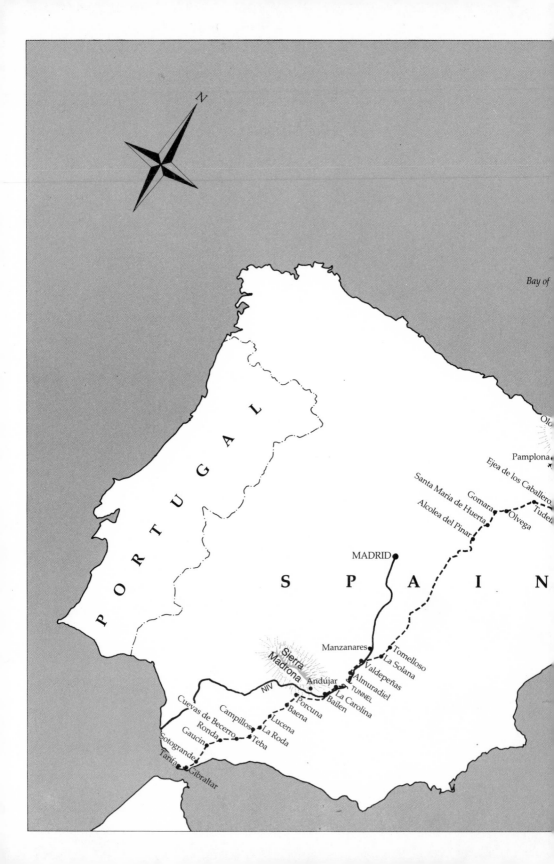

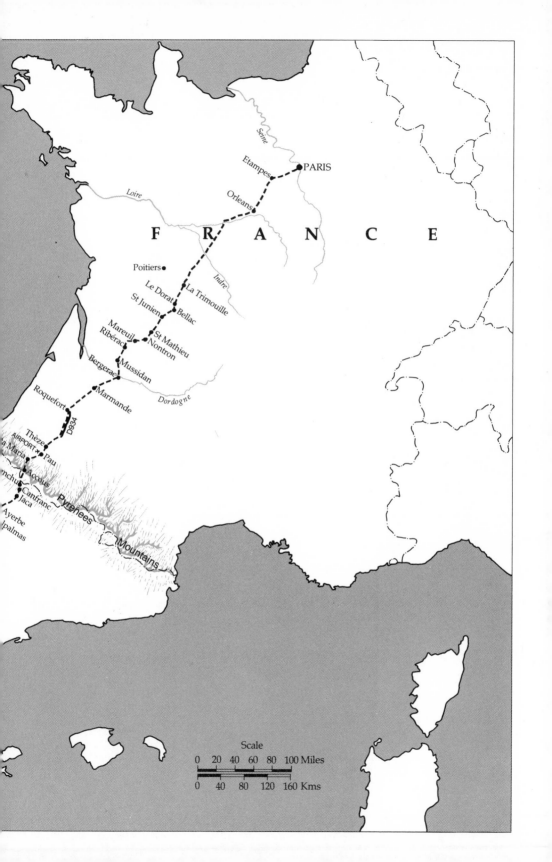

# CONTENTS

# ILLUSTRATIONS

(between pages 110–111)

# ACKNOWLEDGEMENTS

I would like to thank Barbour for their indispensable coat, which doubled as a sleeping bag on many occasions; Olympus for their marvellous idiot-proof camera which produced wonderful photographs in such varied conditions; and Canon for their word-processing equipment, which made the writing of this book a great deal easier.

I would also like to thank the *Daily Mail* for their help and support and for the use of Ted Blackbrow's superb photographs.

Many thanks to my family and friends for their constant flow of letters, to my agent Gillon Aitken, and to Ariane Goodman and Ron Clark for their help with the production of my book.

Last, but by no means least, very special thanks must go to Dragon and Boris, who made it all possible.

# The Beginning

THIS IS THE STORY of a journey across Spain and France – but in fact it all started in South Africa.

I was working at the time for the South African Marine Corporation in Cape Town, and at weekends I would climb into my battered old Citroën, leave the green hills of Cape Town and head for Citrusdal – a vast area of orange plantations cradled by mountains. It was on this beautiful plain that my great friend Louisa kept a couple of horses on her parents' farm.

We'd ride for hours in the hot South African sun, making our way down to Olefants (Elephants) River at the end of the day, filling the dusty silence with our giggles. There is something incredibly fulfilling about discovering new country-side on horseback, and riding with Louisa I came to the con-clusion that sitting in a stuffy plane for fourteen hours was not the real meaning of travel. In fact man's preoccupation with dashing all over our planet in even bigger and faster aeroplanes seems to have led us to neglect the world that exists in between one international airport and another.

It was those sweltering afternoons spent wallowing in Ole-fants River that planted the seeds of an idea which would lead me to ride 1700 miles across Spain and France in the hottest four months of the year.

Living and working in Cape Town I learned a great deal about the countryside and its inhabitants. I began to realize the value of 'living in' rather than 'seeing' a country, and through my work I was able to observe the political situation through new eyes.

Now the fierce sun was losing its strength, the days were getting shorter and it would soon be time to return to England.

Driving to Citrusdal for the last time I felt sad that I would be leaving Louisa, the horses and this vast expanse of sweltering nothing which seemed to offer so much to explore.

We tethered the horses under the shade of an orange tree and sank into the refreshing swirls of Olefants River. When I told Louisa that I was going back to England she bubbled with giggles as usual.

'You could always ride a horse home!' she hooted. 'You could take Mo as a packhorse and tie a fridge to her back!'

'It would be quite something, wouldn't it? I'm not joking, I really mean it. I could take a horse through Europe, maybe.'

It was very difficult for Louisa to be serious about anything but just for a second the giggles stopped.

A couple of hours later we clattered into the yard. Climbing into my old Citroën I waved to Louisa, her blonde hair and smiling face blending into the white sun behind her. As I trundled back towards Cape Town twinges of excitement were tugging at my stomach.

I turned into Rondebosch Main Road; the lights were red. A coloured boy of about nine or ten rushed over, a copy of the *Argus* held high above his head. A grubby hand thrust the paper through my window.

'Det's twenty-five cents,' rasped a husky little voice from beneath the oily red baseball cap. I scratched about in my filthy old Citroën for some change and handed it to the little boy. Green . . . I swung right into Newlands Avenue and the tiny face disappeared.

That evening I gave the idea some serious thought. I had made enough money in Cape Town to cover it, I had the time and no ties. At twenty-one years old, what better could one do with one's time? It was no longer an idea, it was an intention.

I was due to leave South Africa in one month's time and there was a lot of preparation to be done.

One lunch hour I had an extraordinary piece of luck. Dashing back to my office I took a short cut through the market and caught sight of two large leather bags. I rushed up to the man leaning against the counter.

'How much are the leather bags please?'

Pushing back his cap he rubbed his shiny black forehead. 'Ooo, dem's old poost bags, Ma'am.' His wide grin revealed a piano keyboard of bad teeth. 'Dem's thirty rand, Ma'am.'

'Twenty-five?'

'Cool!' Replacing his cap he fished in his pocket for the change.

The following day I took the post bags to the saddler to be converted into saddle-bags. He was already busy adding various rings and clips to an American army saddle for me. Most of the preparation I did myself in the evenings. Every lunch hour I flew round Cape Town trying to get everything together – a sheepskin, five metres of aluminium chain, five and a half metres of canvas strip to cover the chain (which took me a whole weekend to sew), waterproof material to make a bag for my sleeping bag, a tent . . .

It was only at night that I realized how lonely and difficult it might be to take on such an expedition on my own; during the day I was so absorbed by the pressure of time and getting everything organized that I hardly gave myself a chance actually to sit down and wonder whether it was a good idea or not. Having set my mind to do it there was no question . . . except at night.

When I arrived home, I think my family was hoping that the idea of riding across Spain and France had been abandoned, but they underestimated the determination which fuelled my plan.

I desperately wanted to make it a ride for charity and wrote to the *Daily Mail* asking for their help in publicizing my venture. I was disappointed to be told that it would be impossible to organize the necessary paperwork for a scheme of this kind in such a short time. However, they did express interest in covering my adventure and sent a photographer to Sotogrande, the starting point of my journey, to take some pictures before I left.

I arrived in the south of Spain with very little money, no horse and a photographer expecting to take pictures of me and a horse. I couldn't speak a word of Spanish but a friend of a friend had given me a list of horsey people in the area who might be able to help.

The first name on the list was a hotel in Sotogrande with a very smart Spanish yard owned by an English couple. The owner, Mrs Hoskins, led me towards the old cobbled yard where whitewashed stables formed a square courtyard. In the centre, a large stone water trough encircled a palm tree. A faint breeze stirred the palm leaves, causing a slight ripple in the cool water. The reflection of the whitewashed walls quivered for a moment until the water was still. I followed her through an archway to the row of stables behind. I explained that I didn't have much money so I didn't mind what the horse looked like but that it must have sound legs and be a 'good doer', a horse who (like some unfortunate people) stays fat on nothing but air and water. Due to lack of funds and shortage of time I didn't mention the question of temperament. It was something I couldn't afford to be fussy about. Anyway, a 'bad temperament' is usually due to inexperienced or rough handling and can often be ironed out with time.

Having considered my requirements, she walked to the far end of the row and showed me a chestnut mare about sixteen hands high. I have a feeling Mrs Hoskins showed me the mare to see if I knew the slightest thing about horses. At first glance, the mare could have passed as quite a reasonable horse, but I felt a splint (a bone growth) on her near fore and her teeth showed her to be eleven or twelve years old.

'Yes, she's probably a bit old for the job,' said Mrs Hoskins.

She thought for a moment.

'I've got a nice Andalusian gelding who might do you. I bought him from the gypsies a few months ago. He's not being ridden at the moment as he tends to buck.'

We walked back along the row and stopped outside the only door without a head looking out. I peered hopefully into the darkness but after the brilliant sunshine outside I couldn't see a thing. Hearing our voices, a dark shape appeared out of the gloom. He had a lovely head, very slightly concave – a reminder of the Arab blood in his Andalusian ancestry. Mrs Hoskins asked one of the grooms to bring a head collar. '*Pepe, tráigame un cabezón.*'

While Pepe, the groom, was putting it on I asked what the horse was called. 'Dragon,' she replied. 'If you like the look of

16

him you can take him for a spin and I'll ride the chestnut mare.'

The cobbles were quite slippery as we rode out of the yard. I had never sat on a Spanish saddle before so I shifted my position slightly, the strange leather producing unfamiliar creaking noises, and soon found that if I sat like a cowboy it was incredibly comfortable.

Although Dragon was distinctly fat and unfit he instantly felt right: I seemed to be moulded into his back already and the way he carefully picked his way in and out of the sharp stones made me feel wonderfully safe. My imagination ran away with me as I pictured Dragon and me winding our way up the steep mountain paths in the spring sunshine.

'He can put in quite a big buck when he gets excited, so sit tight!' Mrs Hoskins' grim reminder punctured my thoughts and brought me back to reality. There was no point in even thinking about Dragon. There was absolutely no way I would be able to afford him with the little money I had so I might as well just enjoy the ride and stop dreaming. We reached an open grassy patch. Without warning Mrs Hoskins suddenly shot off at great speed; Dragon launched into a series of enormous bucks and followed. Luckily, he was under control by the time we caught up with her, and I was able to cruise up alongside as if nothing had happened. She smiled, obviously pleased that I had managed to stay on board.

'Of course if you were to borrow Dragon . . .'

I didn't listen to the rest of the sentence; she had actually used the word 'borrow'. We clattered back into the cobbled yard and Pepe rushed out of the tack room to meet us. Pepe held Dragon's head while I took off his saddle. I was conscious of Pepe studying my bottom for any tell-tale signs of a fall. I hosed Dragon down. He looked marvellous. Reading my mind Pepe grinned and said, *'Caballo muy noble.'* There was no need to translate. I nodded in agreement and patted Dragon. Mrs Hoskins walked over and gave him a friendly pat too.

'You liked him then?'

'Oh yes, he's gorgeous.'

'You seem to get on well with him, so if you'd like to borrow him, you're welcome to.'

Before I left, Mrs Hoskins told me there was a horse show the following Saturday which I might enjoy.

When I returned the next day to ride Dragon I brought my own tack for a trial run. As soon as I put the saddle and huge saddle-bags over Dragon's door he rushed to the back of his stable in horror at the mere sight of such a huge pile of unfamiliar leather. I held out a carrot to him on the palm of my hand. He snorted in disgust but eventually took a step in my direction. It was such a relief to have found a horse. Even in the gloom of his stable he looked splendid.

When getting a horse fit, especially a young one, it is vital to start the work slowly. Every day I rode Dragon in the hills behind the stables, wading through oceans of brightly coloured flowers in the glorious sunshine. Two weeks was nowhere near long enough and each day brought the boiling Spanish summer nearer. I knew it would be madness to ride through the middle of Spain at the hottest time of the year so although Dragon wasn't as fit as he should have been, I decided to set off. I saw little difference between doing short distances every day in the hills behind the stables and setting off to ride those same short distances in a straight line.

My next problem was to find a dog. Now that I didn't have to buy a horse, I had decided to put my savings towards a guard dog and some insurance. I made a few enquiries and found a guard dog centre in a small village only a few miles away. Although we have always had dogs at home I knew nothing about guard dogs so I wasn't sure what I was looking for.

The guard dog centre was owned by a very nice English couple who at first, quite rightly, were rather sceptical about selling me a dog to walk 1700 miles. I assured them that I would look after him well and never ask him to exceed his capabilities.

Most of their dogs were German shepherds, who would be too heavy for the job and suffer dreadfully from the heat with their thick coats.

'Do you have any Dobermanns?' I asked.

'We prefer working with German shepherds, so we've only got one in at the moment.' A couple of minutes later, in bounced

18

Boris. I knew immediately that he was what I was looking for. He was young, fit and seemed very keen. Being much lighter in build than a German shepherd he would find the long distances much easier.

'Where did he come from?' I asked, wondering who could possibly have had the heart to part with such a lovely dog.

'Unfortunately, he's spent all his life on a chain so he's rather unfit.'

That would make three of us.

They told me to keep him with me at all times for the first couple of weeks, and feed him by hand and let him sleep in my room in order to gain his confidence. If I wanted him to protect me, it was important that nobody else should touch him. He was fifteen months old so I was not expecting it to be easy, but bearing these instructions in mind I took him back to the hotel.

The front entrance of the hotel was down a side street. It was 5.30 p.m. and the street was filled with the happy shouts of Spanish children playing football. The Dobermann, who had been pulling horribly on his lead, stopped dead as soon as he caught sight of the shrieking youngsters. He stiffened, lowered his head and growled. The happy shouts were replaced by terrified shrieks. The Dobermann stopped rumbling and the leader of the frightened children started to giggle, while another began to bark like a dog. The Dobermann bared his teeth and threatened them with a low growl . . . then silence. I took a step forward and the children moved back obediently. Worried that they might suddenly panic, I made the universally recognized sign of a finger against my lips. They understood and remained silent, their backs pressed against the walls of the narrow street.

I walked into the hotel lobby as if nothing had happened. Luckily, the reception desk was busy at the time so when I pointed to the Dobermann and then to my room key the man had far too much on his mind to say no. I led the Dobermann towards the stairs. He was not keen on the idea. After five minutes we had reached the third stair but he refused to go any further. I sat down beside him and tried to reason with him, but he still refused to move. Not wanting to lose his confidence,

19

I was forced to admit defeat and use the lift. He dug his toes in but it was a slippery floor so I was able to drag him inside. Once we were in my room I let him off his lead and made a bed for him in a quiet corner.

When the dog had settled I opened a tin of dog meat. Digging my fingers into the contents of the tin I went through the slightly disgusting process of feeding my new friend by hand. Then I took out a big, knobbly bone and handed it to him, then I lay on the bed and buried myself in a book. I lifted my hand to scratch a mosquito bite and the dog growled. Just to check I wasn't imagining things I moved again. The dog curled back his lips, showing me his fangs. I lay very still, hardly daring to blink. After a couple of minutes I turned my head very slowly towards him. He'd fallen asleep with the precious bone still held between his huge paws – I could be here for days! I slid carefully down the bed until I was able to reach the bag of bones with my toes. It was a bit like playing the crane game at the fair, but on the third attempt I gripped the bag between my toes and pulled it very smoothly up to my hand. I took a piece of meat out of the bag and dangled it in front of the dog. He woke up and sniffed. My heart was racing, but at last he reached up and took the scrap. I grabbed the bone and hid it in the bathroom on top of the loo.

After this little incident I was not very happy about sleeping with him in the same room, but it had to be done so I left the light on and spent a restless night with one eye and both ears on the dog.

Over the next few days I took Boris, as I called him, everywhere. Although he was becoming more and more attached to me, he was becoming increasingly aggressive towards other people, but when I had him on a lead he was much better behaved so I decided to risk taking him to the horse show.

It was just like any English horse show except that at one o'clock everything stopped and everyone walked to a house at the bottom of the field for a three-hour lunchbreak. I tied Boris outside – a safe distance from a pretty Irish setter which was making eyes at him – and walked into the room full of strangers. I was instantly seized by Mariano, the man who had kindly provided me with my list of contacts, and found myself being introduced to an endless stream of friendly English faces. The chatter grew louder as people began to sit down. I had no idea there were so many English people in the area. I found myself sitting next to a charming Englishman called Michael and soon discovered that it was his Irish setter parked next to Boris outside. He was building a hotel in Tarifa, he said; on a completely unspoiled stretch of beach overlooking Morocco. How long was I staying for? It was rather a difficult question to answer, so I told him about my plan to ride to Paris. Almost everyone I'd met so far had told me it would be impossible, but Michael was most encouraging.

After the horse show I went down to Tarifa a few times with Boris. Michael's Irish setter, Boo Boo, was always delighted to see Boris. I was beginning to find Boris rather a problem, though: the longer I had him the more protective he became. He seemed to be able to tell by my tone of voice if the person I was talking to was being friendly, so he was never a problem in Tarifa, but I began to worry whether he was becoming too much of a liability. On one occasion I was taking him for a walk and stopped to ask a man for directions. The man raised his arm to point and the dog lunged at him thinking I was being attacked. I kept Boris with me as much as possible but while I was busy riding Dragon I would tie him up to a railing in the shade. He watched my every move and if somebody came towards me he would growl nastily.

Bearing in mind that I would be staying with complete strangers, reliant on their trust and kindness, he was a dangerous risk. One minute I would look at Boris curled up by the bed and think how I'd miss him if I were to leave without him, then I'd remember how he pinned me down that first night and how frightening he could be. How could I ever forgive myself if he maimed some poor little child? In the end I felt I had no choice but to take him back to the guard dog centre.

My last few days seemed horribly empty without Boris's company, but with so much paperwork to organize I was able to keep my mind off him. Spain revolves around a ridiculous amount of paperwork, all of which has to be stamped, signed and officially sealed. In animal matters, it all hinges on the local vet, when he can be found. With great difficulty I located him at the slaughterhouse: a man in a white coat, standing with his back to me. Hearing my tentative footsteps, the figure spun round revealing a red face to match the ghastly red stains on his white coat. He put out a bloody hand but stopped himself just in time, and beamed at me instead, his bushy eyebrows raised in anticipation.

'*Hola!*' It was one of the only words I knew.

I couldn't hear his reply above the machinery. He waved a hand in the direction of a small wooden door, presumably his office.

Mrs Hoskins had already spoken to him on the telephone so it wasn't as difficult as it might have been. He pointed to a dusty chair, went over to his desk and rummaged through a pile of papers. He surfaced clutching some grubby documents, laid the five official looking documents on the desk in front of me and put his finger where I had to sign. I scratched my name next to the gory fingerprint on each document in turn. One was a piece of paper certifying that the vehicle which would eventually return the horse to Spain had been disinfected and checked by an official veterinary surgeon. He hadn't even seen the vehicle. It seemed unbelievable.

TWO

# Dragon and I

AT 10 A.M. on the morning of 30 May 1985 I loaded up my huge leather saddle-bags and, with Pepe's help, lowered them on to Dragon's back. I led Dragon towards the door of his stable and out into the sunshine, but as we were half-way through the door Pepe started shouting. I looked round to see his anxious face peering over the top of the saddle-bags. Dragon wasn't going to fit through the door! I backed him up, took off the saddle-bags and led him out of the stable before replacing them outside. All the grooms gathered round to see me off. I zipped up my leather chaps, climbed on board and, amidst much waving and shouting, tottered out of the yard. Half-way down the drive I realized that the pretty pair of knickers hanging on Mrs Hoskins' washing line were mine. This would not normally have been a problem but as I only had three pairs I couldn't leave them behind: my extensive Spanish vocabulary of three words didn't run to 'knickers'!

Dragon was quite sure that north was bound to be in the direction of his stable. I pushed and Dragon pulled until we came to a mutual agreement and with Dragon humping and groaning like an old mule we set off across the familiar hills behind the stables. He finally gave in and pricked his ears and we were on the right course for Ronda.

Picking our way through the flowering gorse bushes, we tacked our way across the hills towards our first stop – San Martin del Tesorillo. A stony track led us to the road and I could see San Martin in the distance. Time was passing very slowly.

We had covered quite a long distance in three hours. I decided to give Dragon a short rest and asked him to stand. 'Where now?' he seemed to be saying. I pointed him towards the bank at the side of the road and he clambered up it into the long grass. There were a few trees which gave some shade so I took off Dragon's bridle and tethered him to a tree trunk. I didn't dare take off his saddle and saddle-bags for fear that I might not be able to heave them back on again. I peeled off my leather chaps and zipped them together, one up, one down, into one solid piece to give me something to sit on. Having only been in Spain for a few weeks I wasn't familiar with the local creepy-crawlies.

It wasn't much of a rest; it seemed that the grass was always greener and more delicious on the other side of Belinda as far as Dragon was concerned. Battered and bruised I gave up. 'Sorry, Dragon, time to get moving.' Dragon pushed his way into the nearest oleander bush until only his bottom was visible. The contented swishing of his tail stopped for a moment while he considered the implications of what had been said. 'Dragon?' He edged a little further inside the bush. 'All right, then, five more minutes.'

The munching and tail-swishing started up again. Meanwhile I salvaged his bridle, which he had trodden into the dirt. He'd also made a pretty good job of my boots. I pushed them back into shape, pulled them on and strode over to the large bottom in the oleander bush. 'Time's up.'

The bottom didn't move – it probably couldn't. Just as Dragon had expected, there was no way I could squeeze up alongside him without getting squashed. Thankful for my tough leather chaps I forced my way through the prickly undergrowth, and ducking under the branches, I came eye to eye with him. As a last resort he pretended to be asleep. I gave him a shove . . . he remained stationary but opened half an eye to see if his plan was working. 'You can't fool me,' I said, at which he gave a long sigh and carefully reversed his way out.

Having put his bridle over his halter (which I had decided I should always do just in case his bridle should break or come off), I unclipped the tether rope, coiled it up and tied it to a spare ring on my saddle. One last check to make sure I hadn't left anything behind, and we were off.

I was rather concerned that Dragon might be getting thirsty. The small stream we had crossed earlier had been getting progressively wider and was still running fairly close on our left. It was quite a long way below our present level but the road ahead didn't seem to be gaining much height so I thought we might be able to reach the water a little further up. We plodded on, the dull heat taking its toll. We were now well into the countryside, grassy fields stretching up into the hills on our right. Getting rather bored with riding along the road, I was tempted to ride in the fields alongside, and started looking out for the next gate.

As soon as we started wading through the long grass Dragon perked up a little and quickened his pace. Yes, this was much better. Ten minutes later we arrived at a barbed wire fence. I had no choice but to follow it up the steep hill in the hope that there would be another gate into the next field further up. There was nothing; only the unfriendly barbed wire stretching into the distance as far as I could see. I was so annoyed that I even considered jumping the wretched thing, but I knew only too well that you don't jump barbed wire fences without inviting trouble.

Defeated, we retraced our steps back to the road. Furious that I'd wasted so much time, I squinted into the distance to see San Martin del Tesorillo only a little closer than it had been an hour before.

The road was slowly losing height, gradually getting closer to the river. There was an ugly concrete bridge ahead. It stood well above the river but I thought we should be able to get down to the water. Two small boys were standing knee-deep in the middle, staring into the clear water. As the bridge drew nearer, Dragon slowed down. He didn't like the look of the concrete blocks along its sides. I gave him a reassuring pat and he moved forward, the hollow echo of his hooves ringing on the concrete. One of the blocks had a large chunk missing. It resembled a crouching animal; Dragon spooked at it, slipped and frightened himself. We reached the far end and I gave his neck a friendly tug. I got off and led him towards the edge of the bridge. As I had hoped, a narrow path led down to the cool swirls below. With me in front, we edged our way down the steep path and on to the dry stony edge of the river bed.

Dragon snorted at the rushing water only a few feet in front of us. He was obviously thirsty and instinctively knew that the river meant water, yet never having seen a river before he didn't quite know what to do. Tucked safely behind me his whole body was leaning towards the water, every muscle quivering and taut with anticipation. He looked very funny with his eyes tight shut and his lips straining for contact with the refreshing liquid. I bent down and wet his muzzle with my hand – his eyes sprang open in horror and he gave a high, trumpeting snort. I stood up slowly and Dragon leapt back. There was nothing for it, I would just have to walk into the river with him. Making encouraging noises I waded into the clear water, my boots gushing full of cool water. Dragon followed. Fetlock-deep, he stood still for a moment, trembling from head to foot. Then success: he lowered his head and began to drink. The first battle of confidence had been won.

I let him stand for a while until he was quite happy about the water rushing round his legs – he was almost enjoying himself. Once we were out of the water I climbed back on board and nudged him forward. He seemed greatly refreshed and bounced up the bank back on to the road. We stood on the hot tarmac for a moment while I tightened the girth a hole. Dragon's hooves were shiny and wet, his long black tail still dripping. I could see San Martin del Tesorillo quite clearly now and thought it should only take us twenty minutes or so to get there.

Our road took us right into the centre of the small village. I had eaten my favourite marmalade sandwiches within an hour of leaving the stables so I wanted to buy something for supper. The trouble was that being unable to speak Spanish, I hadn't the faintest clue how to ask for anything. I would solve that problem when I came to it; the first hurdle was to find a food shop. We soon found ourselves in a central square surrounded by screaming children, the old women gossiping and the young boys standing at the street corners gawping at me. There was a butcher's shop on the other side of the square. I rode over to it and, leaning down from my saddle, peered in through the doorway. Dragon was getting agitated by the growing number of people crowding round to look at us. He refused to stand still. Someone inside the butcher's shop pointed at us and everyone turned round. Two old women came out to get a better look. Suddenly somebody realized I wanted to buy some food and rushed into the shop spouting garbled Spanish, of which I understood not a word. The butcher strode out. Poor Dragon took one look and gave a huge snort at the butcher's bloody overall stinking of meat. I felt rather ridiculous having to point at my mouth but it was the only way I could explain what I wanted. The butcher waddled inside and reappeared with all sorts of things, none of which I recognized and all of which looked perfectly disgusting. I smiled at the butcher, my mind racing. How could I begin to explain that all I wanted was a slice of ham? Everyone was watching, waiting.

The silence was broken by a noisy Land Rover rumbling into the square. I groaned; it was the guard dog man.

'Hello again, love, having problems are we?'

Feeling rather stupid, I swallowed my pride. 'Umm, actually I was just trying to buy a piece of ham and a roll.'

'You won't get anything like that here; how about some dried ham? Want me to pop in and get it for you?'

'Yes, that would be very kind.'

He disappeared inside the shop and came out with a small package neatly wrapped in greaseproof paper. Holding the reins in one hand I grappled with the catch on the small bag on the front of my saddle with the other. Feeling the reins loosen slightly, Dragon snatched his head forward and spun round. The crowd scattered. 'Don't worry about the money,' said the guard dog man. 'You'd better get going before he gets you into trouble.'

I thanked him some more and rode out of San Martin del Tesorillo quite a bit faster than I'd ridden in.

The road was rapidly deteriorating into nothing more than a stony track. Dragon's hoofbeats were now gentle thuds. It was late afternoon and I knew that very soon I would have to find somewhere for the night – something I'd been dreading all day. The river curled round to our right, much wider now, and the water was quite shallow. The track we had been following carried on into the river itself. Through the clear ripples I could see parallel tracks flattened into the pebbles of the river bed. I urged Dragon forward, he hesitated for a moment and then leapt into the water with all four feet. It wasn't quite what I had had in mind but it was a start. Feeling rather proud of himself he took one cautious step forward and another and another until he found himself on a sandbank in the middle of the water. The tracks did not cross to the opposite bank but carried on down the middle of the shallow river. They might well have been made by cars, I thought, in which case they could lead to a village. Against the current, we walked up the river a little further, cool water splashing my face. There was a buzzing noise in the distance; a group of boys on mopeds were riding through the middle of the river on the same track as us, probably on their way home from the fields. An ancient Renault 4 was trailing behind them. Dragon stopped dead and stared. I held the reins tight in case he suddenly decided to whip round and run away. But he stood his ground as the fleet of chattering lads buzzed past, their legs held high above the spray. To my relief they hardly noticed us. The battered Renault choked past in its turn and we carried on.

A few houses were perched on the next bend. Perhaps this was Ermita de Rosario – the last village on the map for forty kilometres. I steered Dragon towards the bank.

The tarmac road had disintegrated long ago and Dragon's hoofbeats were now barely audible on the dusty ground. Nevertheless, people seemed to appear from nowhere to watch us ride past. Three fat women stood fanning themselves in the shade, their babies comfortably wedged on their enormous hips and at least ten more playing in the dirt at their feet. One of them gave a slight nod and smiled. I smiled back. Dragon suddenly jerked his head up. Following his gaze I spotted a mule peering over a stable door built into one of the tiny, whitewashed houses.

Leaving the village behind us, we pottered along the bank of the river looking for a good spot to pitch the tent. Every now and then Dragon would glance back, still thinking about the mule. I knew he was right but I hadn't had the nerve to ask there for a stable and I decided it would be much better to find some nice grass for him. We rode through a young plantation and saw a flat grassy patch on the far side of the river – perfect.

Wearily, I lifted my leg over the saddle-bags and slid off

Dragon. I took off his bridle straight away, leaving his halter still underneath, and tied him to a tree. Bit by bit I untacked him until there was a large heap of sweaty leather on the grass. My leather chaps felt horribly hot and uncomfortable, my boots damp and clammy from wading in the river. I sank on to the grass and slowly undid my chaps. Then with a great effort I managed to pull the boots off my sweaty feet. I lay flat on my back for a moment, left boot still in my hand, and gave a long sigh. The evening air was still warm but I wanted to wash Dragon down before his sweat dried so that he wouldn't cool down too fast. I was just about to get up when Dragon suddenly pulled on his rope, panic in his eyes. I leapt to my feet and rushed over to him. His hind foot was caught in a tangle of wire amongst the long grass.

'Just hold still and I'll get you out.' I held his leg and stroked him, trying to calm him just enough for me to get a steady hold on his foot and the piece of wire. He relaxed very slightly and I gave the wire a gentle tug; it seemed to be firmly wedged. I bent down to get a closer look, running the risk of being severely booted. The wire was wedged right under his shoe as a result of his struggles. I wriggled it backwards and forwards until it broke and then by pulling the other end managed to get it free.

Dragon was left with a nasty cut across his heel. He held his foot in the air; it was obviously stinging like mad. I untied him and led him slowly down to the river. The second his foot touched the water he snatched it out. Nudging his front leg, I coaxed him to pick up that foot. In doing so, he was forced to put the tender hind foot in the water. It stung for a moment or two, but when he had relaxed I put down the front one again. We were very fortunate to be by a river; the cool water should clean out the cut, cool the foot and so help to keep down any swelling. We stood in the river for half an hour before I led him gently back to the flat grassy patch and tied him up. I sifted through the grass for any more hidden dangers and then rummaged through the saddle-bags for my box of veterinary kit.

I let the wound air for a while before carefully smoothing antiseptic cream on it. It was much deeper than I had thought

29

and I cursed myself for not having checked the grass properly in the first place. I couldn't see the lid of the cream anywhere and suddenly realized it was nearly dark.

I had never pitched a tent before but luckily I had had a trial run at the stables a couple of days before we left. First peg out the base . . . fine. Fit the guy ropes and . . . Dragon's eyes were on stalks. Like me, he had obviously had zero experience with tents. He gave a low snort of suspicion as I fought with the billowing green monster. I untied him and led him over for a closer look. A few more snorts to which the monster didn't reply, and Dragon decided it was harmless. I noticed his short painful steps and my heart sank; he could be lame for weeks and it was all my fault.

I lay quite still inside the tent. Engulfed by the silence of the darkness which surrounded me I felt terrified, almost frightened of myself. The enormity of what I had taken on was beginning to sink in. Lifting myself up on one elbow I peered out through the tiny mesh window, my eyes searching the blackness for the reassuring shape of Dragon. He was dozing in the gloomy shadow of his tree. I called to him once, desperate to hear a whicker of reassurance. His tail swished through the silence and I lay quiet, petrified of giving away our presence to anything except the surrounding trees.

My imagination began to work overtime on the large animal hole in the undergrowth close to the tent. I had never been someone who had hysterics if they saw a spider, but because I felt tired and unhappy the hole seemed a terrifying thought. Luckily I had parked the tent with the little mesh window pointing towards Dragon, which made me feel a tiny bit safer. There was no moon and the blackness was now heavy and damp. Being so short of space, I hadn't brought a sleeping-bag and now felt pretty cold and miserable huddled under a mound of saddle-bags.

Some unknown time later I opened my eyes. Blackness. My senses then tuned themselves into wakefulness and I was aware of a steady pawing and scraping at the sandy ground outside the tent. My mind still slow, I eventually realized that it was Dragon. I dragged myself from underneath the carefully formed mound so that I would be able to return to its meagre warmth.

I crawled out of the tent and gasped at the chill air. Stumbling over to Dragon I thought I was imagining things: his front end was two feet lower than his back end, as if he was a deflated pantomime horse.

He had walked round and round his tree until there was no rope left and, unable to move, had pawed and pawed until he'd dug a hole like a bomb crater. He eyes me helplessly. I unravelled him, then tied the middle of his tether rope to his head collar and the two ends to the trees on either side of him, so that he was able to lie down but couldn't go round and round in circles. Then I stroked his neck and offered him a piece of grass.

A few hours later I woke up with a groan. Aching all over I burrowed back under the mound of leather for a few more minutes. When I surfaced again the first rays of sunlight had pierced through the mesh window, highlighting the swirls of humidity. Having slept in my clothes I felt horribly clammy. I unzipped the tent, and suddenly realized how stuffy it was as the cool of the outside world poured in. Feeling a little better, I staggered out of the tent to check Dragon and found him happily stuffing his face with good grass. 'Morning,' Uninterested, he carried on munching, so I gave him a pat and tottered down to the river for a wash.

An hour later, my whole world had been crammed into the big leather saddle-bags. Dragon eyed me with suspicion as I pulled on my boots.

It seemed less effort to take Dragon to the pile of tack than to heave it all over to him so I tied him to a nearby tree and rummaged around for the breastplate. The breastplate is a strong leather strap round the horse's neck, attached to the girth at one end and the front of the saddle at the other. It is designed to stop the saddle sliding backwards on a long uphill climb. I had an ex-military saddle of the 'McLennan' type, specially designed for long distances. It looked rather odd as it had a two-inch gap running from front to back and no side panels – the idea being that it would fit any horse's back without pressing on its spine and also allow a good flow of air under the saddle. To make the saddle fit as comfortably as possible

31

the thick saddle-pad was made of horsehair, as foam tends to squash into nothing. I had sewn a sheepskin cover for the girth so that it wouldn't chafe against Dragon's skin.

I wasn't taking any chances with my stirrup leathers, which were made of buffalo hide, the strongest type of leather. The stirrups themselves had rubber treads which are slightly easier on your feet. The English are always terribly supercilious about the dreaded 'crupper', a strap attached to the back of the saddle which loops under the horse's tail to stop the saddle slipping forwards. It's normally used only on grossly fat ponies who due to their barrel-like figures end up with the saddle, plus or minus child, somewhere round their ears. But out of sheer practicality, on it went!

I also used a very soft 'hackamore', a bitless bridle, which works on the nose rather than the bars of the mouth. It made eating and drinking much easier for Dragon, and also had the advantage of weighing very little. I always put the bitless bridle over the top of Dragon's head collar so that I would never have to risk tying him up by his bridle, because if he ever ran backwards in fright, the bridle would most certainly be the first thing to break.

Fully loaded, the saddle-bags were far too heavy and awkwardly shaped for me to lift on to Dragon's back single-handed. Determined to succeed, however, I made a monumental effort and managed to get them half over his back. Dragon took a dainty little side-step, and with a loud thump the saddle-bags hit the ground. He then swung round to the opposite side of the narrow tree trunk looking very smug, almost grinning in fact. 'Ha, ha,' I shouted in frustration. I had no choice but to empty them, and put them on his back before repacking.

When he was fully tacked up and ready to go, I tied Dragon up and gave his foot one last check. It had been a bit tender when I had inspected it first thing that morning so I had given it another half hour in the river. It seemed to have done the trick. The slight swelling had gone down now and it was only a fraction hotter than the other foot. Ideally, I would have liked to have given the cut a couple of days to heal, because being right in the crack of his heel it might easily have caused problems, but with nowhere to stay I decided to carry on very gently, using a good wodge of antiseptic cream to keep it supple.

The far bank looked a little easier, so we waded across to the other side. Dragon leapt up the bank, almost knocking me over. Winding our way in and out of the bushes along the river bank I felt much happier. Dragon seemed full of energy again and, as the heat hadn't yet saturated the day, watching the sunshine on the ripples of the water was an absolute pleasure. Upriver, not far away, the river seemed to disappear off to our right. I took the map out of my small saddle-bag and studied it; the river should take us in more or less a straight line to just short of Ronda, where it seemed to peter out. I could see from the contours that Ronda was quite high, so I would have to leave the river fairly soon and try to gain some height if I was to avoid an impossibly steep climb when the river went dry. I peered at the multi-coloured squiggles more closely. It looked as though a small road crossed the river about three kilometres further on which would take us straight to Ronda.

The banks of the river were becoming more and more dense, and although my legs were protected by the tough leather chaps, my arms were constantly being scratched by gorse bushes. Dragon's foot didn't seem to be causing any trouble so I thought it would probably be all right for me to ride him for a while until we were out of these prickly thickets.

Unfortunately, the undergrowth grew thicker and thicker until we could go no further and were forced to cross the river back to the opposite bank. The banks were becoming very steep in places, making our journey even slower and more tricky. We tried walking in the river but although it was quite shallow, the river bed here was made up of boulders so that it was very difficult for Dragon to get any foothold. We had no choice but to resume our battle along the banks. Finally, the river took pity on us and stretched out its wide inviting swirls and smooth grassy banks. Suddenly, the world seemed beautiful again and I started to keep an eye out for a good place to stop.

I found an idyllic spot with a small flat bank and delicious-looking grass. After last night's experience I certainly didn't want to tether Dragon so I hobbled his front legs and left him loose, in the hope that his interest would not stray too far from the lush grass on the bank. An hour later Dragon started to get bored and on his way to investigate the saddle-bags, trod on his bridle yet again. He was obviously ready to move on so I stood him in the river for fifteen minutes to cool down his bad foot before setting off.

At 4.30, a rather dilapidated bridge blocked our path. I thought this must be the road marked on my map. I was rather apprehensive about leaving the security of the water. It would be a long hard climb up the road and with no water Dragon would find it very difficult. But I took the chance; if nothing else, it would be a change of scenery and we had to start using the roads at some time because we certainly wouldn't be able to follow rivers the whole way.

I jumped off and led Dragon up the bank and on to the broken tarmac of the tiny road. We plodded slowly on up the hill and by about five o'clock the heat was almost unbearable. Without a single building in sight I was beginning to worry about water for Dragon. It was essential that he had water little and often.

He was starting to feel a little weary and as the road was getting steeper I got off and walked beside him. Rounding the next bend I spotted a small well in the distance. As we got closer my stomach felt sick with disappointment and exhaustion. Bright red geraniums were billowing out of the wooden bucket. Dragon didn't know what a well looked like so he was quite oblivious to my frustration.

As we walked past I saw that the top of the well was open and standing next to it was a small plastic bucket on a piece of string. The string didn't look very long and because of the glaring reflection of the whitewashed well I couldn't see the water level. I threw in the little bucket and gasped with relief when I heard the light smack of it hitting the water. Dragon recognized the sound and gave me a hefty shove with his nose. I brought it up very slowly, terrified that the string might break, and we'd lose it. Dragon was desperate and rammed his muzzle into the little bucket. I threw the bucked in a second time. Dragon peered anxiously over the edge. He saw the bucket coming and made a dive for it. After one more helping he

34

seemed fairly satisfied so I gave what he left to the thirsty geraniums.

We plodded on. At last the road seemed to be getting easier. Suddenly Dragon jerked his jead up and whinnied. Horses! There must be horses somewhere. I peered into the distance but couldn't see any animals. The scrub on either side of the road had now been replaced by grass so he was probably quite right . . .

Round the next bend three mares were grazing amongst the bushes on a bank to our right. Dragon's pace quickened. All three horses were loose, not even hobbled, and yet they didn't come rushing towards us. I jumped as a young boy stood up from behind a bush as if to answer my unspoken questions. Glancing over my shoulder I realized that from where he had been sitting he could see the road winding down the mountain almost as far as the river. He'd probably been watching us every step of the way. He screwed up his eyes against the sun to have a better look at us, then smiled and moved forward, only to sit down again in front of the gorse bush. Rather like a dog on a rooftop, he watched us with interest, high above us on his grassy bank.

'Where is water?' was one of the only phrases I had learned before I left. Practising it under my breath I led Dragon across the road towards the grassy bank and stopped when we were standing right underneath the boy. He peered at Dragon, taking note of the saddle-bags and rolled-up tent. I smiled and stumbled through the stock phrase. The boy nodded and came bounding down the bank to our level. He seemed much smaller now, only twelve or thirteen years old. He pointed further up the road and started walking. Dragon and I followed, although Dragon seemed far more interested in flirting with the mares than finding something to drink. He led us down a narrow goat path. I could see a long stone water trough half-way down. Dragon sniffed the water but didn't drink. I splashed it about with my hand and wet his muzzle but he wasn't in the slightest bit interested. Rather embarrassed, I apologized to the boy in English. He seemed to understand what I meant and a second later had disappeared down the path again.

I was sorry he had gone. It was so nice to have company,

even for five minutes. Dragon was tugging at the long grass round my feet. I let him eat for a couple more minutes and then led him back along the path towards the road. The boy was waiting for us on the other side of the road, an old man – possibly his father – by his side. They both gave me a friendly smile. The old man patted Dragon and ran a hand down his neck. He started to speak but soon realized that I didn't understand a word. After a moment's thought, he tried again, this time speaking more slowly. He pointed to Dragon, pointed at his watch and then made a sign for sleep. He seemed to be offering to look after Dragon for the night. I didn't know what to do. I didn't understand the Spanish well enough to be able to recognize genuine kindness and yet I kept thinking of the night before. Dragon was used to a good feed at night, and I felt I must find a stable for him tonight. I decided that it was better not to trust this man and just hope that I could find somewhere in the next hour or so.

I thanked them for their kindness and walked on. We reached the top of the hill and stopped for a moment to admire the valley below us which, as the shadows of the cork oaks grew longer, seemed to develop an increasingly twisted beauty. We began our descent, both of us by now quite weary, and I had a dreadful feeling that there wasn't going to be anywhere else for us to stay. Just as I was thinking I'd made the wrong decision through nothing but cowardice, I caught sight of a very English-looking farmhouse nestled in a hollow down to our right. Its long drive led to our road. Five minutes later we stopped outside the high wrought-iron gates. A mare and foal were nibbling at the grass at the edge of the drive; I wasn't sure if I could walk Dragon down the drive without upsetting the mare and almost certainly the farmer as well. The mare walked forward, purposely putting herself between her young foal and us. She seemed calm enough, so I unhooked the chain and led Dragon through the gate. I led him slowly up the drive towards the farmhouse, giving the mare and foal a wide berth.

The farmhouse sat quietly in the middle of its neatly fenced grassy paddocks, engulfed by the surrounding mass of orange trees. A tall woman was collecting her washing, which was strung between two orange trees. Catching sight of this stranger plodding up the drive she stood quite still, the basket of washing resting on her hip. Then she put it down and hurried into the farmhouse. The mare and foal had not followed us so I opened the second gate and went into the farmyard. The woman reappeared. To my great surprise she was coloured; I had never seen a coloured person in Spain. She didn't smile. I walked slowly towards her and stopped at polite distance. '*Hola*,' I said as convincingly as possible. She nodded in recognition and a brief smile crossed her lips. I decided to begin by just asking for some water. She lifted her hand, asking me to wait, and disappeared inside again.

While I waited I loosened Dragon's girth and gave him a scratch behind the ears. When I turned round a huge man stood in the doorway.

'Are you English?'

With huge relief I said 'Yes'. In a strong German accent he introduced himself as Ernst and the coloured woman as Bertha, his wife. He led me into the farmyard where a large bath stood at the far end. Dragon was very thirsty. Half an hour had passed since we arrived at the farm so I let him drink as much as he wanted. If a horse drinks a lot of water too soon after work he can easily get colic. Having quenched his thirst he felt all itchy and nearly pushed me over trying to use me as a scratching-post. I asked Ernst if he would mind if I used the hose to wash him down. He wandered over to the tap and connected it up. With great difficulty I heaved the heavy saddle from Dragon's back, feeling it sliding off his back he stepped sideways, leaving me staggering under the combined weight of the saddle and saddle-bags. I hoped that the novelty of this new trick would quickly wear off! The underside of the saddle felt hot and sweaty against my bare arms. Leaving Dragon to scratch his head against the edge of the bath I leant the saddle against the wall. I then drenched his sweaty body with the hose. He wasn't too keen on it but I knew he would feel much better afterwards. I then rubbed him all over with the side of my hand to get rid of the excess water and walked him round for a while to dry off in the warm evening air.

Ernst was admiring Dragon who despite such a long day

looked magnificent with his coat still wet and shiny. I asked him about his mare and foal and he reeled off the mare's pedigree with great enthusiasm. Now that he was in a slightly brighter frame of mind I asked him whether he had anywhere I might leave Dragon for the night – a stable, or the field perhaps? As the mare and foal were brought into the yard at night he offered me the field and a feed for Dragon.

'Do you have a tent or something?' After last night I longed for a bed to sleep in but if they weren't offering me a room I didn't think I could say I hadn't got a tent when there was something looking remarkably like one rolled up behind my saddle.

'Yes, tied to my saddle-bags over there.' Just looking at it reminded me of the damp misery of the night before.

A groom was leading the mare and foal towards the farmyard so I would be able to let Dragon loose in the field. Ernst held him while I fetched the hobbles. I walked Dragon down to the field and tied him to the gate while I put his hobbles on. He made it very difficult, hopping from foot to foot and yelling sweet nothings at the mare, who had disappeared from sight into the yard. Dragon's padded hobbles had been made specially in England and were pure luxury compared to the twisted ropes the Spanish use, which leave dreadful sores round the poor animal's fetlocks. I had never seen Dragon free in a field before. It was wonderful for him to have such a huge space with lots of lush grass to nibble. He made a bee line for the low branches of the nearest orange tree and, with the finger-like twigs digging into his back, spent the next ten minutes giving himself the most heavenly back-scratch. His long neck was stretched forward, his head slightly to one side and his eyes glazed in pleasure. His top lip curled forward in ecstasy like a tiny elephant's trunk. He moved back a bit and started to have a go at his mane. 'Dragon! you'll pull it all out,' I shrieked.

Someone was calling from the gate. It was Ernst. He said they were having a barbecue for the farm workers in an hour or so, and that if I wanted to join them I would be very welcome. I had completely forgotten about food all day and at the mention of the word 'barbecue' I suddenly felt starving. I thanked him and said I'd join them as soon as I'd put up the tent and sorted out my things.

It took me at least ten minutes to find a remotely flat piece of ground, but having settled for a patch right in the middle of all the orange trees I picked up as many stones as I could see and pitched the tent. I crawled inside and changed into my one other shirt. I longed for a bath but it hadn't been offered so I took my tiny wash-box and wandered over to the bright yellow hose.

Worried about my jeans reeking of horse, I walked through the orange trees towards the barbecue. I could see the coals beginning to glow in the warm evening light, their reflection dancing on the windowpanes of the old farmhouse. Bertha offered me sangria in a white paper cup. The farmhands sat in a line along the wall and mumbled a greeting to. '*Hola,*' was all I could say in reply. I went over to Bertha who was fiddling with the barbecue. Chatting to her for a while I discovered that she had met Ernst, who was Swiss-German, in Kenya. They had decided to settle here in Spain but as they hadn't been living here for very long she spoke very little Spanish and was finding it rather lonely. Understanding my problem with the language, she did her best to teach me the couple of phrases she knew. My stomach was tying itself in knots watching her prodding the juicy chicken with a long fork and I found it excruciatingly difficult to concentrate on what she was teaching me. Nevertheless, the three phrases which did sink in proved to be invaluable: 'I want', 'I have', and 'Where can I buy . . .?'

Having consumed two pieces of chicken, I went over to Ernst to ask how far it was to Ronda. I soon discovered that the road I had been following was in fact quite a long way before the one I had intended to take. The village just beyond the farm was Gaucin, about thirty-eight kilometres from Ronda. My heart sank; it was miles further than I thought. So far we had only managed about fifteen kilometres a day, though admittedly the river had made progress much slower and more difficult. With a long way to go the next day I made my apologies and, feeling distinctly light-headed from the sangria after so little to eat all day, I staggered back to the tent.

I changed back into my old shirt but took off my jeans and

soon looked something like a leather armadillo with all my tack piled on top of me to keep me warm. Happy in the knowledge that Dragon was comfortable, safe and well fed, I slept much better than I had the night before and didn't wake up until 7.30 a.m. I peered through the wire mesh and found that my view was blocked by a herd of cows. The nearest jumped as I unzipped the tent and crawled out of my green cocoon. Her large brown eyes blinked in calm amazement as I jumped up and down trying to shoo her friends away.

I rolled up the tent and hung everything as high as possible in a nearby orange tree in case the cows trampled all over it. I found Dragon down by the gate waiting for his sleeping beauty to emerge from her slumbers.

The kitchen door was wide open and delicious smells of toast and bacon were wafting towards me. I paused for a second just short of the door and dared to let myself breathe in the familiar smells. Not for the last time, I longed to be at home. Bertha must have heard my thoughts for the next moment I was sitting in the middle of the old farmhouse kitchen at a huge table with a large mug of coffee and a plate piled high with bacon, eggs, sausages; in fact everything I had let myself dream about. Absolute heaven – she even managed to produce a big pot of marmalade!

So it was thoroughly well stuffed, squeaky clean and greatly refreshed that we turned out of the drive and set sail for Ronda.

# THREE

# The Road to Ronda

THIRTY-EIGHT KILOMETRES was a pretty daunting prospect so I was glad Dragon seemed so full of energy; he pranced along very skittishly. The road to Ronda is a memory I hold above all others. The road itself is perched right up on a mountain ridge with a breathtaking view of the valleys tumbling down on either side. Occasionally I would catch a glimpse of the river we had been following through a chink in the velvet green so far below us. The valley itself had a raw beauty, an almost untouched feel about it, as if by walking through its emerald forests one might leave a ghastly scar in its delicate weave.

Almost an hour had passed since we turned on to the high mountain road and the sun was just beginning to penetrate the cool swirls of morning mist. Quite unexpectedly we found a small bar perched on the next bend.

It was a small whitewashed building. Two ancient Fiats were waiting patiently in the sparse shade offered by the vines, which were twisted round a rickety metal frame. With not a tree or a bush in sight, I tied Dragon to the metal frame above our heads. I pushed through the plastic fronds in the doorway and into the bar. I was greatly relieved that not one of the three men drinking even bothered to look up as I clomped through the door in my heavy boots and leather chaps.

After using one of my new phrases I was thrilled when an ice-cold bottle of Coke appeared on the bar; I had not had to resort to a single bit of sign language. However, my next request would not be so easy . . .

I managed to say that I had a horse, pointed outside and

41

asked for some water. The man's eyes widened and he peered incredulously through the plastic fronds. His head suddenly started nodding up and down while he scampered about looking for a bucket. He found one and filled it with water. I pointed to it. He looked at me; perhaps he had misunderstood? I had no idea how to ask what it was called so I used '*Qué?*' ('What?') instead. '*Cubo, cubo, señorita!*'

Thanking him very much, I lugged the heavy bucket out to the car park. Dragon was resting in the shade. I put the bucket down in front of him and let him drink half the water. Putting it out of reach I loosened his girth a little before letting him have the rest.

I sat at a small table inside and ate an ice cream. One more Coke, then time to move. I sifted through my little red purse and left a tip on the bar. Walking into the air on the other side of the plastic fronds was like walking into a hair dryer. Dragon was waiting for me just outside the door – not where I had left him – and one look at the mangled remains of the metal frame explained why.

I rescued a tattered branch of the vine from the roof of one of the old Fiats and balanced it on the only surviving piece of framework. I thought we probably ought to move on fairly fast.

Despite my apprehension yesterday, travelling along this quiet mountain road was proving to have many unforeseen advantages. Although the road was worn and slippery in places, it was generally very easy-going for Dragon in comparison with the thick undergrowth of the river banks, and certainly far better than the awkward rocks and pebbles of the river bed had been.

We jogged along at a comfortable pace, enjoying the view, and after a couple of hours we had covered 14 kilometres, which was a great improvement on the day before. I am able to tell you exactly how many kilometres because every kilometre was marked by a large white three-cornered stone. We even passed a garage where I was able to borrow a hose and wash down Dragon's legs.

By four o'clock we had covered 29 kilometres but Dragon was starting to tire. Riding along a road, I hoped we would stand a much better chance of finding a stable. I was right. Round the next long bend I saw a big farm, though it was quite a distance from the road. We plodded on until we came to the stony track falling away from the high road. Dragon found it quite tricky getting all his feet organized on his way down the steep slope.

As we got closer I could see at least ten stable doors in one of the whitewashed barns. Tonight shouldn't be so difficult, I thought. Having sat in the saddle for nearly six hours I was getting rather stiff and uncomfortable so the thought of trudging round in the gloom desperate to find somewhere filled me with dread. I rode towards the ugly square farmhouse, which didn't look very different to one of the big modern barns. Dragon's hooves made nothing more than a soft patting sound on the sun-baked earth. The place was silent, empty, and yet the flowers growing outside the aluminium front door must mean somebody lived there. Flowers like that couldn't survive the blistering heat without someone to look after them. The absence of a dog barking started to give me that creeping feeling of disappointment. Farms are never left completely unattended, I told myself. But the whole place was deserted. Perhaps I could use one of the stables, just for tonight.

My feet hit the ground with a heavy thump, jarring my ankles. The weight of my heavy, sweaty boots and chaps made me feel suddenly slow and cumbersome. I walked slowly towards the barn door, my heels scuffing up the dust behind me. Dragon snorted. With great difficulty I managed to heave open the barn door; with a low rumble it slid back just enough for me to squeeze through the gap into the darkness. For a couple of seconds I couldn't see a thing which made me doubly aware of the musty, unused smell. When my eyes were accustomed to the gloom I moved forward to investigate. A large concrete feeder ran the length of the wall and there were two stalls at the far end. I put my hand on the cool clammy concrete and peered into the feeder. Mouse droppings and the odd dusty oat husk were all it could offer. There was no straw anywhere, and nothing for it but to carry on.

Two kilometres further on I caught sight of a building with a stone wall in front of it, forming a corral. Nestled in a slight hollow in the valley down to our left, it had enough shade from the surrounding cork oak trees to have some fairly good grass around it. Just next to the large white stone marking kilometre 66, a bumpy farm track ran down towards the little empty building. Dragon seemed keen to move off down it; he had been quick to learn that stony tracks often led to a good rest.

The corral was completely horse-proof so I was able to let Dragon loose. The tiny stone building had a peat floor, and I moved my saddle-bags and other kit inside so that they couldn't be seen from the road. Luckily Dragon's dark bay colour camouflaged him very well.

Having removed everything from my waist downwards I put on my shorts which felt fantastically light and cool. Taking my folding plastic bucket from the heap of tack in the corner of the little barn, I went outside and into the corral to catch Dragon and lead him down to the stream for a wash-down and a drink.

It wasn't as easy as the river because even though it was summer, the banks of the stream were rather mushy. Not only was it difficult for us to stand near the edge, but it was also almost impossible to find a place where one could get near the stream in the first place because both banks were overgrown with huge rushes. However, we found a good spot and while Dragon made the most of the delicious marshy grass I scooped up bucketfuls of the crystal-clear water and gave him a bath. When Dragon was thoroughly soaked all over I washed out the bucket, refilled it and stood it a little way from Dragon while I immersed my hot and aching head in the wonderfully cool water.

Unfortunately, grass alone doesn't provide enough protein for a horse doing a lot of work like Dragon, so I was going to have to go and find him some hard feed; some oats or barley. I wasn't very happy about leaving him alone in the corral so I put his hobbles on just to be safe and bound the gate up very tightly with both his lead ropes before climbing back up the hill to the road.

I had never hitched a lift in my life. I stood on the side of the quiet country road and waited, and waited some more, until at last I heard a distant buzz coming from behind the hills round the bend on my right. I stuck out my thumb in anticipation as the sound grew louder. The inevitable Fiat lurched round the bend and into view. I took a slight step nearer the road, confident that it was going to stop. It didn't . . . nor did the next car or the next. It was half an hour before someone gave me a lift and then it was only by chance; a herd of goats poured across the road towards us just as a bread lorry appeared round the bend. There was a screech of brakes and it came to a halt a little way from where I was standing so I rushed up to it and shouted 'Ronda?' through the open window. To my relief the driver leaned over and opened the door.

With one hand resting on the small red purse in my pocket I sat back in my seat, which felt very comfortable after sitting on a saddle all day. I sat right up against the window with the cool air rushing past, leaving as much space as possible between the hairy-looking driver and me.

He dropped me right in the centre of Ronda. I looked around for a moment or two to get my bearings. It was now a quarter to seven and as the cool evening air breathed on the ancient town, its inhabitants poured out of their homes and on to the cobbled streets. With no idea where I was going I found myself swept along by the jostling faces, all foreign, all different. I was so interested by all the different faces and expressions that even if I had known where I was going in the first place I certainly would have forgotten by now.

The crowd dispersed as the narrow street opened out into a beautiful square. Without thinking I stood still for a moment just to look at this lovely scene. Almost immediately I was very nearly sent flying by some old woman's basket; I let out a yelp as it crunched against my head. Everyone around started squawking and shrieking at the old woman although I couldn't be sure whether they were reprimanding or congratulating her. I moved hurriedly out of her line of fire and wandered into the square.

On the opposite side of it was a magnificent stone building. Bright red geraniums billowed out of ancient wrought-iron balconies, cascading down in a torrent of brilliant colour. Hundreds of white pigeons fluttered round the eaves enhancing the sound of the gentle voices of the old men who sat in small groups at the pretty white tables far below. It struck me as slightly odd that there were no women. The square was edged by large orange trees, the ripe oranges providing a wonderful contrast to the rich green leaves. In the centre was an enormous fountain covered in blue and white ceramic tiles. Every edge and corner of the fountain had an ornament or a curl of some kind so that the whole fountain was octagonal and opposite every face of the octagon was a well-worn bench – and there sat all the ladies who had been missing from the large building on the other side of the square. A teeming mass of happy children were playing on the cobbled stones around their feet while the women of all generations caught up on the day's gossip.

I walked slowly along the edge of the square in the shade of the orange trees. A small shop of some sort was perched on the corner of a tiny passage leading off the square. I wandered over to it, breathing in the wonderful smell of oranges as I went.

It was a little cake shop with *'Pastelería'* written in large curling letters across the faded canopy. I hadn't eaten a thing all day and the sight of all those delicious cakes was just too much. Inside the shop it was quite cool despite the amazing smell of hot, newly-baked cakes wafting through the plastic fronds in a doorway which presumably led to the bakery behind. I peered at the rows of cakes. Pointing to a sticky almond one I fished out my purse for some money. Before I had opened my mouth the large woman behind the counter realized I was foreign and wrote the price down on the glass counter with a stick of chalk: 'PTAS 30'. I laid a few coins on the counter and trusted her to pick out the right ones.

Regardless of where I was going I wound my way in and out of the maze of ancient streets until at last I found what I was looking for: a wide street lined with shops of every description. Peering in all the windows as I went along I came across a book shop which reminded me that I was desperately in need of a good dictionary. Unable to speak a word of Spanish I couldn't explain what I was looking for to the kind assistant who was doing his best to help. He gave up and left me in peace to browse along the shelves until I found a section with some maps and a few geography books and there, in between a book on Andalusia and a Bible, was a copy of *Berlitz Spanish for Travellers*. Perfect, exactly what I wanted. It was rather an old copy but it would have the basics which was all I needed.

Until I could speak a little more Spanish I decided it would probably be easier for me to grab a bite to eat in a cheap café rather than try to explain what I wanted to dumbfounded shop assistants. The whole town seemed full of cafés – every third building had a sea of chairs outside – so the next one I came to I sat down and pointed to one of the omelettes on the menu.

By the time I had finished it was just after eight o'clock so I would have to hurry back to Dragon before it got too dark. It was really too late to hitch a lift so I found a taxi. But how on earth was I going to explain that I wanted to be dropped at the side of the road in the middle of nowhere and I didn't even know which direction it would be in? 'Gaucin,' I said hopefully. The driver nodded and set off. As we left the outskirts of Ronda we passed a big farm. 'Stop!' I called to the driver. He slammed on his brakes. I pointed to the farm just behind us. He reversed back towards it and drove into the main yard.

I had been rather worried that all the farmworkers might have gone home but hearing voices from one of the barns, I got out of the taxi and motioned to the driver to wait.

Four men were shovelling feed into a nearby trolley. '*Hola*,' I said. One of the men turned round, nodded and carried on. Unsure what to do next, I stood and waited until all four turned round together. I pointed to the feed bin saying, 'I want to buy,' at the same time. They looked at me carefully, making sure they understood me correctly. To make things a little clearer I said, '*Tengo caballo*,' which means quite literally, 'I have horse'. Suddenly the penny dropped and one of the men rushed off into the gloom at the other end. By the rustling of paper sacks I realized he was finding me something to put the feed in.

Having skimmed through my *Berlitz Spanish for Travellers* in the taxi, I was able to ask 'How much?' He wrote '300' in the dust on the floor. The gold coloured coins were worth 100 pesetas so I was able to pick out 300 straight away. With endless '*Muchas gracias*', I retreated to the taxi clutching Dragon's feed under my arm.

As we turned right out of the farm entrance I leaned forward and said to the driver, '*Kilometro seis seis*.' I didn't know how to say 'sixty-six', so 'six six' seemed to be the next best thing.

*

As I ran down the track towards the stone barn, I called out to Dragon. I thought the light must be fading fast because I couldn't actually see his dark brown shape against the tawny warmth of the stones which formed the corral. I reached the soft marshy ground by the stream and stopped dead. To my horror I saw that the corral gate was open! I dropped the bag of feed and ran.

The corral was empty. I dashed into the barn but there was no Dragon. He can't be far away, I thought, trying to reassure myself. He's probably eating the marshy grass somewhere down by the stream. I ran down to the stream where I had dropped the feed bag, calling him, but the still night air remained unbroken.

Dragon takes care of his stomach before anything else so I rattled the feed bag in the hope that he wouldn't be able to resist the thought of food . . . I strained to hear above the sound of the stream trickling through the silence but my senses told me there was nothing out there among the twisted oaks. Dragon had disappeared.

I refused to let myself panic so I picked up the bag of feed and went back to the corral for my torch.

Standing by the stream, I shone the torch at a horse's eye level, turning very slowly in a full circle. A horse's eye, like a dog's, will shine very brightly from quite a long way if it catches a beam of light from a torch or headlight. I walked further downstream, always keeping to the sweet marshy grass, stopping every ten minutes or so to make another circle with the torch. Having thoroughly searched the flat area of good ground within half a mile of the corral I was convinced that he was nowhere within earshot. As it was now pitch black and getting on for midnight, I thought it best to try and get some sleep and start looking again as soon as it was light. He wouldn't move far in the dark, I reasoned; he was probably asleep under a cork oak on the other side of the hill.

With my torch nearly dead, I stumbled through the darkness back to the corral, too upset to both about my tent. I huddled into a corner of the barn and, leaning against the damp stone wall, shivered myself into a fitful sleep.

*

I woke up at about 5 a.m. lying with my face on the dirt floor of the barn. For a split second I had forgotten that Dragon was missing. Then I leapt up and dashed outside, expecting to see him standing in a corner of the corral, quietly resting a foot. But it was still empty. I went back into the barn, pulled on my boots and prepared myself for a major search. Through the door, a shaft of light cut across the musty gloom of the barn. Tiny particles of dust danced in the luminous rays. Looking down I noticed that the dusty floor wasn't peat at all, it was dried goat muck broken down over the years until it was nothing but dust. I suddenly became aware of millions of the tiny particles inside my shirt, jeans, hair, even my ears seemed full of the revolting stuff. Taking my plastic mug with me, I headed straight for the stream. I took off my jeans and shirt and kneeled over the stream. It was freezing cold, but I needed to feel clean again and refresh my mind ready for the hunt for Dragon.

The stone barn nestled in a long, narrow hollow, along which ran the stream. The steep hill on my right led up to the road and I doubted very much that he would have gone in that direction, so I set off at a brisk walk towards the rocky slope on my left.

It was a long, hard climb, but I could see a few cork oaks on a flat area a bit higher up. From up there I would be able to see most of the surrounding area. Thinking of snakes, I wasn't very happy clambering amongst all those rocks, but at last the ground became easier as the rocks gave way to the short tufts of elephant grass. I stood under the shade of a huge cork oak tree and peered into the distance, searching for that familiar brown hump. When horses go wandering they usually head in the direction of home, which in this case, as far as I could work out, would be roughly south-east of where I was standing. Shielding my eyes with my hands, I scoured every hump and bump in that direction. A long way further down on the other side of the hill was a cluster of small buildings. A few goats were grazing along the outside wall. Horses sometimes make straight for other animals if they wander off and become lost and hungry so I felt there was a chance that Dragon might be there.

49

Half an hour later I arrived, sweating and filthy, at the nearest of the stone buildings. I could hear sounds of activity coming from inside the sturdy stone walls. There were about sixty goats, all different colours and sizes milling round the yard. Moth-eaten chickens scratched about in front of a big wooden door. That, I thought, must be the feed room. There was no one about so I walked across the yard and opened the door. The chickens clucked in disapproval at my interruption of their breakfast and studied me with their unnerving sideways stare.

Inside the barn, about six stalls were built out of the wall. There were five rather bony black-and-white bottoms and there on the end was a fat brown hump. My heart leapt with excitement. 'Dragon?' His head shot up above the line of partitions, his ears going round and round like radar transmitters, trying to locate my voice. I felt like a mother who'd found her lost child, I didn't know whether to be angry or happy. I decided it was my fault for not tying up the gate well enough, so I gave him a big pat and he leaned round to snuffle shamelessly in case I'd brought him a reward.

The chickens scattered as I closed the wooden door. I wandered round the yard trying to find one of the kind people who'd given Dragon a stable. I was beginning to learn how to make myself understood without being able to speak the language so the prospect of explaining who I was, where I'd come from and that the brown horse belonged to me didn't worry me at all.

I couldn't see anyone in the yard so I decided to have a look in the other buildings. As I turned the corner, I bumped straight into an enormous woman carrying a bundle of washing which, luckily, cushioned the collision. The woman jumped back in amazement, holding her pudgy fingers over her mouth. '*Madre Mía!*' she exclaimed. I apologized and pointed in the direction of Dragon's barn. Sighing with relief, still muttering under her breath, she led me towards one of the houses.

A man was sitting on the steps of the front door sorting long spiky palm leaves into piles. He climbed to his feet as we approached and gave us a wide, toothless welcome. The fat woman spoke to him and went inside. The old man nodded and shuffled off towards Dragon's barn, beckoning me to follow.

He picked up a long piece of string from the floor of the barn and in two seconds had made a makeshift halter, which he gave to me. He gave Dragon a friendly pat and began to speak. I could only presume that he was telling me how he had found him wandering about outside either late last night or early this morning. Every time he paused I smiled and thanked him. I led Dragon outside, insisted on paying him 300 pesetas and walked out of the yard, trusty steed in tow.

It was a long climb up the hill and then down again to the barn. Dragon found the rocky terrain much easier to cope with than I did and kept pushing past me in his haste to get back to the little corral. The next large rock we came to, I clambered on top, jumped on to Dragon's back and left it to him to take us safely back to the barn. Being an Andalusian horse, he picked his way up the rocky slope as easily as if it had been a snooker table.

By the time we reached the corral it was almost eleven o'clock. I led Dragon down to the stream for a drink, then tied him very tightly in the corral and closed the gate while I packed my saddle-bags.

Half an hour later I was ready to go. Feeling very hot and uncomfortable after my search I thought I'd have a quick splash in the stream before we left, so making sure Dragon was tied with a double knot rather than the quick release knot, I took my wash-box out of the saddle-bags and wandered down to the river.

On my way back, I saw a man standing by the corral. My heart sank; it was probably the farmer wanting to know what this strange horse was doing on his land. I walked up to the man, pointed to Dragon and then to the road.

He started to speak and as usual I didn't understand a word, so as I thought I was probably being dished out a few stern words, I nodded my head in silence. The next thing I knew, the man was starting to unzip his trousers! I said 'No' as fiercely as I could, with which he grabbed me and held my arms in a vice-like grip. Thrashing the air with my hands, I forced him to hold me slightly further away from him, so that I had just enough space to give him an almighty crack on the shins with my boot. He let out a yell and still gripping my arm with one hand, rubbed his aching shins with the other. Seizing my opportunity I kicked him in the groin as hard as I could. He let go of my arm and I ran for the corral. I flew through the gate and grabbed Dragon, forgetting he was still tied up. The man was on his feet again, waving his fist at me. It was no good, the knot was too tight, and the more I tugged the tighter it became. It was like one of those awful horror films when the monster is closing in and the poor woman can't start her car. Just as the man started lumbering towards us I realized I was being incredibly stupid – all I had to do was to unclip the rope at the halter end. We were away, out of the corral and across the stream in a matter of seconds. I didn't look back until we reached the top of the hill by the main road. Only then did I stop to make sure, and to my relief I saw the man sitting by the stream nursing his sore shin.

Dragon thought it had all been quite fun and snorted to himself in amusement. A white kilometre stone stood a little way ahead of us; '67' was painted in large black letters on all its three sides. Whizzing along in the lorry last night I had no idea how many kilometres it was to Ronda, but we had left the farm in Gaucin at kilometre 98 so we must have covered 29 of the 38 kilometres to Ronda, leaving us only 9 kilometres left to go. The day before we had been travelling at between 6 and 8 kilometres per hour so I calculated that it would probably take us a little over an hour.

Spanish towns don't have endless outskirts with just one more house stuck on the end of a sprawling line of modern boxes. One minute you're in the country, the next minute you're surrounded by houses, shops and bars. I'd dropped in at the farm where I bought the feed the evening before to ask if they knew of a place I could stay in Ronda and they had given me the name '*Posada Maraga*'. I asked Dragon to walk and got out my dictionary to look up *posada*. *Portugués . . . porvenir . . . posada*: inn, lodging, boarding house.

There were so many things for Dragon to spook at he didn't know which one to choose. Eventually he settled for a sweet shop with fluorescent windmills hanging from its canopy and danced past; it was the perfect excuse for a loud trumpeting snort. I patted his neck, which was taut with excitement and mock fear.

Then we came to an ancient-looking bridge. The ironwork set into the stones had been worn absolutely smooth by generations of anxious hands clinging to it for safety. The bridge crossed a spectacular gorge or *tajo* which seemed to divide the town in two. The gorge was nearly 1000 feet below us and seemed even more alarming when one was perched on top of a horse. Dragon was so busy looking for something else to shy at that I don't think he noticed the vast chasm on either side of the bridge. With a good firm hold on my reins I kept his head straight in case his eyes wandered beyond the railings of the bridge.

A butcher's bicycle overtook us on the outside and Dragon immediately hopped sideways in disgust as the bicycle's gory load drew level with his nose. Prancing and jigging, we slowly made our way into the centre of Ronda.

When we passed a bar, its tables and chairs almost spilling out onto the road, I stopped to ask directions for '*Posada Maraga*'. Everyone seemed eager to help and although I couldn't understand most of what they were saying, I had taken the trouble to learn the words *derecha* and *izquierda* (right and left). So following the arm signals and the odd right and left we turned right up the next street, left a bit further on and then had to ask again. The same rules applied; I took note of the direction of the first arm signal and the first *derecha* or *izquierda*. I repeated this exercise until somebody pointed to two very large doors on the opposite side of the road which resembled an English coach house.

I jumped off Dragon and ticked him off when he nearly pushed me over trying to use me as a scratching-post for his itchy head. I led him across the road to the large doors. A normal-sized door was inset into one of them. I knocked; the door was so solid that my knock produced nothing more than a gentle thud. I gave it a good thump and waited . . . Presently, the small door opened, a man looked at me, then at Dragon, closed the small door and slid back the bolts of the huge wooden doors. The tired hinges complained bitterly as the heavy doors slowly creaked open. Once we were inside, they were firmly locked behind us. The old man took Dragon's reins from me and led him towards a dilapidated whitewashed building on the far side of a cobbled yard.

It was as if I had stumbled into history; I had no idea that horse inns still existed in Europe. Here I was in the middle of a tourist town, and yet behind the scenes of modern shops it was just as it had always been: whitewashed buildings with stalls for thirty horses and a tired old nagsman who knew his job. But there was a certain smell in the stalls which told me that a horse hadn't passed through this place for years.

The old man motioned for me to sit on the bench in the shade outside. I never thought he'd be able to work out how to undo all the extra buckles on the saddle-bags, but I didn't want to hurt the old man's feelings so I peeled off my leather chaps and, laying them down on the bench beside me, did as I was told.

To my amazement the old man reappeared ten minutes later carrying my saddle-bags over one arm and my saddle and bridle over the other. He must have been as strong as an ox to carry it all at once. He jerked his head in the direction of the gatehouse. I followed him through the doorway and into a tack room. There was saddlery of every description: bits, hobbles, whips, a driving harness, a few old-fashioned bits of tack that I didn't recognize and about twelve saddles. Beyond the tack room were three very small rooms, completely empty except for five hooks along one wall and a saddle-horse in the middle. He carefully laid my saddle-bags across the saddle-horse, put the saddle in front and then hung my bridle on the hook, neatly looping the reins through the throat lash. He nodded proudly in acknowledgement and ushered me out of the door before him, he touched his cap and motioned towards the door of the tack room. It felt good to be in the fresh air again.

He then led me into the feed room and took a raffia basket, scooped up a couple of kilos of whole oats, added some chaff (finely chopped hay to stop a horse eating too fast) and walked steadily across the yard to Dragon's stall. I followed, and was surprised to see that Dragon had been washed down. I must have dropped off for a few minutes while he was being untacked. The old man shook the oats and chaff out of the basket along the length of the stone feeder.

He showed me into the gatehouse, introduced me to his aged wife and found a chair for me to sit on. His wife put a large mug of hot milk on the table with a couple of sponge cakes. I can't bear drinking hot milk, but I didn't want to appear ungrateful, so with the help of the sponge cakes I just managed to finish it.

It was getting late and I wondered whether they might have somewhere for me to sleep. They seemed so kind and helpful that I felt confident they wouldn't turf me out with nowhere to go, so for the next half-hour I sat back and enjoyed their kindness and the warm security of their little kitchen. It felt wonderful to be able to relax with human beings again. I always found it very difficult to cope with never being able to trust anyone, always feeling vulnerable and terribly alone and unable to communicate.

Crouched over the kitchen table, the old man reminded me of a tortoise. His tired old face hung in folds over his scrawny neck. His slightly hooked nose seemed to study me more closely than his eyes, or perhaps I was just exhausted after a long day in the sun. Anyway his wife noticed me fading and clucked at her husband.

He led me across the road to a small boarding-house, said something to the woman behind the counter and was gone. She smiled kindly, took my passport and showed me to my room – long and narrow with a very hard bed, a wooden chair and a tiny sink on the far wall. A leaky pipe dripped small, slow drops onto the lino floor, but apart from that it was bright, clean and perfect for a good night's sleep.

# FOUR

# Losing Weight

IT WAS THE FIRST time since I had left Sotogrande that both Dragon and I were somewhere comfortable and safe for the night. The first thing I did was have a bath and I found the bathroom on the other side of the landing. In it was a towel slightly bigger than my own tiny one, so with that and my own bar of soap I enjoyed a long soak albeit in lukewarm water.

I lay on the hard bed and went over the last three days in my mind. My journey so far had not been at all what I had expected and now that I had found somewhere comfortable to stay for a few days I would have a good chance to rethink the whole journey and the equipment I would be needing.

My biggest problem was the unnecessary weight of my saddle-bags. Being made of strong leather they weighed quite a lot before I'd even started to load them up. I had done my best to make them as comfortable for Dragon as possible by lining the centre-piece with sheepskin. It tended to make his back rather hot, but without it his spine would be tender and sore.

As I laid the contents of the saddle-bags on the lino floor, most of my stuff seemed to be an unnecessary luxury or unlikely to be used at all. Being as strict with myself as possible, I put only the absolute essentials on one side.

The most important consideration was weight, so even things weighing as little as toothpaste hit the 'out' pile. I chopped my bar of soap in half with a penknife, ripped my small towel into half its present size, chucked out a tiny plastic bottle of instant coffee granules and replaced it with shampoo. The shampoo, still in its original bottle, joined my gas stove on the 'out' pile, along with the spare water bucket, spare shoes for Dragon, cooking things, a book for me to read, my painting things and lastly a hot water bottle!

By the time I'd finished there wasn't much left on the 'coming with me' pile. Given the fact that I was only wrapped in a small towel, it consisted of the following: one pair of jeans, one pair of shorts, two shirts, three pairs of knickers, two pairs of socks, one bra and a pair of shoes (for when I took my boots off), half a toothbrush, half a bar of soap, one tiny bottle of shampoo for hair and clothes, one very small towel, deodorant, sun-block, lipstick and a comb (my hairbrush was too big). A very small collection of veterinary stuff which would have to do for me as well as Dragon came on to the pile as well: disinfectant spray, wound powder and antiseptic cream. I included a couple of tail bandages which would be useful for anything ranging from serving as a spare rope to giving some support to Dragon's tendons; one fold-up plastic bucket for Dragon's water and one bright green plastic mug for me; a not particularly sophisticated penknife; a hay-net in case I needed to carry hay on board; my personal hi-fi and four music cassettes. I was also going to need something to keep a record of my journey so I had included my dictaphone, ten tapes and a notebook for written notes along with two Biros. I didn't want to take my address book so I wrote a few important addresses in the back of the notebook. Lastly came my long waterproof Barbour coat. Although I wasn't expecting any rain until I reached France it was the only thing I had to keep me warm and was also surprisingly light.

As far as Dragon's tack was concerned, there was really very little I could cut down on, but I could do without a few things such as his tether collar; I would clip the tether rope to his head collar instead. The head collar was nylon and the bridle didn't have a bit, so they were also light. I had made his tether rope out of a light aluminium chain, with a cotton cover to prevent it chafing if he got it caught round his legs. Even so, the chain was still too heavy so I decided to find a hardware shop in the morning and buy a strong rope instead.

I turned my attention to the saddle-bags once more. Apart from their great weight, they were coming unstitched from the central piece of leather holding them together. On my way into Ronda I had seen a couple of saddlery shops so I decided to visit them first thing in the morning to see if they had some sensible alternative.

The following day I was up quite early and went straight to see Dragon. I found him thoroughly well fed and rested, gleaming with health. He, like me, was still distinctly over-weight but another few weeks and it would all have turned to muscle. I could have stayed at the Sotogrande stables for another couple of weeks in order to get us both a bit fitter but as the days ticked past and the hot summer drew nearer I still felt it made more sense to take things slowly and do our fitness work day by day.

Dragon had buried a hole right down into his hay box and had shoved his nose in until the hay was level with his eyes. He hardly bothered to look up when he saw me leaning over his door so I decided to leave him in peace and go for a wander round the town to find some breakfast and the few bits and pieces I needed.

I turned round to find the old man just behind me. I smiled and pointed to Dragon saying, 'Very happy,' in an appreciative tone of voice. The old man beamed with pride and said some-thing I didn't understand. I wanted to ask him about the old coach house, how long it had been since a horse had stayed here and how long he had worked here, but unable to speak any Spanish, I could only ask the simplest of questions.

Having walked round the town for a while the day before, I found it a little easier to find my way this time and in half an hour I had managed to buy the length of rope. I also bought four square plastic boxes to keep my things dry as I found that even through the thick leather sides of the saddle-bags, everything got slightly damp and smelled of horse sweat.

Next stop was one of the little tack shops I had seen near the old bridge on my way into town. I was now fairly well practised at asking where something was so having looked up the word for a bridge it was fairly easy to find.

The little shop turned out to be rather more of a tourist attraction than a real tack shop, but I caught sight of a pair of small cloth saddle-bags hanging on a beam above my head and a young man who was stamping eyes into a piece of coloured material kindly brought them down for me.

As soon as he realized that I wasn't a tourist looking for something to hang on my wall at home he was very helpful. The saddle-bags he had brought down were a bit small and were open at the top, which was no good because all my things would fall out. Making a bigger sign with my hands I asked if he had anything larger. He disappeared and came back with four or five cloth saddle-bags hung over his arm. Unfortunately they were all open at the top. I picked out a pair which were roughly the size I wanted and pointed to the gap. I looked up 'rain' in my dictionary and he understood what my problem was. He went over to his workbench and came back with a loose piece of the same material, which he held over the open bag. I nodded my head in approval and he took it one step further by suggesting in mime that he could sew heavy duty poppers on each corner to hold the flaps down. I asked how much and he wrote '1500' on a pad of paper. It seemed nothing for all that work. He said he would have them finished '*mañana*', tomorrow.

Feeling very pleased, I headed in what I thought was the direction of Dragon's stable. It wasn't, but it didn't really matter as I had plenty of time. My long detour happened to take me past a vegetable shop, so I bought two kilos of carrots for Dragon.

I arrived back at the stables exhausted and rather regretting having bought two kilos rather than one of carrots, but Dragon was far more attentive than he had been earlier once he spied the delicious bundle under my arm.

The following morning I found the old man leaning over Dragon's door. He wished me good morning and then, pointing at Dragon, explained that he would be happier with other horses. Mentioning the name Señor Barea and putting on his cap, he beckoned me to follow him.

Despite his years, I had difficulty in keeping up with the old man as he trotted nimbly in and out of the bustling crowds until we arrived in the street where I had bought the dictionary the day before. The old man moved from bar to bar nodding his head as he edged his way through the sea of tables and chairs from one group of old men to the next. Each time,

59

he would introduce me, exchange a few words then ask the whereabouts of Señor Barea.

We found him sitting in the middle of a particularly large group of old men. He stood up, took my hand and with a slight nod of his head, introduced himself to me in the traditional manner. The old man from the inn told him everything he knew about me and Dragon. Señor Barea listened intently, his head cocked on one side like a wise old bird's. He asked me a question and I recognized the word *'donde'*, 'where', so presuming he was asking me where I had ridden from I replied 'Sotogrande'. He looked puzzled and asked *'Donde?'* once more. Sotogrande had only been developed in the last ten years, and perhaps he had never heard of it, so I said 'Algeciras', the old port. *'Ah, sí, sí!'* he replied and patted me on the back in hearty congratulation.

He excused himself from the muttering gaggle and strode off down the wide cobbled street with the old man from the inn just behind and me bringing up the rear. People seemed to appear from nowhere to touch their caps in recognition as the fine old man marched past, his long stick worn smooth from the years of tapping on the uneven cobbles as he walked.

We reached a triangular area, its ancient cobbles carefully arranged in intricate patterns, well polished by time; the mellow tones of grey had a rich glow. Señor Barea raised his stick in the direction of a vast curved wall. I had been so busy studying the cobbles that I hadn't noticed the fabulous construction stretching up towards the clear blue sky. *'Plaza de Toros'* he exclaimed proudly. The bullring. As we walked nearer the high stone wall, I could see large posters depicting a charging bull, its powerful shoulders streaked with red from the savage wounds made by the brightly coloured spears. It was only a rough painting but I still felt the pain and confusion in the animal's eyes.

Underneath the posters was a line of four wooden sentry boxes, presumably ticket offices. We walked away from them, following the sweeping curve of the wall to the back of the bullring, and came to a large wooden door set deep into the thick stone wall. Señor Barea shouted something and there was an instant patter of feet on the dust as someone rushed to open the door. Stepping through that door was like walking into another world. An area of about two acres was full of horses of all shapes and sizes, some being washed, some groomed and one or two were being schooled Spanish-style in the large expanse of dust. The whole place was built between two curves; the outer wall of the whole complex and an inner wall almost as high which I thought must surround the bullring itself. A makeshift roof jutted out of the inner wall providing shade for the horses resting in their stalls underneath. The stables, temporary stalls and exercise area must take up about an eighth of the space in the outer ring, the remaining seven eighths being used to seat the spectators. Just in front of the high wall of the actual bullring was a maze of lower whitewashed walls leading to a very heavy wooden door made of railway sleepers. Strong ropes ran from the door to a pulley above and from the sturdiness of the door and the maze of walls I thought these must have been built for the bulls.

Surrounded by all this activity I was completely unaware of being in the middle of a crowded tourist town. It seemed that whatever happened on the other side of those awesome walls, all the old traditions of training and preparing for the bullfight would remain as they had always been since the 1770s when the fabulous bullfighter Pedro Romero founded the bullring in Ronda.

I followed Señor Barea and the others across the dusty exercise area and into a shabby-looking building which housed the finest horses for the picadors to ride. There was one empty stable and Señor Barea seemed to be offering it to me. I was thrilled; it would be wonderful to stay inside such magnificent walls and watch all the training and preparation for the bullfight.

That afternoon I tacked up Dragon with just his saddle and bridle and rode him over to the bullring. He was almost on springs as he pranced from foot to foot with excitement at the sight of all those horses. It was as much as I could do to hold him. He was absolutely dying to go and say hello to them all. As most of them were probably stallions I had to speak to him quite sharply to make him behave, as a large stallion could have gobbled him up for breakfast.

61

The old groom came out to meet me and squawked at a young lad to take Dragon from me. Once again I was only allowed to watch while Dragon was carefully untacked, washed down and led into his new bedroom. As soon as he was let loose, Dragon made a beeline for the young grey stallion in the stable next to his, shoving his nose right up against the bars and pleading with him to come and sniff hello. The stallion sidled up to the bars and let out a series of short indignant snorts, Dragon arched his neck slightly and the other horse let out a loud squeal. '*Hombre!*' shouted the old groom. The young stallion retreated to the back of his stable but Dragon remained where he was, his muzzle pressed hopefully up against the bars.

I stayed to see Dragon well fed and watered, and happy that he was in good hands I let myself out through the small wooden door. On my way back to the boarding-house, I dropped in at the tack shop to see how my new saddle-bags were coming on. To my surprise I found that the young man had finished them. I examined them closely, checking the stitching and strength of the material. He had done them beautifully. Unlike my old leather saddle-bags, these weighed almost nothing.

That evening I spent in the boarding house reading my phrase book. The basics were at last beginning to come naturally, and now that I had numbers too my life was becoming much easier. Every time I came across something I would need for my journey I would ask its name, make a mental note and write it down in the back of my notebook as soon as I could. These words, such as 'bucket', 'oats', 'hay', 'water', stable', 'hose', 'boarding-house', 'rest', formed an essential part of my vocabulary, which was increasing by the day.

That evening I concentrated on questions – 'how old?' 'where from?' 'how many?' 'when?' 'why?' – so that I would be able to find out a little more about the bullring the following day.

The short walk to the bullring was marvellous early in the morning. The mountain air breathed fresh life into the sleepy backstreets of Ronda. I wandered through the square which had captured my attention the other day. At that time in the morning it was almost silent, vacant. The pigeons still fluttered about the eaves as I had remembered, but the café was closed, the elegant tables and chairs dull with morning dew. The benches stood cold and silent round the fountain. I could almost hear their old timbers creaking in preparation for the coming onslaught. I walked on. The cobbled street with all the bars seemed much wider without the masses of jostling people fighting their way from one shop to another. The bullring was just round the corner. I crossed the road towards it and marvelled at its magnificent splendour as it stood like a fortress in the delicate morning light.

I knocked on the door and waited for the patter of feet. They didn't come. I knocked again, louder this time. A minute or two later, solid steps approached and the door opened. It was the old groom. He gave me a nod, muttered *'Buenos días,'* and returned to his work.

I found Dragon positively cooing with pleasure at being surrounded by all these horsey sounds and smells. His head shot up when I walked through the door and I thought I heard him murmur a welcome. I went in to give him a pat and was promptly frisked by a well-trained nose. 'Come on, if I had something I would have given it to you by now so don't be so silly.' He didn't believe me, so I held both hands out to the side and let him give me a thorough examination before he was satisfied. I asked the old man for my head collar so that I could lead Dragon round the exercise yard for a while. It's not good for a horse to do a lot of exercise and then suddenly stop; one should always keep it going, even though in Dragon's case he could do with a good rest.

Today was Thursday, and there seemed to be far more activity than there had been the day before. I was just about to try to ask the young lad looking after the picadors' horses why everyone seemed so busy when both of the enormous wooden doors were swung back to let in a big lorry. It rumbled across the exercise area towards the maze of solid walls built up against the inner circular wall. As it drove past me, I saw a small beady eye peering through the side of the lorry. It could only have been the eye of a bull. I walked a bit closer to get a better look. I had never seen a fierce black bull before.

Men seemed to appear from nowhere, shouting and waving at each other to get the lorry in exactly the right position for the ramp to come down. A man was positioned on each side of the hefty timber gates. The tremendously thick walls of what I can only describe as the maze had a narrow gulley running along the middle which I hadn't noticed before. The floor of the gulley was about ten feet above ground level, and five or six people who had no particular job to do crept along it to get a better view of the proceedings. The old groom, who seemed to be in charge of the whole operation, noticed me watching and pointed in the direction of the gulley. Very excited, I joined the others. Then there was silence. They must be about to let down the ramp, I thought, peering anxiously over the edge of the whitewashed stone. A hand came down on my head telling me to keep out of sight. I did as I was told. All seven of us, including two small boys, remained absolutely motionless, waiting . . .

I heard the bolts of the ramp slowly sliding back. Suddenly, there was a loud clang as the ramp came down on target and a terrific thunder as the bull leapt out of the truck and into the maze. I was dying to catch a glimpse of the fearsome beast but everyone else was remaining perfectly still and silent so I thought I had better do the same. I heard a heavy thud as the first gate was heaved shut by the two big grooms who were manning the ropes. The others in the gulley began to rise slowly and carefully until the tops of their heads were just visible. I followed their example and caught a glimpse of black as the bull thundered backwards and forwards, up and down the maze. Thud, down came the second gate; this one was lined with steel. The bull was getting angry and snorted with rage as he charged along the narrow run and hurled his great weight against the steel plate. I felt the vibration through the stone under my feet.

It was an incredible beast that had jumped out of that lorry, and yet already he was being tricked into unnecessary fury. Suddenly the horrors of tales of bullfighting and the pain of the poster outside the bullring came flooding back to me. The magnificent shine on the bull was drenched in sweat, his eyes rolled with fury and confusion at being unable to find a way out. Finally he stood still, his sides heaving. Once again a hand came down on my head and somebody muttered *'Peligroso'*, which I later looked up and found to mean 'dangerous'. Five minutes went by and all I could hear was the agonizing panting of the bull. I was getting cramp in my legs and I didn't want to see any more. The steel door was drawn up and the bull trotted through into the next chamber. The steel door hit the ground behind him, barring his escape. He didn't seem unduly angry at being shunted through one more section of the maze so the signal was given for the last gate to be opened. To my surprise I saw a miniature bullring beyond the final gate. The bull galloped round and round it, relieved to feel free again.

Now that the bull was out of the maze, everyone stood up straight and scrambled along the gulley to the edge of the mini bullring. It had sleeper screens four sleepers wide positioned at north, south, east and west. A red handkerchief was waving from behind the one on the east side. I couldn't see who it was. A moment later the old groom danced out from behind the screen, waving the handkerchief at the puzzled bull as he made the dangerous crossing to the screen positioned south. Without warning, the bull charged, reaching the old groom only a split second after he had disappeared behind the safety of the screen. A moment later he reappeared and stood behind the bull while it waited on the other side of the screen. Sensing the old man's presence, the bull seemed to hesitate before it swung round and headed straight for him. I was terrified; there was no chance of his running for refuge behind the screen before the bull reached him. But I had underestimated the old man. Apparently unflustered, he ducked neatly out of the way as the enormous hulk of the bull galloped past.

It was only when I understood a little more about the ancient tradition of bullfighting that I realized the skill behind what I had seen the old man doing with the new bull. In a bullfight the poor animal has the tendons in its neck severed by those brightly coloured spears that I had seen in the poster. Unable to raise its head, the bull is far less dangerous for the matador. The bulls, like the one I saw arriving, are selectively bred for one thing – courage – and weigh anything up to half a ton. Even the mothers are bravery-tested before being allowed to conceive. The bulls which I saw jump out of the lorries over the next couple of days had been brought straight from their breeders, so they were still full of arrogant confidence, knowing no fear whatsoever.

What I saw of that bull and the others like it in the days before the fight saddened me. They were given only enough food and water to keep them alive, nothing more. They were baited in the way that I had witnessed, albeit with great skill, until they were desperate and confused, ready to charge anything which came into their sights; especially the matador on the big day.

I had seen enough, and leaving them all hanging over the side of the small bullring I crept back along the gulley, said goodbye to Dragon and let myself out of the small wooden gate, back into the world of thriving cafés, bright sunshine and pink tourists in summer dresses.

Seeing the manic expressions on the faces of the men watching the bull reminded me that I must go back for Boris. I longed for his company and security. It had been nearly a week since I had taken him back to the guard dog centre so I could only pray that they hadn't found a home for him already.

I was lucky to pass a sign saying AUTO-ESCUELA just before the cake shop in my favourite square. 'Auto' had to be something to do with cars, I thought, as I climbed the three stone steps up to the door.

The long, narrow room was crowded with young people. There didn't seem to be any sort of queue so I battled my way through to the counter at the far end. Once I had reached the young man standing behind it, I wasn't quite sure what to say other than, '*Car, por favor?*' Understandably, he wasn't quite sure what I wanted so his only reply was, '*Inglesa?*'

'*Sí, sí.*' I nodded.

'*Maria!*' he called. '*Ven aquí.*' A tall girl pushed her way towards us.

A few words with the young man, then she turned to me and in rather shaky English asked, 'What wanting please?'

'I want to borrow a car.' My answer was translated and the young man's face lit up in a way that only Spanish faces can when at last the penny drops.

66

*'Sí, sí señorita, cuando lo quieres?'* Recognizing the word *'cuando'*, meaning 'when', I replied, *'Ahora,'* – now.

And so it went on, with the tall girl translating for me when necessary and also explaining to me that this was really a driving school but they would be kind and let me borrow a Fiat Panda for twenty four hours. When all was settled, she led me to the street behind the shop where the sum total of three driving school cars were parked.

I drove off, more than a little puzzled about what was going to happen about all the driving lessons that should have been given in this particular car. Still, this is Spain, the world of *mañana*.

I had never driven a car with left-hand drive before so I found it exceedingly difficult to get my co-ordination organized to start with. Driving in Spain one never stops to ask directions or find the way – with hundreds of Fiats tooting away behind you, you must just keep going. Desperately clinging to my vague sense of direction I drove up and down the one-way streets, most of them at least three times, before I eventually saw the familiar sign of the boarding in yellow lights, high up on a wall to my right.

That evening I decided to sample some Spanish cooking, so after a bath I put on my newly washed jeans and only pair of shoes, then wandered down into the town. After only four days I was already very conscious of the Latin tendency to give a low hiss at any passing female. It was a habit which I found very tiresome and slightly unnerving, so I kept a very low profile.

I went straight to my favourite square and found a quiet café where mostly families were eating, so I felt safe to go in and sit down. Feeling ravenously hungry I ordered a *gazpacho* and *ensalada* to start with and *estofada* (stew) to follow.

Gazpacho is cold tomato soup made with finely strained tomatoes, vinegar, olive oil, finely sifted breadcrumbs, a little pepper, paprika and some water. Just before it is put on the table, a few chunks of chopped cucumber, green pimentos and croûtons are sprinkled on the top. The end result is quite delicious and well worth sampling. My *ensalada* was mainly tomatoes with a very strong oily dressing. The stew turned out to be chicken with a few other unidentifiable bits and pieces thrown in which tasted good as long as you didn't examine them too closely; the chicken's feet were almost certainly thrown in!

The next morning I was up very early in order to ride Dragon before I set off to collect Boris. Just as I was about to leave, I had a sudden brainwave: Michael, who was building the Hurricane Hotel in Tarifa wasn't far from the guard dog centre, so when I went to pick up Boris I could leave my unwanted equipment and old saddle-bags with him. I staggered down the stairs with them to the car which was parked just outside the door. The road seemed so twisty as I sped along in the car. On a horse one doesn't really notice the bends as each one takes about three minutes. It was fun passing all the places which had been the cause of so many difficulties over the last few days; today, they were of no importance, they had very different meanings. We passed the little barn in the valley on my right. It looked so perfect, nestled in its little hollow, the glimmering thread of the stream curling round it, catching the light of the fresh morning sun. It hardly seemed the same place that I remembered, where I had woken with my face in the dirt and faced the horrors of the farmer the next morning. Still, all that was behind me now and with Boris everything should be much easier. I only hoped that he was still there. I put my foot down as much as I dared, spurred on by the awful possibility of someone taking him away that very morning. The guard dog people didn't have a telephone so I couldn't ring up and make sure.

I turned into the bumpy track leading to the guard dog centre. Three or four Alsatians were lying outside the house. There was no sign of Boris. I parked the car and went towards the house. It was Tina, the wife, who opened the door. Rather breathlessly, I explained that I wanted to take Boris after all. He was on the point of being given to someone else, she said. I had only just come in time.

I ran up the slope and found Boris asleep in the shade of a big eucalyptus tree. 'I thought you'd be back,' said a voice from behind me. It was Tony, Tina's husband. Boris seemed thrilled to see me and covered me in licks.

'Probably not such a bad thing for him to have been on his own for a week because he now really thinks of you as his boss. Why don't you untie him and bring him down to the house, and we can all have a cup of coffee while you tell us about the last few days.'

Trying to squeeze Boris into a tiny Fiat Panda when he's not very keen on cars wasn't easy. Finally we got him settled on the back seat but he was so long that his legs had to dangle over the edge.

By the time we reached Algeciras, Boris was sitting up and sniffing the fresh air through the slightly open back window. Every time we stopped at traffic lights and a motorbike buzzed past his nose, he growled, giving the rider an awful fright.

When we reached the hotel, Boris trampled all over me in his effort to escape from the cramped little car. He had been here before and knew Michael so he rushed up to him to say hello. Michael was rather surprised to see us, especially driving a car, but kindly gave me some lunch while we caught up on the adventures of the last few days. Boris had fallen in love with Michael's Irish setter, Boo Boo, so we were able to let him loose confident that he wouldn't stray far from her backside. It was marvellous to be back in civilization again, speaking English and eating good food in such idyllic surroundings, but it couldn't last long as it was a three-hour drive back to Ronda, so leaving my saddle-bags in Michael's care, I bundled a protesting Boris on to the back seat of the car and said goodbye.

Once I had dropped off the car at the driving school, I put Boris on his lead and walked back to the boarding-house. I rang the bell on the reception desk and the landlady shuffled through the plastic fronds to the desk. I pointed at the dog and then towards my room. She sighed and looked rather irritated, then asked me something about the dog. I could only presume she was asking me either if he barked a lot or if he bit. I took a chance and shook my head, stroking his back as if to say how well-behaved he was. She peered over the desk for a better look. I stroked Boris' head, desperately hoping he wasn't going to bare his teeth at the large face leaning towards him. She brought her head up again and nodded just as I felt a faint rumble under my hand. She hadn't noticed, so I thanked her very much and crept up to my room.

Just as before, I made him a nest in the corner using my long Barbour coat. Boris seemed quite happy curled up on his bed, but when I moved to the other end of the room to go through my remaining pile of stuff, he got up and followed. I was thrilled. Only a few weeks ago he had been so wary of me and yet now he didn't want to let me out of his sight. I picked up the Barbour coat and put it down next to the things I was going through, then patting the bed with my hand, I asked him to sit down. Being close to what I was doing, he was happy to oblige, and watched with interest as I packed my bits and pieces into the small plastic boxes and put them neatly into my new saddle-bags.

It was seven o'clock. The shops would be open by now but the people wouldn't start flooding the streets for about an hour so now would probably be a good time to take Boris out for a walk and buy him some dog meat.

He was still rather nervous in crowds so it was good practice for him to walk in a town. I remembered the name '*Carnicería*' and bought him a kilo of meat. Then I sat down on a bench by the fountain in my favourite square and emptied Boris' meat onto the ground. He wolfed it down and gave me a smelly kiss to tell me he'd finished. I sat for a while longer, looking up at the busy doves fluttering round the eaves. Boris was a changed dog; he stood quite still next to me on close guard, watching everyone who walked past very carefully. I got up and headed towards the bullring; Boris could do with a bit more exercise and I wanted to check on Dragon.

By now it was getting quite late so I was amazed to find the bullring still full of people beavering away. Dragon was very comfortable with a deep bed of clean straw and a bin crammed full of alfalfa. The old groom came into the stable and Boris gave a low growl. 'It's all right,' I said, stroking his head. The old man seemed to be telling me about the fight tomorrow. It was so frustrating not being able to understand. He paused for a moment as if waiting for an answer. Realizing I didn't understand, he pointed to me, then to the bullring and said,

'*Mañana*', a word which I knew well. '*Quieres?*' *Quiero* means 'I want' so *quieres* could mean 'do you want?'

'*Sí, sí, Señor, muchas gracias.*' I had guessed right.

He said, 'Four o'clock,' then walked out of the stable to carry on with his work.

I wasn't really sure whether I wanted to witness a bullfight but the main object of my ride was to learn about this beautiful country and as bullfighting plays a very important part in its traditions it seemed wrong not to have seen a bullfight for myself.

# FIVE

# The Bullfight

I KNOCKED on the little door as usual and heard footsteps coming to open the door but instead of opening the door, a voice demanded '*Quién es?*' (Who is there?)

'Belinda, *Inglesa,*' I replied.

The door opened just a crack and a suspicious eye peered through the gap. I was allowed in. Quite a sight met my eyes. The yard had been transformed into a mass of colour. Horses and men walked round and round the dusty exercise area waiting their turn, their brightly decorated costumes in brilliant contrast to the dust. The mules were hitched up in teams of three, scarlet and yellow ribbons tied to their well scrubbed manes and tails. A group of matadors stood huddled in the corner by the main entrance to the ring, all of them smoking. Their fabulous costumes shone in the warm afternoon sun.

I noticed Señor Barea coming towards me. I would hardly have recognized him in his smart navy-blue suit. It was the first time I had seen him since he had kindly given Dragon a place in his yard. He seemed pleased to see me, and taking me by the arm led me towards the main ring. I found myself sitting with Señor Barea on one side and a fat jewel-encrusted female on the other. We were sitting fairly high up in the centre of the shade in what I imagine were some of the best seats. We certainly had an excellent view, but I was thankful that being so high up we weren't going to be able to see the details too closely. The sweet-smelling silk dress of whoever was sitting behind me kept wafting into my hair, reminding me how terribly underdressed I must look, but at least my clothes were clean and my hair tidy – they would just have to take me as they found me.

Thousands of excited people talked and shouted noisily in anticipation of the coming bullfight. Most of them had come armed with five gallon containers of wine and huge picnic hampers crammed full of cold meats and long loaves. Some had even brought their own cushions to sit on. The bullring itself was on a much larger, grander scale than the one I had seen used a couple of days ago when the bulls arrived in the yard. But I was interested to see that it had the same heavy wooden screens set slightly forward from the edge of the ring. I leaned over to Señor Barea and asked what they were called. '*Burladeros*,' he replied.

There was a flutter of excitement from the crowd and I turned towards the large tunnel leading under the stands; the matadors and their assistants were starting to congregate ready for the preliminary procession. I suddenly realized that the dark patch on the floor of the ring, which I had presumed to be a shadow, seemed to carry on into the tunnel. It was not a shadow at all, but the blood shed by thousands of brave bulls over the years. There was a sudden silence as a long line of officials trooped in and took their seats. One balcony was marked 'GUARDIA CIVIL', another 'POLICIA' and the rest were words I didn't recognize. One balcony had the Spanish flag draped over the railing in front. The man sitting directly in the centre placed his handkerchief over the edge of the rail in front of him.

Almost at once the drums and bugles relayed the signal and the crowd's heads swivelled towards the tunnel again. Two sinister-looking riders led the procession wearing black medieval costume. '*Alguaciles*,' whispered Señor Barea. Behind them were three proud matadors riding abreast, their *trajes de luces* or 'suits of light' shimmering with reflected sunlight. To add to his splendour, each matador carried a heavily-embroidered parade cape across his shoulder; this would be used for the procession and nothing else. On his head each wore a black '*montera*', with the '*coleta*', the dark pig-tail (the hallmark of the Spanish bullfighter), hanging just below.

Slowly and carefully, Señor Barea explained that the matador on the right was the 'first' matador, the one whose name appeared at the top of the list on the posters. The matador on the left was the 'second' and the novice was in the middle.

Behind the line of matadors were their assistants who, I was surprised to see, were also wearing *trajes de luces*. Then came the mounted picadors, wearing beaver hats. Bringing up the rear were the ring servants and the old faithfuls, the team of mules.

The whole team moved slowly across the middle of the ring, and when the front members of the procession reached the wall at the far side they bowed, wheeled round and dispersed, leaving only the matadors in the ring. Although there was no bull, the crowd down below was going mad. I then saw why; the matadors had peeled off their parade capes and were toying with the crowd. Eventually, they handed the capes to a friend in the *Callejón* (the narrow passageway encircling the ring), who passed each a yellow and magenta 'working cape' or *mozo de estoque*. All three of them began to make elaborate swerves and passes with the utmost control. I watched, fascinated, for about five minutes until they gave a short bow and left the ring.

Silence once more, then the handkerchief appeared over the railing, the drums and bugles bashed away and amid deafening applause, the first bull thundered into the ring. Its eyes were wild as it bucked and galloped round the vast ring with the crowd still waving and cheering. I looked around briefly and noticed that picnic hampers were being opened and great hunks of bread passed round. The wine began to flow; the fight was about to begin.

The first matador watched from behind the barrier just below where I was sitting as the assistants pranced nimbly from one *burladero* to another, baiting the bull as they leapt cleverly out of its path. The purpose of this exercise is for the matador to assess the bull's little tricks and vices. When they had finished the bull was left to thunder round and round the ring once more, his temper up, searching the arena for something to charge. The handkerchief signalled once more and in came the picadors. Their big sturdy horses looked like medieval chargers with their heavy armoured skirts, which protected them from the bull's ten-inch horns.

The picadors were two huge men, also covered in heavy armour. Each picador wore a white legging on his right leg for added protection. As a result of both horses' and riders' protective clothing they were only able to move at a slow jog round the ring. With their *'picas'* (a *pica* is a long pole with a sharp spike at the end) held high they shuffled off in opposite directions.

The bull stood still for a moment, not quite sure which one to go for. The picadors' horses were blindfolded so that they wouldn't be able to see the approaching bull, in case they panicked. The bull focused his attention on the nearest picador. He lowered his head and, travelling at full speed, butted the unsuspecting horse just below the saddle. The horse hardly moved and as the bull struggled to free his horns, the picador dug the long, cruel spike into the bull's neck muscles. I stiffened with disgust as the huge picador gouged the long pole a little further into the poor animal's neck. With a hearty grunt, the bull managed to pull himself free and, his head held low as a result of the damaged neck muscles, cantered back into the centre of the ring.

A matador leapt out from behind one of the screens to distract the bull while the picadors prepared themselves for another go at him. This time, it was the other picador, even bigger than the first, who took on the charging bull. The instant the bull's long horns made contact with the horse's side, the picador rammed the *pica* hard into the animal's neck. The bull was still wedged right underneath the horse and was slowly pushing the horse into the side wall of the ring. The bull gave a sudden upward jerk with his head and tipped the horse over. The crowd went mad as the bull repeatedly buffeted the poor horse in the stomach. The matadors and their assistants rushed on to the scene to draw the charging bull away from them. As soon as the bull's attention had been diverted a team of ring servants rushed to help. The picador was trapped by his leg under the massive horse. Until the great leather skirt, which came down to the horse's feet, had been unbuckled, the poor horse couldn't put his feet out in front of him to get up. At last they succeeded; the groaning picador was dragged free and helped out of the ring. Thankfully, the horse wasn't hurt and was led out of the ring through the tunnel. The first picador gave the bull one final jab in the neck with his *pica* and leaving the bull hardly able to lift his neck at all, rode out of the ring to great applause.

'*Ahora, los banderilleros,*' shouted Señor Barea above the screaming crowds. The bull was no longer galloping endlessly round and round the ring. He was getting tired, and with nothing to charge he stood in the middle, his sides heaving, and waited. A slim, colourfully dressed young man sprang out from behind the wooden screen. Instead of a cape, he held two decorated sticks, about two and a half feet long, with barbed steel points. I shrank back into my seat. The nimble little *banderillero* danced in front of the bull until, with its head hung low, it charged. To my surprise, the *banderillero* ran towards the bull, but he ran diagonally, forcing the bull to change direction so that he couldn't gather speed. I hung on to the edge of my seat, convinced there was going to be an awful collision but not quite sure whose side I was on. Just as the bull reached the man, he thrust in the barbed sticks and leapt away to safety. The bull lashed out with his heels in pain and trotted across the ring with his impressive shoulders now drenched in blood.

The 'first' matador then strutted jauntily into the ring and raised his hands, welcoming the thunderous applause from the crowd. He was a hero before the fight had even begun. It seemed unfair that no matter how noble a fight the bull put up, he would never leave this ring a hero like the proud man who stood gloating before his troubled eyes.

With his back to the waiting bull, the matador walked calmly over to the barrier where he was handed his hat and sword and, most important of all, the *muleta*, a red cloth much smaller than a cape. His tunic was emerald green, heavily embroidered in gold. Older and more experienced, this matador had a slightly stouter figure than the 'second' and the novice. He had probably worn his stunning attire when he was a novice himself, judging by how tight it was.

The assistants came into the ring and began to entice the bull while the matador paced round the ring until he was facing the balcony with the Spanish flag. The crowd was silent. He said something to the man with the handkerchief, bowed to the crowd and laid his hat gently on the sand behind him. The assistants disappeared behind the heavy wooden barriers and watched from the *callejón*, ready to leap back into the ring if they were needed to divert the bull at any stage. There was a hush as the crowd waited for the first charge. It was amazing to watch the poise and control of every movement as the matador moved across the sand as if on air, edging his way closer and closer towards the bull. He stopped and lowered his head to stare right into the animal's eyes. There was a murmur of excitement from the crowd as he fluttered the *muleta* across his emerald body. The bull began to scrape at the sand with his hoof, sending up a cloud of dust. There was a grunt as he surged forward, his huge body powering him towards the matador at great speed. The matador turned his side to the bull and, with one foot stretched out behind him, held the *muleta* out in front, allowing the terrifying beast to charge through it quite harmlessly. The crowd were starting to shout and cheer again.

His second pass seemed to follow quite quickly. This time, he let the bull rush through the *muleta* while he held it close to his chest. There was a slight pause; the bull stood in the middle of the ring, almost aware that he was fighting an impossible battle. I found it hard to understand how anyone could derive pleasure from watching such a magnificent beast, soaked in sweat and his own blood, being put through this useless test of bravery.

The fight continued. The matador was now holding the *muleta* high in front of his face, inching his way towards the bull until he was just a few feet from the heaving body. He fluttered the *muleta* very gently; the bull didn't move. The crowd was transfixed as he swayed it slowly from side to side, but still the bull didn't flinch. The noise grew louder and then the bull charged. Only a few feet from the matador, he came fast and straight, his eyes fixed in fury on the red cloth. Displaying astonishing skill and judgement, the matador seemed to lead the bull round his body in a slow swing of colour, wrapping the bull around him in an almost complete circle . . . and a second time. He then threw back his head, snatched away the *muleta* and, with his back to the confused bull, strutted off across the ring. The crowd loved it. Señor Barea leaned over and said, '*Buenísimo.*' I nodded, not sure whether I agreed with him or not.

The matador walked to the side of the ring and was handed

the killing sword. I was not looking forward to this, but I couldn't walk out; having come to witness a bullfight, I must see the whole thing. Señor Barea demonstrated that the bull must be standing straight with its front feet together as the sword went in between the shoulder blades. If not, the sword would hit bone and fly out; Señor Barea shook his finger to say that this would be a bad display of swordsmanship.

The matador now held the *muleta* in his left hand and the sword in his right. He moved towards the bull, a little more purposefully than before. There was no need for him to be quite so wary because the bull was by now very tired and weak from loss of blood. He moved the *muleta* diagonally across his chest, holding it slightly away from his body. Holding the sword straight out in front, level with his eyes, he sighted the bull down the length of the sword. There was a quiet hush and the bloodthirsty crowd waited in anticipation. The exhausted bull lumbered towards him and the matador sprang up on his toes and thrust the sword deep into the animal's body. '*Perfecto!*' screamed the jewel-encrusted lady. The crowd stood up and cheered, mad with excitement as the assistants rushed out to turn the bull this way and that, their mustard-coloured capes held out in front of them. It was terrible to see the bull slowly but surely sinking to his feet in agony and despair. It seemed a barbaric waste of life. By now, the bull had dropped to his knees, blood streaming out of his nose. It was horrible to watch as the matador paraded round the ring, to be swept up on to his comrades' shoulders amid a snowstorm of waving handker-chiefs. One of the assistants handed him the bull's ears which the matador threw in the air for everyone to see. The crowd responded by showering their hero with flowers, hats, shoes and leather *botas* filled with wine.

Nobody seemed to notice as the teams of mules were hitched up to the bull's horns and the true hero's lifeless body was dragged out of the ring.

# SIX

# On the Road Again

ONCE DRAGON was tacked up and ready to go, I brought Boris into the stable to say hello. Boris didn't seem particularly bothered by Dragon, who was about eight times his size, so I led Dragon out of the stable and tied him up outside while I clipped Boris' lead on to the girth buckle. I had given Boris quite a long lead to start with, until he became used to the horse's feet.

Señor Barea and the old groom had come to see me off. I thanked them for all their kindness and paid the old groom for my stable. I said goodbye to Señor Barea and he handed me a small envelope with the words '*Picadero*, Campillos' written in old-fashioned curly writing. *Picadero* is an extraordinary word. It refers to a man who keeps horses, as in this context, but also to his yard and his round, fenced schooling ring. This letter would serve as an introduction to the horseman in Campillos. It meant that I wouldn't have to worry about finding somewhere to stay the following night.

'*Muchas gracias!*' The huge gates swung open for the last time.

I made a slight detour to say goodbye to the old man at the *posada* and trotted out of Ronda on the quiet country road towards Cuevas de Becerro. It felt good to be on the road again having spent nearly a week in Ronda. Today was a good first day to have Boris on the lead as there wasn't much traffic. The road out of Ronda was downhill and rather slippery so we just walked. Boris was making life very hard for himself by constantly pulling against his lead. I tried giving the lead little jerks but it didn't make him any better and as he seemed to be quite happy I left him to do it his way.

The landscape on this side of Ronda was very different to the difficult and mountainous terrain we had encountered on our way in. Although I could see a small ridge of mountains in the distance, the immediate landscape was one of gently rolling hills. When the road began to level out we broke into a gentle trot. Bearing in mind that Boris was very unfit I was only planning to go as far as Cuevas de Becerro today with a few long rests in between.

We were about a hundred kilometres from the coast now and I could feel the rising temperature as we moved further away from the sea breeze. When we came to a ford, Dragon bent his head and snorted, but having successfully negotiated the river at San Martin del Tesorillo he walked through it with very little persuasion.

Before I had even put my feet in the stirrups, Dragon gave a sharp tug at the reins and was off. Although it had only been a short break for him, Boris seemed full of energy again. Soon we passed an orange grove. I stopped for a moment to look for a gap in the hedge or a gateway. There were only about twenty orange trees but each was heavy with ripe fruit. Lots of overripe oranges had fallen and were scattered on the ground like gold pebbles. There were so many that he couldn't avoid treading on them. Dragon was slightly unnerved by the squishy sensation under his feet and darted forward like a cat on a hot tin roof with poor Boris towed along behind. Boris looked at Dragon as if to say, 'Stupid horse, haven't you seen an orange before?' I patted Dragon on the neck to reassure him and brought him to a halt underneath a particularly large orange tree. Holding the reins with one hand, I stood up in my stirrups and gave one of the oranges a tug, and another. I put them both in the small saddle-bag on the front of my saddle and retraced my steps back on to the road.

Eventually the road straightened and I could just make out a small village in the distance, though it was a long time before it seemed any closer. Distance is deceptive when you are going at horse speed, but at last the houses grew bigger and I could see the church spire and the whitewashed houses built all around it.

It was nearly six o'clock by the time we walked into

Cuevas de Becerro. Unfortunately, there were no farm buildings and nowhere which looked even remotely possible for us to stay. I walked on through the village; it was quite a bit larger than I had thought.

Walking through the charming cobbled streets, I began to feel worried. The families were sitting in groups along the pavements outside their houses. The children, as usual, shouted and screamed in excitement at this amazing spectacle as Dragon, Boris and I plodded slowly on past their homes. It disintegrated into nothing more than a dusty well-used track, which I thought might lead to a farm. We walked past the last of the smiling, toothless faces and on out of the *pueblo* (village), and along the track. There were hedges along the sides of it; something which I had not seen before in Spain. The fields beyond the hedges on either side had both been recently harvested and were standing stubble.

A few minutes later we came across some men loading bales of straw on to the back of a lorry parked in a field. I couldn't see a gateway so I shouted to them across the hedge. One of them looked up and began to walk slowly and steadily towards us. At that moment, a car appeared, going in the direction of the *pueblo*. I moved over to let it pass but its young occupants motioned that they were quite happy to wait while I stumbled along in Spanish, trying to explain to the man on the other side of the hedge that I was looking for somewhere to put my horse for the night. I didn't seem to be making any headway whatsoever. At last, one of the young men in the car got out and came to my rescue. He waved the man away and explained that his uncle had a stable I could use. He pointed to Cuevas de Becerro and drove slowly back towards the village as I followed behind. It was another ten minutes before he stopped the car and told me to wait.

Children seemed to appear from nowhere, and before long we had attracted a crowd of at least twenty-five. They all wanted to come and pat Dragon. I didn't know Boris well enough to trust him with children yet so I let them come forward one by one and pat Dragon on the opposite side to him. Boris was not happy about all these suspicious-looking mini-people and bared his teeth. The front row of children shrieked and ran back.

Understandably, none of them wanted to come and pat the horse any more.

I was relieved when the car reappeared and the same young man signalled for me to follow. I walked beside Dragon as we followed the old Fiat through the streets to the other side of the village. We arrived at a line of dusty old wooden shacks. I tied Dragon up to untack him and tied Boris well away so he wouldn't be a nuisance. The young man first introduced himself as 'Pepe', and then the old man (who appeared from inside the shack) as his uncle, but I don't think he told me his name. Pointing to myself I said 'Belinda' as I undid Dragon's girth.

All Dragon's tack was left in a small room inside. The uncle beckoned me to follow him through the narrow doorway with Dragon. The door was so narrow and low that I wasn't sure that Dragon would fit. I walked through myself, with Dragon just behind. By now it was nearly dark and it was only when I walked forwards that I realized that Dragon was going to have to negotiate a small flight of steps. Dear old Dragon, it was no problem. There was a loud clatter as we stepped on a sheet of corrugated iron and the chickens scattered. It was a very narrow passageway so Dragon had great difficulty in turning his long body to manage the left turn into his stable. Boris was whining outside. Pepe and his uncle heaved three long timbers into place and bound them with wire to keep Dragon in his stable. I took off Dragon's head collar and let him loose. There was very little straw so I hoped he would be able to have a roll; there had been no hose for me to wash him down and he must be feeling horribly itchy, so I was very pleased when the uncle climbed through the timber partition clutching a couple more sections of straw. He handed one to me and just as I was about to shake it out on to the floor, he put all his along the feed manger. I was amazed. In England one covers the straw in all sorts of disgusting potions to stop the horse eating it in case it makes him cough and yet this man was giving it to Dragon in place of hay. I caught myself just in time and spread it out along the manger.

The old man gave him some whole oats, handed me my saddle-bags and padlocked the door behind us. It's not usual practice to feed whole grains of oats. In England we tend to crush the oats before feeding them so that they can be more easily digested.

I untied a very over-excited Boris and followed the young man back into the centre of the village. Although he was doing his best to talk very slowly, I could only understand the odd word of what he was saying. He stopped outside a garage, through which we walked to a door on the far side. He let us go first up the narrow staircase. I felt so much better having Boris with me. Three days ago, I would rather have slept with Dragon than follow a stranger into an unknown room but although I couldn't be sure whether Boris would protect me, I knew for certain that nobody would dare to try anything with a Dobermann of his proportions around. He led me up one more flight and showed me a small bathroom with a cracked sink and no loo seat. Down the stairs again and along a passage we came to another door. This was where Boris and I could sleep for the night. There were two beds with one grubby sheet each and nothing else. An ugly wardrobe stood against one wall, its doors wide open, casting an asymmetric shadow on the lino covered floor. Pepe seemed to be apologizing for the state of the room, but I was lucky to be given a room at all. I assured him that it was very comfortable and he shrugged his shoulders, handed me the key and left us.

Boris was pacing round the room looking for somewhere to lie down, and I put my Barbour coat in the corner for him. The sheets on the bed were filthy and muddy and looked as though a dog had been sleeping on them. I took the sheet off one bed leaving just the bare mattress.

There was a loud clang as someone knocked on the metal garage door. I wasn't sure who it was, so taking Boris with me on the lead, I went downstairs to have a look. It was Pepe with a couple of friends. Pepe pointed to the centre of town and then to me, asking if I would like to join them. I nodded and gestured to them to wait a moment. Keeping Boris with me I dashed upstairs to get my purse and the key. I was still very wary of strangers, even these kind boys, so I decided to take Boris as well under the pretence of taking him for a walk. 'And you'd better behave, Boris.'

They asked me if I was hungry. '*No mucho,*' I replied. As we walked through the humble little streets, everybody stopped to say hello to us. Cuevas de Becerro's square was very lowly in comparison to the elegance of my favourite orange square in Ronda, which had been just one of at least six in the town. It was rather dark, but as we walked nearer I saw that the square was filled with rows of children on wooden chairs. They were watching a cartoon film projected on to the whitewashed wall on the far side of the square. Within five minutes, at least ten more of Pepe's friends had joined us. All of us, including Boris, went on to a small café where we had, of all things, beefburgers!

Feeling rather tired after a long day I soon made my apologies and headed back towards my garage. Unlike the warm hostel where I had been staying for £4 per night for the last few days, this room was cold and musty, and with no bedclothes I was going to have to sleep in my clothes to keep warm. I fumbled my way down the corridor, up the little staircase and into the tiny bathroom where I washed my other shirt in the small cracked sink. Then I felt my way in the darkness back to the unwelcoming lino floor of my room. I opened the door and Boris covered me in licks, greatly relieved that I hadn't left him again.

I unfolded my map of Spain and spread it out on the floor. I found Sotogrande and was horrified to see that Cuevas de Becerro was only a couple of inches away. If it took one week to do a couple of inches, I wouldn't reach Paris until Christmas! Looking at the intricate weave of tiny roads threading their way backwards and forwards across the paper I decided to make a definite route plan using these tiny roads. I unfolded the map of France and placed it carefully above Spain, the Pyrenees overlapping, so that the two maps fitted exactly. With one finger on Paris I lay on the floor with my face level with Cuevas de Becerro and, rather as if I was staring down a billiard cue, estimated a straight line towards my finger on Paris. My straight line would take us across the border at Col du Somport. I folded the map of France until I was left with one long straight edge and lined it up against Cuevas de Becerro and Col du Somport. I drew a light pencil line along its edge, running the length of Spain. I leaned closer and studied the small roads which ran close to my pencil line. Some criss-crossed it and others ran parallel to it or even along the pencil line itself.

Following the path of the pencil line as closely as possible, I marked dots against all the villages on it. Tomorrow I would buy a fluorescent pen to trace the line of the actual roads I would be following. I didn't bother to draw the first basic pencil line across France; it seemed so far away that I didn't even want to think about it.

I had a miserable night with very little sleep and when I did eventually manage to close my eyes, there was a loud knocking at the garage downstairs. Sensing that we were about to leave, Boris insisted on coming too and on the way back, did an enormous pee on a frondy plant. 'Boris, how could you!' I shrieked as the steaming yellow liquid dripped off the green fronds and crept across the floor. There was nothing for me to wash the poor plant with so I made a feeble attempt at chucking a few handfuls of water over its steaming leaves. I found a piece of newspaper and soaked up the remainder.

'Hola' called a voice. It was Pepe. I dashed back to the room, grabbed my things and, with Boris in one hand, flew down the stairs to open the garage door. He started speaking rather fast but I caught the word 'caballo' and followed him towards Dragon's stable.

It was much further than I thought, but at last we came to the shabby buildings which I recognized. I could hear someone shuffling around inside. It was the old man feeding his chickens. Looking at Boris, not at me, he muttered a greeting. I thought I'd better tie Boris up outside so that he wouldn't be a nuisance. I went back inside the poky little building to say hello to Dragon. The old man pointed to the grain he had been feeding to the chickens and then pointed to Dragon.

As Dragon had only just been fed, I wouldn't be able to set off for at least an hour.

'Quieres desayuno?' (Do you want some breakfast?) asked Pepe.

'Muchas gracias,' I replied, suddenly realizing that I felt very hungry after eating not much more than a beefburger the day before. I untied Boris and took him with us.

At that moment I made a conscious decision to have at

least one big meal every day because after only seven days of insufficient nourishment, I was beginning to lose my stamina. I chomped my way through an enormous heap of food and felt acutely embarrassed when Pepe insisted on doing the gentlemanly thing of paying for it all. In Spain, a woman is never allowed to pay for anything, however small, if she is in the company of a man. I had learned my lesson; in future my big meal would always be consumed in private.

Pepe chuckled to himself as I staggered back to Dragon. Desperate to explain my amazing display of early-morning piggery I used the few phrases I had picked up recently. Pepe nodded thoughtfully, not quite sure that he could imagine forcing oneself to eat just in case one didn't get another meal for days.

We arrived and found that the old man had already put Dragon's saddle on and was now struggling to work out how the bitless bridle worked. He watched, fascinated, as I slipped the light bridle over Dragon's ears and buckled the throat lash. Puzzled, the old man pulled on Dragon's right rein. Dragon bent his head round to the right obediently. The old man was impressed. '*Es bueno,*' he exclaimed.

I turned to the old man and asked, '*Cuánto por un noche?*' (How much for one night?)

'*Mil pesetas,*' he replied.

'Five pounds! *Es mucho, Señor.*'

'*Tres cientas,*' he said. The speed of his reply assured me that he had expected me to contest the figure.

I climbed on board and Pepe asked, '*Dónde vas?*' (Where are you heading?)

'Campillos,' I replied, feeling in the pocket of my jeans for the precious letter.

'*No es posible en un día,*' muttered the old man, shaking his head.

Oh dear, this would mean yet another unknown destination. I hated not having anywhere to go. In the hot sunshine it was easy to feel happy and secure trotting alongside the pretty fields as the tiny tarmac road stretched on and on into the distance. The trouble came when the shadows grew long, the animals grew weary and the three of us would begin to plod with slow steps towards the nearest village, searching for somewhere suitable to rest. Sometimes it came, sometimes there was nothing. As the months of trudging from one village to the next went by, my early feelings of happiness and excitement evaporated. It became a matter of survival.

It wasn't difficult to find the road to Campillos; there were only two roads leading out of the village. A sign by the side of the road told me CAMPILLOS 42. As we walked along, I took the map of Spain out of the small saddle-bag to see if there was a village between Cuevas de Becerro and Campillos. There was a small *pueblo*, Teba, 18 kimometres away.

For a long time the road appeared to curve round the back of the mountain but as we drew closer I could see that it went through a deep cutting in the middle.

It was rather daunting riding through that cutting. Dragon and I seemed minute in comparison to the vast sides of white rock, stretching high above us on both sides. I was normally very conscious of the loud clip-clopping of Dragon's hooves on the tarmac but although the air was quite still, there was only the faintest tapping, the squeak of the saddle and Boris' panting to be heard.

On and on we rode in the searing heat, on past the mine at the far end of the cutting and away into the open again. Not a living thing in sight. The heat was so fierce that the shimmer in the distance made it impossible to make out one shape from another.

I was disappointed to find that Teba was nothing more than a cluster of about five houses; there wasn't a single outbuilding between them. There was no point in stopping here as it obviously had nothing to offer us so I rode on a little further towards Campillos. The fields on either side of the road were corn, which produces grain and needs harvesting, so I felt confident there must be a farm not too far away. Most of the fields around us had already been harvested so there should be a good stock of grain for Dragon's supper that evening.

It was another eight kilometres before we eventually came across such a farm and to my utter disappointment it appeared to be deserted. Its huge iron gates were firmly locked, so I couldn't see into the farmyard. I assume it was deserted because the buildings were in very bad repair, there were no tyre marks, and the surrounding grass grew long and uncropped, which most certainly would not have been the case had there been animals inside. Dragon picked his way over the tumbled stones which lay hidden in the long grass as we walked once round the whole building. We were in luck. At the back of the farm there were two goat sheds, one of which had a twenty-foot square enclosure surrounded by a high whitewashed wall. I led Dragon through the wrought-iron gate and untacked him. Although it was such a small area, it was good for him to be loose. A long, wide water trough was built against the high farmyard wall. Stumbling across the hidden stones to look at it I remembered how easily Dragon had coped with them a few minutes earlier.

Fed by a lead pipe, the water running through the trough was cool and clear. I had taken the precaution of bringing a few water-purifying tablets with me, so I filled my blue water bottle and waited while they dissolved. I was dying for a drink, and although the water tasted dreadfully of chlorine, I gulped it down. I went back for Dragon and Boris. It was not good for them to drink too soon after we stopped somewhere, so I usually gave them fifteen minutes to settle down before giving them a drink.

Dragon was so thirsty that he laid back his ears and refused to let Boris have a drink. Much to Dragon's annoyance, I let Boris loose to find his own way to the trough at the far end. He stood on his back legs and stooped down towards the water. He lapped it up for about two minutes and then took one huge leap into the water trough itself. Boris hadn't realized that the water was only three inches deep, nor that the bottom was green and very slippery. The result was Boris landing upside-down in the trough right in front of Dragon's nose. Dragon was amazed; first the dreadful creature had tried to take his water and now he'd stirred it all up so that it was murky.

It was only three o'clock and the sun was still hot so I would have time to wash my shirt and jeans.

I picked my way over the stones back to the enclosure and found Boris waiting at the gate. I let him in and tied it up again.

Dragon came to investigate, wondering whether I had brought him any food. With no clean surface to put down the clean wet clothes I balanced them on one hand while I fished out my octopus clip with the other, then I hooked one end of the octopus clip to the wrought-iron gate and the other end to a thin strip of wood underneath the low roof tiles of the goat shed. The octopus clip made an excellent washing line as it could be stretched to any length. I found that leaving things to dry on rocks or branches left them as filthy as when I'd started. And hanging clothes on bushes snags and tears them and you may well have the added bonus of it being a berry bush, in which case your clothes will be covered in overripe splodges, so beware!

I had no food for Boris so I would have to walk or hitch into Teba to find him some. I tied the gate shut very securely, not wanting a repeat of the Ronda episode. I walked up to the main road and, with my thumb stuck out, set off in the direction of Teba. Presently I heard the soft chug of a car engine.

'A dónde?' the driver called through the open window.

'Teba,' I replied.

The door opened and I stepped inside. Slowly we drove past the first two houses of Teba. We turned left and the road climbed up to an extraordinary rise. On the other side was a mini *pueblo* with four or five shops, a post office and a dear little square, all hidden from view by that small rise in the middle of nowhere.

In the butcher's shop I could only point at things as I hadn't a clue what everything was called. All the women in the shop were staring at this stranger in their midst. I smiled as pleasantly as I could and explained, 'Esta por un perro.' There was hardly any fresh red meat and what little there was seemed rather expensive to use for dog food or was unsuitable because it was dried and spiced. Eventually I bought a chicken for Boris and two *chorizos* (spiced sausages) for me. She chalked up '320' (about £1.50) on the marble counter. I fished the change out of my purse and moved on to the next shop, where I bought a yoghurt, two apples and an orange.

I hitched successfully back to the farm and was greatly

89

relieved to find Dragon and Boris safe in the walled enclosure and the gate still firmly shut. Boris wagged his stump with great enthusiasm as I walked towards them, and licked my hands through the bars as I untied the rope. Other than my clean clothes, which either Dragon or Boris – probably Dragon – had tweaked off the line, everything seemed to be much as I had left it.

I took refuge inside the goat shed while I sorted out the food. The goat shed had a tiled roof which was about eight feet high at the back and sloped down to a height of only three feet at the front to enable the smaller animals such as goats, sheep or pigs to go freely in and out while excluding the larger ones such as horses and cattle, who might bully or squash them. I sat on the edge of an ancient feed trough which had been carved out of a large flat stone. Boris moved in, his enormous snout pushing insistently at the bag. To get rid of him, I pulled out the big white chicken. It still had its head. Boris looked at it rather carefully, wondering whether I really expected him to eat it. Poor Boris was really not very keen on uncooked dead chicken.

There was a large woolly head peering under the low roof at the front of the shed. It was Dragon. I'd brought him an apple, and his lips flapped at the air asking for it. He bit it in half, making a terrific scrunching noise as all the juice foamed out of his mouth. I felt guilty about not being able to give him proper feeds morning and night, but it was very difficult to find proper horse feed unless we were staying at an animal farm.

If a horse isn't doing any work and is just sitting in a field all day, providing there is enough grass it doesn't need anything else to eat. Just like an athlete, a horse needs protein as well as roughage to keep him going when he is using a lot of energy. Dragon had not really been getting as much hard food (corn) as he should during these first couple of weeks and every day I would be eaten up with worry trying to find him some.

I tied the gate behind me and made my way round the high outer wall of the farmyard, trying every door and solid, high gate that I found. They were all firmly locked. I found a tractor trailer on the far side, and wondered whether I might be able to clamber up the high wall if I stood on it. It was rather dangerous but I succeeded in reaching the top of the wall. Before I jumped eight feet down into the farmyard I had a good look to see how I was going to get out again. Fortunately the small door on my right seemed to be locked from the inside with a sliding bolt.

It was a gorgeous place. The wonderful stone buildings were built round a cobbled courtyard with a dilapidated well standing in the middle. The farmhouse ran along one side of the court-yard, twisted vines clinging to a rickety wooden framework nailed to its uneven stone walls. The whitewash had faded to a soft streaky grey, suggesting that it had been deserted for quite some time. I walked across the courtyard towards what looked like a cow shed. The sun felt warm on my back as I walked through the doorway. Inside, the building was com-pletely open with no partitions for the animals. A stone manger ran the length of the far wall, and iron rings were bolted to the wall at regular intervals. One of these rings still had a leather head collar and chain attached to it. It felt hard and desperately in need of some oil.

The manger was empty, of course, but if I was lucky, I thought I might find a couple of feed bins with a handful of corn left. I walked into the small feed room. The cobwebs covering the windows made the room rather dark, but I found the feed bins and raised the heavy lid on the one nearest to me. I dropped it in fright, for it was full of dead rats and mice. I wasn't sure how they had got in there but they obviously hadn't been able to get out again. I opened the second bin more slowly, but to my relief there weren't any more corpses. On the contrary, one side of the bin was a quarter full of grain. I looked around for something to put it in and found a small raffia basket hanging on a horseshoe nailed to the wall. I filled it to the brim, closed the bin and hurried back out into the sunshine again.

Dragon was thrilled to have a few kilos of corn and buried his nose happily into the contents of the raffia basket. Boris appeared from underneath the low roof of the shed. I gave him a pat and crawled under the low roof. To my great annoyance I found that Boris' greedy snout had raided the bag and he'd eaten not only my yoghurt, but the *chorizos* as well. I couldn't be angry with him because I shouldn't have left them there in

91

the first place and I wanted him to have as much energy as possible, but it didn't alter the fact that all I had left to eat was an orange.

Presently I heard a car draw up outside and then voices approaching. It sounded like three or four men and a woman. I stayed put and waited. Boris was watching them through the bars of the wrought-iron gate. His head was low; he was trying to look as frightening as possible. The footsteps stopped. '*Hola*,' said a voice. Boris growled.

'*Sí, uno momento*,' I replied, and like a caged animal at the zoo moved foward out of my lair. I was somewhat taken aback to find that it was the *Guardia Civil*. I had been warned about them; a cross between the police and the army, they can cause a lot of problems for someone like me. I smiled politely. I could see that he wasn't quite sure where to start, so I motioned for him to wait while I went to get my phrase book. '*Solamente un noche*,' I said to the fierce-looking men in starched uniforms staring through the bars – 'Only one night.' One of them leaned closer to have a better look at Dragon. Boris gave a vicious snarl; he must have sensed my nerves and was all set to chew whoever it was that was upsetting me into tiny pieces.

'*Su caballo?*' asked the uniformed man, pointing at Dragon. He withdrew his finger rather sharply as Boris snapped his teeth. He must be asking what every policeman was bound to ask: 'Was it my horse?'

'*Sí, Señor.*'

'*Sus papeles, por favor.*' Papers, papers; yes, in my saddle-bags. I scrambled back under the low roof and rummaged for the precious papers.

While he studied them I flicked through my phrase book to find 'I'm going tomorrow.' '*Voy mañana*,' I said helpfully. One of them grunted.

When they had finished with my papers I put my hand through the bars to retrieve them, just in case Boris took some-one's arm off. I didn't want them to think he was dangerous or they might prevent him from coming with me. Satisfied that I was just a harmless foreigner and bonkers with it, they gave me a short lecture which I didn't understand. Then they touched their caps and picked their way back across the buried stones towards their car. The woman trailed behind, her unsuitable shoes teetering from one solid-looking patch to the next.

I wondered who had told them about me. The only person it could possibly have been was the man who gave me a lift back to the farm from Teba; he must have reported me.

I decided to sleep that night outside on the grass. It was such a lovely warm evening I did not bother to put up the tent. I pegged out the groundsheet so that I wouldn't be lying on the damp grass all night. The darkness came quickly and it wasn't long before I was lying huddled under my Barbour coat with my saddle-bags heaped up on top of me. Boris insisted on lying right next to me, which wasn't very pleasant because the *chorizos* were making him fart. 'That's the last time you have *chorizos* for supper!'

After an hour or so, Dragon stopped eating, plodded over to where Boris and I were lying and bent his knees to lie down. Boris growled in protest. Dragon put his ears flat back and made a face at Boris, who barked in retaliation. Poor Dragon desperately wanted to lie down next to us but Boris felt that Dragon looked after me during the day and it was his job at night. Boris won and Dragon had to go and lie down in the corner. Boris began to get restless and kept moving about, which made him fart again.

I lay flat on my back with my eyes open, looking at the stars. I wasn't frightened with both my animals so close at hand. Dragon had originally belonged to gypsies and they say that Spanish gypsies (*gitanos*) train their horses to attack like guard dogs. I'm not sure I believe it but I liked to imagine it was true.

# SEVEN

# Picadero Hospitality

It was a pleasant ride from Teba to Campillos although every day seemed at least five degrees hotter than the day before. The rolling hills of corn were beginning to give way to olive groves. In the morning we had forded a river and in the lush grass along the banks a young boy was looking after a herd of about twenty brood mares and their foals. Dragon didn't notice them for a while and then let out a shrieking whinny, announcing his arrival to the lovely ladies. They took no notice so Dragon pretended not to either. By the early afternoon I had become so hot that when we at last found a water trough, I put my whole head in. I no longer needed to get off and show Boris the water; he knew all about water troughs now, and as long as Dragon had his right side towards the water trough, Boris could stand on his back legs and have a drink. Dragon spent more time playing with the water than actually drinking it. He would put his head in up to his eyes, blowing bubbles through his nose so that the water didn't flood up his nostrils.

Campillos was quite a large place, and as we rode through the town I kept an eye out for a bank. I tied Dragon to the railing outside and leaving Boris still clipped to the girth buckle, went inside in my leather boots and chaps. I could see a crowd gathering outside, but I didn't need to worry; Boris would keep them all at a safe distance. He was an amazing dog. He would allow people to cluster round, but the second somebody reached out a hand to touch either Dragon or my saddlery, he would give a warning growl and everyone would spring back a few feet. Boris loved to be in charge when I was away. Dragon, on the other hand, was quite happy to go to sleep.

94

We found the picadero of Campillos without any trouble: a small house with a schooling ring in front. A man who was cantering a young grey horse round and round the ring came to an abrupt halt and touched his cap in greeting. Dragon pulled forward, anxious to say hello to the grey. Dragon is a very friendly horse and greatly missed equine company. To be polite, I dismounted and led Dragon up the stony drive.

I took the now rather scrumpled letter out of the pocket of my jeans and handed it to the man. He read the curly hand-written letter and handed it back to me. It read something like this:

> Dear *Picadero*,
> This is a friend of mine. She has travelled from
> Cadiz. Please take care of her and her animals,
> both of which are very noble.
> Your grateful friend,
> *Picadero*, Ronda

He introduced me to his wife and mongol daughter, who were standing arm in arm outside the small house waiting for us. He asked me to wait while he put his horse away and instructed his daughter to give my horse a drink. She smiled and gave Dragon a big pat right on the end of his nose (something most horses absolutely hate). With an unco-ordinated jerk of her arm she asked me to follow her. The water trough was at the far end of the small cow shed. I was slightly worried about how Boris would react to her; I was terrified that he might bite her as she stared right into his eyes only a few inches from his face. I showed her how to stroke his back and she copied by giving Boris rather heavy bangs on his head. I was amazed that dear old Boris seemed to understand.

The *picadero* reappeared and took Dragon from me. I held on to Boris and asked the *picadero*'s wife where I might tie him up. She pointed towards the stable. I led Boris into the small whitewashed building and the *picadero* suggested that I should tie him up in the stall next to Dragon. Loli, the daughter, went over to Dragon and stroked his tail lovingly. Had it been any other horse, she might well have been kicked as Dragon was well stuck in to his corn. He was still a little sweaty so I picked

95

up a handful of straw to rub him down. '*No, no señorita,*' said a voice behind me. I turned to see the *picadero* looking most offended at what I was doing. I realized that I was being rude by not leaving him to look after my horse. Loli put a huge arm round me and led me out of the stable.

The house was built out of stone, rendered with mud and then whitewashed, giving it a bumpy, cock-eyed appearance. Loli took my hand and pulled back the plastic fronds in the doorway for me to walk through into the kitchen. The *picadero*'s wife, like most Spanish women, was dressed in black. From a distance I had thought her to be at least sixty but when I studied her more closely I saw that she couldn't have been much more than forty-five.

Her ample figure rolled towards me and she started to say something, then stopped almost immediately, realizing that I didn't understand a word. But she adapted to sign language very well and asked if I would like to have a wash. I nodded and smiled appreciatively. She said something to Loli who galloped up two steps and through the curtain on the far side of the room. '*Venga, venga!*' she called, waving her arms at me. I waved back thinking she was saying goodbye to me. '*Venga,*' she said more insistently. I jumped up and followed her.

She led me through one room and past a dung-coloured curtain into a smaller room beyond. The walls were painted a sickly green colour, emphasizing the bumpy, mud-rendered walls. A small bed was pushed up against the wall, its ancient horsehair mattress bulging high above the rickety wooden bedframe. A pile of cowbells toppled against a single chair on the far side of the room. A string of garlic hung over the back of the chair, scattering fragments of white peel on the concrete floor. A well-loved rag doll sagged with exhaustion on top of the chest of drawers. Loli's eyes lit up as she followed my gaze. She leapt forward and took the sagging doll by the hair. She offered it to me. I took it with exaggerated admiration. The girl grinned, her tiny eyes sparkling to see her beloved possession the object of such attention.

The girl's mother entered the room carrying a large wash bowl, a clean towel neatly folded over her arm. 'Loli,' she scolded.

'*Nada,*' (It's nothing) I said. I wished I could explain that I enjoyed the girl's childlike happiness.

She rested the bowl in its place on the washstand and sent Loli off to get a bar of soap and a candle. The mother glanced round the room quickly and, as there were no doors in the three-roomed house, drew the faded curtain behind her. When I came back to the kitchen, Loli grabbed my arm to claim me as hers and led me to a chair. I thanked her and then asked the mother if I might go outside and see my horse. '*Mi caballo?*' was all I could say but she understood what I meant and asked Loli to take me.

Dragon was in Heaven, with a deep bed of straw and a manger bulging with alfalfa. The *picadero* had been very brave and given Boris a blanket to lie on. He had given my animals the very best of everything he had and I did my best with the little Spanish I had to thank him accordingly. He beamed with pride. There was still the problem of feeding Boris and I didn't want to ask for food for him because, from what I had seen, the family had little enough for themselves without giving precious meat to strangers. As if reading my mind, the man pointed at Boris saying, '*Comida?*' (food?)

'*Si, esta un problema,*' I replied hopefully.

'*No es problema aquí,*' he said kindly and walked out of the stables to an old lorry parked outside the house.

On the back of the lorry were four or five fifty-gallon drums which stank terribly. He jumped on to the back of the lorry and asked me to pass him the plastic crate which was lying by my feet. He rolled up his sleeve and put his arm inside one of the stinking drums. I then realized it must be pigswill for a moment later he brought his hand out of the barrel holding a few pieces of old meat. They hit the plastic crate with a splat and he put his arm back in the barrel again to look for some more. It was rather a disgusting form of Lucky Dip with equally revolting prizes. '*Muy amable,*' (Very kind) I said over and over again. It was one of the first and most important phrases I had learned.

Boris wolfed down the first mouthful of his meal and was a little hesitant about the second. I can't say I blamed him; the stench was perfectly dreadful.

97

In the kitchen, a single place had been laid on the small table in the middle of the room, and the mother asked me to sit down. The *picadero* walked through and bade me *'Que te aproveches'* (*bon appétit*) before going into the only other bedroom to change. Then his wife brought me a glass of hot milk and a small sponge cake. Having had no supper the night before and only a sandwich and an ice-cream for lunch I felt ravenous and had great difficulty controlling my desire to wolf the whole thing down in one.

Then followed a plate of food for which I had no such desire whatsoever. It was a small, very fatty piece of meat which I didn't recognize at all. Either it was a piece of the animal which is seldom eaten or it was derived from an animal not usually eaten at all. I tried not to let my imagination run away with me and, with Cheltenham Ladies' College training behind me, put it in my mouth and thought of England. When I felt it safe to open my mouth, I complimented the cook on her culinary skills. Possibly a mistake – she promptly produced another piece. With a constant supply of warm milk I was able to gulp down the offending article without too much difficulty. As I ate each plateful, the mother sat quietly on the plastic sofa, her children on either side of her, and watched. As soon as my knife and fork touched the plate, she jumped up and took my plate away, replacing it moments later with greasy peppers and more unidentified objects. There was absolute silence as I shovelled each fork-load into my mouth.

When I had finished and the plates had been cleared away, the *picadero* reappeared through the curtain. Perhaps it was considered rude for the man of the house to watch a visitor eating. He sat down at the table and the two children joined us, then asked me where I had come from. When Loli got up and began to lay the table, I wondered whether I should perhaps leave the room while the family was eating, but they insisted I sat down and had a glass of wine while they ate.

After dinner, I followed the family outside and we sat in a line against the whitewashed walls of the house. They asked me endless questions about England. Is it green? Does it have mountains? Are there lots of people? Are there farms, and cows? Is it hot? Struggling with my appalling Spanish, I did my best to answer.

The *picadero* went inside and reappeared carrying a well-thumbed book and a candle. It was a book written by a friend of his, he said proudly. There were many photographs of horses doing the Spanish Walk, Capriole, Passage and many other trained leaps and jumps. '*Es el picadero de Lucena,*' he announced, and offered to write me a letter of introduction if I was going anywhere near Lucena. Now the mother noticed I was weary and asked if I wanted to go to bed. Loli led the way and her father gave her the candle.

I was asleep in two minutes.

Loli's head appeared round the curtain at 7 a.m. precisely. She cocked her head sideways, wondering if I was still asleep. '*Buenos días,*' I said as brightly as I could. She walked up to the bed and pushed her rag doll at my face, then she patted my head and left the room. She returned moments later carrying my second shirt. It was a lovely surprise. Her mother must have washed it while I was giving Boris his supper. It felt marvellous to wear a clean shirt first thing in the morning. I gathered my belongings together and went through to the kitchen.

Just before nine o'clock I tacked up Dragon and walked him out into the sunshine before clipping Boris on to the girth. The *picadero* had written a note to the *picaderos* of Lucena and La Roda as well, and they all stood waving as I walked out of the gate.

It was another hot day and the countryside was deserted. The fields on either side of the road were no longer of corn, but sunflowers, their huge yellow heads quite still in the shimmering heat. Boris trotted happily alongside, leaning on his lead as usual. Being a male dog, he loved to pee on everything within range. Not easy when you're tied to a horse, but he soon found a way round the problem. He would run ahead of Dragon and lift his leg for the second it took Dragon to catch up; it was jolly funny to watch.

It had been two hours since a car had passed so I thought it was safe to let Boris off his lead for a while. He went dashing off through the sunflowers, making the heads quiver as if an unseen current was flowing through their roots. He reappeared panting. He had completely exhausted himself and trotted from one patch of shade to the next, desperate for some relief from the sun's punishing rays. Dragon had long ago given up bucking and he was now the perfect hack, plodding on and on at just the pace I wanted. Being Andalusian, he held himself with such elegance that I found him effortless to ride. My only problem at the moment was my saddle which I found increasingly uncomfortable. It was much better if I folded a blanket over the seat that the *picadero* had given me, but then it became dreadfully hot. By midday I was sweltering in the heat. I sometimes wished I could ride in shorts but I knew I would get pinched by the saddle and probably terribly sunburned.

By the early afternoon the sunflowers, like us, had begun to droop. I was starting to get worried about finding water for Dragon and Boris. Every now and then I would see a white-washed stone trough in the distance but when we got closer we would find it was broken and cracked.

For a while we took an earthy track which ran along the edge of the field. It was a little easier for Boris because he could walk in the shade of the sunflowers. Tarmac radiates a lot of heat, so I too found it considerably cooler to walk on the soft earth.

We didn't find any water so by the time we reached La Roda all three of us were very tired and wobbly. We walked along the main street, where the women stopped sweeping and the old men pushed back their caps and sucked a little harder on their tobacco as they stood and watched us jog past. I was getting used to it and even Boris no longer took any notice of the sinister figures hanging in the shadows, watching.

The whole *pueblo* seemed to be built along one long street. Neat rows of whitewashed houses sat arm in arm with the small shops; the *panadería* (bakery), *carnicería* (butcher), *ferretería* (ironmonger) on one side and the *correos* (post office) and *farmacia* (chemist) on the other. I stopped at the post office, unclipped Dragon's head-collar rope from underneath his chin and tied him up to the railing. I stomped into the tiny room and the line of women waiting in front of the window jumped back in surprise. I smiled and the women looked at each other and shuffled a bit. One of them smiled back. I took a step forward and they parted, anxious not to upset the strange beast in their midst. I wanted to say 'You first', but didn't know how to so I said, '*Gracias*,' instead and took my place at the back of the queue. The women resumed their chatter, but a little more cautiously than before and with one eye on me. At last it was my turn, and the woman before me waited to one side, dying to know what this foreigner wanted. I held the letter up to the window and asked, '*Dónde está el picadero, por favor?*'

The woman leaned round in her chair and pointed behind her. '*Cuarenta metros a la derecha*,' she replied. They all watched me leave and I smiled.

As we set off down the road, there was a lovely dark bay coming down behind us. The rider touched his cap and I waited for him to catch up with us. With such a tremendous neck and beautiful long mane, the horse had to be a stallion. When he was almost level, I said, '*Buenos días*.'

He nodded and smiled.

'*Quiero el picadero, por favor?*'

'*Es me padre.*' (It's my father) he replied. He rode up alongside us.

He stopped outside a large door, leaned out of the saddle and gave it three loud bangs with his stick. The great door swung open and that familiar smell of horse wafted out to meet us, breathing new life into Dragon. A large, red-faced man walked towards us and patted his son on the shoulder.

'*Esta Senorita Ingles monta caballo de Algeciras.*'

'*Sí?*' said the father, his eyes widening. '*Como te llamas?*' (What is your name?) he asked.

'Belinda.'

'*Que bonita.*'

In Spain all girls must have Maria (Mary) included somewhere in their name, so 'Belinda' must sound refreshing to Spanish ears. By law, the boys must be named after a saint, resulting in vast numbers of men with the same name, especially the more popular ones such as Pedro (Peter), Juan (John), Miguel (Michael) and Carlos (Charles). The only advantage is that one rarely calls someone by the wrong name.

Dragon had a good-sized stall next to the bay stallion. I was

101

surprised to see that the horses' beds were deep litter – just the droppings, not the wet straw, are taken out of the beds daily and clean straw is put on top so that the bed remains dry on top but becomes thicker and more solid as the well-rotted straw underneath becomes more tightly packed. This gives off a tremendous amount of heat which, providing the animal doesn't stir it up, makes a nice warm bed for ponies in the cold English winter, but it seemed strange in the Spanish heat. Still, Dragon seemed blissfully happy on the top of his mountain, up to his eyes in the alfalfa which billowed out of his manger. I gave Boris a drink, put the blanket on the floor in a corner and tied him up. He was given dog nuts for his supper.

The *picadero* and his son showed me their horses. The barn we were standing in served as a garage, bar and general meeting-place for the locals, leaving just enough room for five horses including Dragon and the bay stallion. We went through to a further barn at the back where the *picadero* housed another eight horses. None of them was as grand as the bay stallion, but with their tumbling manes and tails they still looked quite impressive. The horses stood quietly in rows with only a single bar to act as a partition between each stall. The *picadero* reached a dappled grey bottom and gave it a friendly pat. 'Caballo!' he said, and the horse moved over, allowing him to slide up alongside and give it a pat on its neck. '*Esto es un caballo muy noble,*' he said as he slid past the horse into the aisle. I was quite surprised when the *picadero* told me they were all '*semental*' (stallions), because in England we only keep the very best animals as stallions and those that are kept 'entire' are treated with great care; they can be unruly beasts if not kept under an experienced hand. One would certainly never dream of keeping them in close proximity to each other and yet these stallions were just as well behaved as any English geldings. In fact I don't think I had seen a gelding since I left Sotogrande; they had all been entire or '*entero*', which is a less polite Spanish word for an uncastrated horse.

As we walked back towards the first barn where Dragon was I heard a young woman's voice bubbling away above the dull speech of the old grooms. The *picadero* heard it too and his face lit up. '*Ah, Maria, venga aquí, tengo una amiga.*' There was a clack of fine shoes as the voice came towards us. A pretty young woman appeared round the corner, her dark eyes full of happiness, fine tanned skin in beautiful contrast to her flowery pink dress. The *picadero* introduced her as his daughter: '*Esta es mi niña, Maria.*' He went on to explain where I had come from and what I was doing there. Her dark eyes widened. To a Spanish woman it was incredible for a female to sit on a horse and they would certainly never dream of going anywhere alone; to do both together was incomprehensible. Women were for cooking and making babies, nothing more.

The *picadero* asked me if I would like to have a wash and something to eat. I nodded gratefully and followed Maria.

She stopped outside an impressive, fortress-like house and took a large key out of her handbag. The house felt very new and unlived-in. It was so clean and tidy that I felt thoroughly out of place standing in her immaculate modern kitchen in my filthy jeans and cowboy boots while she floated around in a pretty summer dress making coffee. She was not much older than me and although we didn't really understand each other, we smiled and chatted, using the few words common to both of us. When we had finished our coffee she handed me two pink towels and a flannel out of the warm airing cupboard. Holding them reminded me of home and I realized that after only two weeks I was living on the bottom line as far as soap and soft towels were concerned. My life now revolved round the bare essentials; of necessity, or I was never going to make it.

I sank into the bath and enjoyed a long soak in the warmth of my old world. Just for a moment, sleeping in goat sheds and washing in water troughs seemed miles away. I stepped out of the bath on to the white cotton bath mat which sat comfortably on the expensive tiles. There was a clean sink with a large mirror. I dried my hair, still dreaming. There was a knock at the door. 'Belinda?' It was Maria.

'*Si, uno momento.*' I wrapped myself in the large pink towel and opened the door.

She asked me if I would like to put my clothes in the washing machine. I would! I picked up the pile of clothes which I had

103

cast off like an old snakeskin in the corner of the bathroom. I was just wondering whether Maria realized that I had no other clothes when she reappeared carrying a pretty summer dress, a cardigan and a pair of sandals for me to wear.

I found Maria downstairs cooking lunch. The Spanish tend to eat very late. It varies from one family to another, but lunch can be at anything from two o'clock to five o'clock and dinner sometimes as late as half-past eleven. She produced some fried peppers, pork and the usual quantity of bread. Using my dictionary, I was able to ask her a little more about herself. She told me that until recently she had lived in the family house with her five brothers but eight months ago she had married a wealthy man from Seville and moved into this house. I asked her how she had met him, as it was unusual in these small country communities for a girl to marry someone outside her home town. She explained that he had been working in the bank in La Roda for three years and was then transferred to Seville. Was I married? I smiled and shook my head. A *novio* (boyfriend) perhaps? I told her about Michael. 'So you will marry him?' she said.

'I don't know.'

She looked at me quizzically. '*En España*,' she said, 'all the girls marry their boyfriends.' Then she added thoughtfully, 'How else would they have a house, a husband and lots of babies?'

I couldn't explain the answer to a Spaniard. We laughed and cleared away the plates.

The next morning we set off for Lucena at about ten. Despite his good rest, Dragon felt a little weary. At first, Boris was his usual self, padding along beside us, happy to be coming too. But as the temperature rose I could see him beginning to suffer from its fierce rays. I got off and clipped him on to the other side of Dragon so that he would be in the shade. I tilted my hat against the sun and rode on.

This was the part of the day I dreaded. The half-way mark; when the sun was at its hottest, all three of us had lost our early morning spark and there was nothing to do except trudge on and on into the distance, a distance which never seemed any closer, any brighter, just a road disappearing into forever. Dragon seemed to be able to switch off but Boris found the intense heat difficult to cope with. I had music to listen to which did break the monotony of it all, and there were always the kilometre stones to look out for every ten minutes or so, depending on whether we were walking or trotting.

Walking pace was five kilometres an hour, trotting seven kilometres an hour and cantering ten to twelve kilometres an hour, but I found that cantering took far more out of the horse than it was worth, even for short distances. Once Dragon was properly fit, I would aim at a more or less steady trot because he could sustain it for long periods of time and a slow trot seemed to minimize the bounce of the saddle-bags.

Olive trees surrounded us on either side, their small twisted trunks reaching out of the harrowed earth. Although there was hardly a breath of wind, the cornfields had seemed to breathe and sigh as we rode past, but these ancient olive trees were haggard and lifeless in comparison. They stood quite still, row after row, mile upon mile in the shimmering dust.

The surrounding hills were closing in and we had a steep climb before we arrived in Lucena. Riding down the main street I didn't feel the apprehension that I had felt only a few days ago. I rode up to a well-populated bar and without getting off my horse, asked where I might find the *picadero*. Various men all started shouting directions and waving their arms. One stepped forward and walked right up to us, offering to show me the way. The others fell silent and went back to their sherry. The old men leaned forward on their sticks and peered at us through old, uncomprehending eyes. The man asked me where I had come from and when I told him he gave a low whistle of amazement. I found it very satisfying that we had now come far enough for it to be considered a long way. Suddenly people were beginning to take me seriously.

We came to a halt outside a high, solid metal gate. It was painted a dull grey. The man rang a bell on the right-hand side and we waited. It reminded me of the bullring as we stood there in anticipation, listening to the sound of hooves on the dust, the horsey smells filling our nostrils. It sounded as though

105

someone inside was cantering a horse in a circle; perhaps there was a schooling ring? Then the cantering stopped and the hoofbeats came towards us. There was a thud as the rider jumped off to open the gate. '*Hola?*' said a man's voice.

'*Soy Paco,*' replied my companion. A greased bolt slid back and the door opened. The man holding the horse looked at me and touched his cap. '*Esta señorita . . .*' Dragon surged forward before he could explain further.

Half an hour later, Dragon was in a good-sized stable and Boris was tied up in the tack room making eyes at a large Alsatian who prowled round him. The *picadero* was showing me round his horses. It seemed that the further I ventured into this wonderful country, the more impressive the horses became. The *picadero*, another Pepe, opened the next door and a very grand bay stallion stood before us. I asked how old it was and found that although it was only three, it was already doing some quite advanced dressage or '*doma*'. The Spanish horses look rather like the horses one sees in Renaissance paintings and are considerably stronger than their English counterparts, with their powerful limbs and long flowing manes. '*Es muy noble,*' said Pepe as he went up behind the stallion and pulled its tail. A figure stood in the doorway and Pepe introduced Carlos, his brother.

The tour of the stables over, the three of us went through a small door at the back of the stables to a tiny bar opposite, hung with photographs of horses dipping and swerving to avoid the bull's horns. Pepe followed my gaze and pointed to one in particular of a small boy riding a very tall horse performing the Spanish Walk, front leg thrown right out in front, chin on its chest. '*Es mí,*' said Pepe, proudly pointing to himself, '*Siete años.*' For a boy of seven years old it was a quite a feat, especially in front of thousands of people. There was no bull in the photograph so I asked '*El toro?*' and he explained that it was the parade before the bullfight in Madrid.

Pepe and Carlos sat comfortably on the rickety bar stools like a pair of cowboys; one foot on the stool and the other resting on the tiled floor. My legs were too short so I stood next to the bar and rested my elbow on the ridiculously high stool.

We went back to the stables to bed the horses down for the night. Señor Porras senior, the famous old *picadero*, came out to meet us. Carlos introduced him as his father and the woman standing beside him as Anna, Pepe's wife. Anna kindly invited me to stay in their house. I thanked her and went to help Pepe put down the straw beds for the horses.

Pepe and his wife lived on the other side of Lucena, so the three of us climbed into their tiny Fiat and spluttered off down the street. It made me feel much more at home with my surroundings being on the inside of one of these amazing contraptions for a change. The bubble car heaved its way up and down the narrow streets, beeping at anyone who crossed its path, almost sighing with relief as it free-wheeled down the ramp of the underground car park below the block where Pepe and Anna Maria lived.

We walked up a grubby staircase to the third floor. Pepe stopped outside a wooden door with a metal plate saying 'Pepe Blanxart de Porras'. The door opened to reveal a child's beaming face. Pepe introduced me to his two children: Alfonso, aged seven, who was still swinging on the door handle in shyness, and Rosanna, aged nine, who stepped boldly forward to say hello. She had long blonde hair, very unusual for a Spaniard.

The flat had three small rooms so I wondered where they were going to put me for the night. Anna Maria swept the homework books aside and put a glass of hot milk in front of me. The children had lots of questions to ask and I was interested to discover that I found them far easier to understand than adults. A child has a much smaller vocabulary and uses basic language. If I didn't understand a word, he would automatically use another simple word until I understood. When I didn't understand adults, they would try and explain what they meant rather than changing just the one key word.

After supper, Pepe and Anna Maria took me into the centre of Lucena. Spanish towns come alive after dark. The shops open, cafés buzz and the shouts of happy children fill the warm evening air. I noticed how clean all the streets seemed to be; not a piece of litter in sight. The Spanish are very gregarious by nature and we saw people gathered in ever-increasing

107

numbers as we neared the central square. We went into a large and rather elegant building where groups of old men sat in leather chairs in the vast rooms. This was the *casino* (the term used by Spaniards to describe the men's club).

Pepe handed Anna Maria and me a glass of fino each, then a large man rolled towards us and engulfed Pepe in a bear grip. I was thrilled to find that the man's daughter Elisa spoke English.

Through Elisa I told them all about my journey, and in turn I could answer their questions. It was getting late and time to go home, but before we left, Elisa invited me for lunch the following day.

I was happy to give Dragon and Boris a quiet day's rest with plenty of good food so I watched Pepe and Carlos schooling the young stallions for a couple of hours before Elisa arrived. I sat on the wooden bench in the makeshift gallery above the indoor school and absorbed the amazing elevation and grace of the animals who danced and pirouetted before me. Pepe handed the dappled grey he had been working to the old groom who promptly produced the three-year-old bay stallion I had been so impressed with the previous evening. I was enthralled as this young animal performed canter pirouettes, Spanish Walk and Piaffer, where the horse springs lightly from one foot to the other in an elevated trot on the spot. Elisa arrived at midday, and Pepe and Carlos promised to take care of my animals for me while I was away.

We drove out of Lucena and into the rolling hills. With Lucena behind us, I saw olive trees everywhere I looked. Their well-ordered lines stretched into the distance as far as the horizon where they blended together to form a mass of dull green. Over the next rise a large white house came into view. We'd be there in about five minutes, said Elisa. Moments later we bounced off the road and down a bumpy track. I could see the dust flying out behind us as we roared through the silent olives in Elisa's ancient station wagon.

It was almost one o'clock and the heat shimmered above the dry, cracked earth. A dog came out to meet us from its kennel under a huge fig tree. The poor dog could only jump up and down and yelp while rushing backwards and forwards in an arc, straining desperately against its rusty old chain. Surprisingly, Elisa took no notice of it. I went over to it and looked at Elisa, expecting her to warn me if it was fierce. The dog was delighted and lay on its back with its legs in the air, waiting for a tickle. The next second it was up, dashing about again. I patted it once more and then followed Elisa into the house.

As we stood in the cool hallway I could hear happy shouts coming from the garden door at the far end. Elisa beckoned me to follow. 'Mama,' she called, and almost immediately the shouting stopped and a row of heads appeared above the side of the pool. Elisa introduced me to everyone.

'Are they all your brothers and sisters?' I asked incredulously as I met Manolo, 24, Carmen, 22, Luis, 20, Paco, 19, Juan Angel, 17, Pepe, 16, Marie Dolores, 14 and Marie Araceli, 12. At 23 Elisa was the eldest girl.

She laughed and said, 'Everyone has lots of children in Spain.'

After a delicious lunch we sat in the shade on the grass while the boys played a rather rough and noisy game in the pool. Carmen was studying English at a college in Malaga and seemed very pleased to speak English with me as all her teachers were Spanish. After a while they made an attempt to improve my Spanish. While they were trying to explain the basic grammar to me, we discovered that they found it virtually impossible to say the word 'adverb'. They just couldn't pronounce the 'v' straight after the 'd' which resulted in a very poor 'adwearb'. We all collapsed into a heap laughing and Marie Araceli insisted that I try to get her brothers to say it. The boys found it just as difficult and pulled Marie Araceli into the pool.

Elisa suggested that we go for a dip in the pool. When I asked whether she had a bikini I could borrow, I was amazed to hear that her father didn't allow the girls to wear bikinis in front of their brothers. She went on to say that it was only in the last five years that she and her sisters had been allowed to swim in the pool at all. My first impression had been one of a modern European family, but it seemed that in Lucena old traditions would take a little longer to dissolve.

\*

I pressed the rider-height buzzer at the side of the Porrases' yard door. There was a short pause before little Alfonso heaved it open. He took my hand and smiled up at me proudly as we walked through the dusty yard towards the stables. As I went into the tack room, I was bombarded by a large black body, shaking with happiness. Boris held my wrist in his teeth, 'piano-biting', as the guard dog man called it; scrunching my arm in his teeth little by little up to my elbow and back. Alfonso ran out of the tack room in fright; he thought Boris was attacking me.

I went over to Dragon's stable. The door was so high that I had to balance on the brickwork in order to peer over the top. The familiar brown bottom was facing in my direction. He had pulled most of his bedding out from under the manger and had obviously had a wonderful day picking his way through it for any delicious morsels of spilled oats that it had to offer. He tilted his head slightly, pretending not to notice me, his nose sifting through the straw with slightly more urgency just in case I was about to take it away or tie him up. I tied him up. I went round his feet, looking at his shoes. They were getting rather thin and I couldn't be sure how long it would be before I came across another *picadero*, so it was probably best to try and have him shod here in Lucena.

The blacksmith didn't have a telephone, of course, so it was a matter of doing the rounds in all the local bars until we finally came across him. The procedure seemed to be that one bought the bent old man four or five sherries and only then did one broach the subject. He sucked his teeth and shook his head. He looked at me and grumbled under his breath. I smiled hopefully and patted him on the shoulder, the old man lost his balance slightly and mumbled again. Pepe winked at me and I breathed a sigh of relief. It cost us another round of sherries before we could part good friends.

The next morning we set out to take Dragon to the black-smith's shop. Despite his wonderful shine, I was sorry to admit that Dragon looked rather small and insignificant next to Carlos' fabulous beast. We walked towards the gate. Alfonso shouted to us to let him open it. As we stood waiting, Dragon did his best to make up for his size by leaping four feet in the air in a

I didn't realize what I'd let myself in for

Dragon and Boris, my faithful
friends and companions, whom
I have to thank for everything

Feeding time, but water wasn't
always available. My
full-length Barbour doubled as
a sleeping bag

Setting off. After three days I abandoned three-quarters of my luggage

Asking directions in Bailoo while Boris rests in Dragon's shade

Dragon and I found the small towns a welcome diversion

The open road. Dragon's ears are back, listening to the lorry

A well-earned rest

This shady wood made a pleasant change from the hot tarmac

I often slept with the animals in dusty old barns and out-houses

Swimming in a river in the Pyrenees – a wonderful escape from the heat

Dragon testing a new set of shoes at the military fort in Jaca

Cutting corners

Chateau Reglier – a haven on the road to Paris

Heavy traffic on the Champs Elysées

A drink to celebrate our arrival

Journey's end

spectacular buck. The large stallion glared at him, amazed by his strange behaviour. Seeing that the gate was now open, Dragon blinked a large brown eye and surged forward in a very rude fashion. I tried to explain to Carlos that he was rather excited as he hadn't been out of his stable yesterday. Luckily Carlos was smiling. Alfonso thought it was wonderful. All his father's horses were so well trained that they never did things like that.

The old blacksmith gave Dragon a hearty slap on the shoulder and ran a hand down his foreleg before picking up his hoof. He cast an eye over each hoof in turn before getting to work. English blacksmiths work on their own, but the Spanish have an assistant to hold the foot for them while they work, in addition to at least five ancient bystanders. The old blacksmith shuffled off to get his pincers. He tweaked the nails all the way round to ease the nailheads straight before wrenching the worn shoe off the hoof. He cleaned the sole and began to cut back the foot. '*No mucho,*' I said, anxiously. When an old set of shoes is removed, it is normal practice to cut back the foot before the new set is nailed on. But as Dragon was doing so much road work his shoes had worn out very quickly. His hooves had not had a chance to grow and were therefore quite short enough already.

I had asked the blacksmith to leave the foot with the wire cut until last as I suspected the Dragon might be rather badly behaved with it. The man holding Dragon's head wasn't concentrating when the assistant put his hand on the tender back foot and so when Dragon jumped forward in fright, he trod on the man's foot. '*Caballo!*' shouted the blacksmith in a gruff voice. Dragon stood still, his eyes twitching nervously, wondering which side the assistant would approach from. I patted Dragon on the neck and talked to him but again he leapt forward when the assistant tried to pick up his sore foot. The bystanders stopped their conversation to watch the little drama; things were looking up this morning.

The blacksmith's apprentice stepped in and took over. He gripped Dragon's foot very hard but after a valiant attempt he too was shaken off. They were getting angry and short-tempered and called for some rope. This was exactly what I had

111

hoped to avoid; if you give a horse a fight and start tying it up you are likely to have problems for as long as the horse's memory lasts, which is usually a very long time. I desperately tried to explain to Carlos, who persuaded the blacksmith to let me have a go before they tied up his feet. It's not women's work,' I could hear them say.

Eventually they agreed. Time was on my side, because while they had been messing about with ropes I had been calming Dragon down, so when I stroked his bottom and slid my hand down his leg he stayed relaxed. When I reached his fetlock I could feel him tense so I left it alone and started from the top again. This time he was better and allowed me to pick it up. The blacksmith approached and Dragon waved his foot about, so I kept a firm but relaxed hold with my left hand and stroked his bottom with my right. Once he had relaxed, I moved his foot about a bit and then passed it back to the assistant without Dragon noticing. Carlos smiled, obviously amused.

I handed a 2000-peseta note to the blacksmith and climbed on board, praying that Dragon would still be sound. As we rode home, Carlos commented on my American army saddle; was it comfortable? I scrumpled up my face and pointed to my bottom and then, standing up in my stirrups, knocked my fist against the hard seat. He laughed and sank into the comfortable folds of sheepskin on his own Spanish saddle. '*Sí, es mejor,*' I replied.

I untacked Dragon and received a wet welcome from Boris as I hung the saddle and bridle back on the hooks. Carlos came in with a saddle under his arm. He dumped it rather heavily on the saddle-horse in the middle of the room and patted the dust off it with his cap. It took him five minutes to explain that I could borrow this old Spanish saddle and leave mine with them if I wanted to. The stitching was rotten and the leather parched and dry, but with a little saddle soap it would be fine – the Spanish never oil their leather. There were various small rings which would be useful for hanging things, and being so broad it should be immensely comfortable. I thanked Carlos and offered to clean it with my saddle soap.

An hour and a half later, the dusty old saddle had been transformed. All that remained to be done was the stitching.

Carlos' father had given me the name of a saddler in Baena, my next stop, who would be able to patch it up for me. So now that Dragon had been reshod and my equipment was in good order, I was ready to move on.

# EIGHT

# The Heat of the Day

I RODE OUT of the Porrases' yard on my new saddle at about 6 a.m. Pepe had shown me how to find the road to Baena in the car so although it was still dark I found it quite easily. I had decided to leave so early as an experiment to see how much easier it would be to ride in the cool of the morning, because in the last few days Boris had been finding it difficult to cope with the heat. It was surprising just how cold it was at that hour, but there was no doubt that both Dragon and Boris were more comfortable.

I began to feel worried as we plodded further and further on into the silent blackness of the countryside with no light attached to either myself or Dragon. With the comforting lights of Lucena now far behind us, I was acutely aware of the danger of oncoming traffic; my ears were straining for the sound of an engine so that I would be able to leap up the bank for safety. Despite the blackness Dragon appeared to have no difficulty in looking where he was going. I couldn't see the kilometre stones so I had no idea how fast we were going but we reached a little place called Cabra, which I knew was ten kilometres from Lucena, just before half-past seven. It was a new experience for me to see one of these little country towns starting its day. We passed three or four mules with empty panniers, their owners sitting sideways across their backs. A group of women chattered away as they washed the pavement outside their line of houses. One woman was splashing water out of a bucket over the dirt road in front of her house to keep down the dust. We passed women dusting the outside walls of their houses and even the orange trees which grew along the pavement!

It was getting lighter so I didn't need to worry about the

114

traffic any more. I got my Walkman out of the small saddle-bag and listened to Vivaldi's 'The Four Seasons' for a while. With the early morning sun warming up the world, the rhythm of my horse through a comfortable saddle and a happy dog trotting alongside, life was good. With nothing but olive trees to look at I studied every twist and curl of their trunks with interest as we passed them one by one.

The whitewashed houses of Baena covered the top of the hill like a blanket of snow in contrast to the changing browns of the hillside, streaked with the dull green lines of the olive trees which engraved the surrounding countryside.

We rode in at a gentle walk. I was lucky; the first person I asked was able to direct me to Señor Enrique Luque Triguero. His shop was on a busy corner in the centre of Baena. A young boy understood my predicament and, as if by telepathy, leapt across the road to hammer at the saddler's door. A short fat man rolled across the road to meet us, and I handed him the letter from Señor Porras. He fumbled in his grubby jacket pocket for his glasses. He wound them round his ears, then slowly and carefully read the letter out loud. Satisfied, he shook my hand and pointed to a side turn behind me. I followed him up the long hill, feeling rather worried as his face grew redder and redder with the exertion. At the top of the hill was a vast water trough like a swimming pool with about eight pipes to feed it. The old man rested on the stone step of the trough while the animals drank. Dragon was being most unfair, making horrible faces at Boris every time he tried to put his front feet on the side of the trough in order to drink. When they'd finished, we followed the man behind the houses.

Dragon was going to have to share his bed with four goats and some chickens. The owner of the stable brought some clean straw and a bowl of oats from the loft above. One of the chickens perched on the edge of Dragon's food bin. Dragon took a swipe at it with the end of his nose, oats spilling from his mouth onto the floor. Hearing the oats sprinkling into the straw, chickens appeared from nowhere, eagerly pecking and chattering at their good fortune. The goats cowered in a corner of the stable, not quite sure what this terrifying creature would do next.

115

Boris' bed was just as far from the saddler's shop in the opposite direction. By the time the saddler and I arrived back at the shop, I was exhausted, but happy in the knowledge that both my animals were comfortable and well fed. My saddle suddenly seemed to weigh a ton as I dumped it wearily on the saddler's workbench. He fished out his glasses and cast an experienced eye over it. He rubbed the grey bristles on his chin and tugged at the girth straps held in place by rotten stitching. He pored over the saddle like a grizzly bear, but at last his face lit up. Then he patted me warmly on the back, ushering me out of the back of the shop and into the house for his wife to look after me.

I must have been very tired because I hardly remember anything about that evening apart from shovelling down a bowl of greasy soup and a few slices of *chorizo* and taking a cold bath. I slept in the daughters' bedroom at the top of the house. It was a boiling hot night and the tiny windows did little to lower the temperature.

I must have drifted off eventually because I felt someone tugging at my arm and when I opened my eyes I found it was four o'clock already. I was surprised to find my clothes clean and folded on my chair. It made a wonderful change to pull on a clean pair of trousers. Still half asleep, I made my way down to the kitchen. I was rather embarrassed to find that the whole family had got up to say goodbye to me. I thanked the saddler's wife for washing my clothes. Only in a hot, dry climate like this could one dry a pair of jeans in such a short length of time.

When I was ready, the saddler and his family led me into the shop. My saddle was propped up on the pitted surface of the workbench. He'd done more than just repair the stitching; he'd managed to find a thick piece of sheepskin for the seat. '*Mucho mas còmodo*,' he said proudly, pressing his fat fingers into the thick fur. The saddle had been in a very poor condition so he must have spent hours on it. He reached over the workbench and lifted a smart red and yellow head collar from his chair. He handed it to me and seemed very pleased when I noted the '*Colores de España*'. The previous afternoon I had bought a big torch which the saddler had mounted on to Dragon's crupper. I had taped some red tinted plastic over the light, so now that it could be permanently fixed on to Dragon's bottom, I had a

116

large and very effective rear light. I said goodbye to the saddler's wife and two daughters and then went with the saddler to pick up Boris who had spent the night in his curing barn.

Hearing our voices, Boris strained against his chain in anticipation, the rusty links groaning. It was still dark. The old saddler fished in his pocket for the key. My heavy saddle resting on my hip, I held the torch attached to the crupper out in front of us as we entered the barn. Boris' feet skittered against the dusty floor as his black body shook with excitement.

There seemed no end to these people's thoughtfulness and kindness. The couple who owned the stable, or should I say 'room', where Dragon had stayed the night were fully dressed and waiting for us. They led us quietly through their tiny cottage and into Dragon's 'room'. It was quite an amusing sight to see him sitting in the middle, the chickens roosting in a line along the manger and the nervous goats still cowering in their corner. He blinked his eyes, put out his front legs and pulled himself to his feet. He shook himself and then, tucking his chin on to his chest, he pointed a hind foot right out behind him like a ballet dancer and enjoyed a momentary stretch.

With everyone anxious to help, tacking up took no time at all. I threaded Dragon's black tail through the crupper and they all admired the new rear light. The saddler glowed with pride.

Once Boris was clipped on there was nothing left to do except to say thank you as best I could in my poor but ever-improving Spanish. Having already given the saddler something for all his kindness, I pressed 200-pesetas into the hand of the woman who had given Dragon somewhere to stay. She protested but I quickly mounted Dragon so that she couldn't give it back.

I found it sad, always having to leave friendly, smiling faces and ride off in search of others, never quite knowing what I might find. Would there be a stable, even a courtyard for Dragon? If there were no animals at all then where would I find food for him? Would there be someone I could trust to look after us? I always felt the same mixture of uncertainty and a sense of loss as I rode out of each village.

It was only five o'clock in the morning and still very dark. The road to Porcuna was narrow and winding which made my progress rather slow because although I now had a rear light, I could not find a way of fixing a similar torch to the front. I had bought a much smaller bicycle torch which could be attached to Dragon's breastplate but as it did not give much light, I could only travel at a walk, carefully following the ragged edge of the tarmac.

Time seemed to drag terribly as I waited for the wisps of the daylight to pierce my boring, dark world. I felt as if the three of us were walking a treadmill inside a large black box. It wasn't until about six o'clock that the first rays of light streaked the sky ahead of us, outlining the shape of a large hill. At last it was just light enough for me to see the new countryside. The rolling hills of the previous day had changed overnight into an undulating mass of hillocks.

It was while I was studying these unusually shaped hillocks, which almost seemed to be carved out of the earth, that I noticed three or four fine plumes of smoke curling upwards from some a little further on. It took us at least ten minutes to come level with them and during that time I was most puzzled as to what they might be. Now that I could see them properly, I was surprised to find that the hillocks producing the smoke seemed to have had a slice cut out of them, and what could almost have been a door set into each earthy wall. Surely they couldn't be houses? I thought to myself, and yet I could think of no other possible explanation. A little further on, we came to a few more little wisps of smoke emanating from the humps. This time, however, my questions were answered, for stacked neatly outside what I had previously supposed to be a door was a large pile of wood. I had spent the last few hours feeling quite safe in the knowledge that I was miles from anyone or anything, but for all I knew we might have been riding alongside these inhabited humps all the way. The thought of those strange dwellings bothered me all the way to Porcuna.

It was 37 kilometres from Baena to Porcuna so Dragon and Boris were feeling quite weary. We rounded a bend and I suddenly became aware of the incredible beauty and tranquillity which surrounded us. A field of bright yellow sunflowers fell away to our left, their beaming faces framed by three fir trees which grew alongside the road. On our right, a man was

118

trudging slowly behind two mules as they plodded up and down a small field ploughing one furrow at a time. He eased the mules to a standstill and rolled a cigarette as he watched us go by. I waved and he gave a nod in reply.

The little road seemed to be taking us into Porcuna through the backstreets of the town. A woman was dusting her front door. I called to her and she sighed, turning her grossly fat body to face me, her pudgy hands resting arrogantly on her hips. *'El picadero?'* I asked without too much hope. She pointed further up the town and returned to her door. At least I now knew that the *picadero* existed.

Once I'd found his house, the *picadero* himself was out, and I waited nearly seven hours for his return. He arrived, to my relief, with a friendly-looking chap in tow, and they helped me carry my saddle into the tack room. They seemed fascinated by my weird and wonderful variety of equipment, especially my leather chaps. Spanish chaps are beautifully cut and very ornate but are really nothing more than an elaborate piece of leather down the outside of the rider's leg, offering no protection to the inside whatsoever. The Spanish only wear them when they are parading with their horses at the local *feria* (fair), whereas mine were like those of an American cowboy, wrapping themselves round my whole leg and offering real protection. The *picadero*'s friend was so impressed with this design that he asked me what time I would be leaving so that he could come and take a pattern of them in the morning.

I was rather lazy about getting up at the boarding-house the *picadero* found for me, and didn't reach the stables until it was almost five o'clock in the morning. I was amazed to find the *picadero*'s friend waiting for me standing on the wall in full feria dress, complete with Spanish chaps and sombrero, brown paper and scissors in hand. I had completely forgotten that he was coming.

Once he'd finished I climbed on board and asked him which road I wanted for Andujar, but he waved his hand and jumped into his car as an escort. This really was too kind.

I followed the little car through the sleepy streets of Porcuna until we reached a signpost saying 'ANDUJAR 30'. He stopped the car and waved his arm in the direction of the signpost. I stopped Dragon level with his window and thanked him for his help. He pointed out a small house which sat on the crossroads: '*Casa del picadero*,' he said. I urged Dragon forward and waved goodbye to yet another friendly face. As we clip-clopped quietly past the *picadero*'s house, I wondered whether he heard us pass. He'd said he would be listening.

We spent the next night in Andujar. From there we would follow the main road to Madrid for 130 kilometres until we reached Valdepeñas where we would cut across towards the border using the small country roads again. Dragon was still not very good in traffic so I didn't relish the thought of such a busy road, but with the Sierra Madrona mountains cutting across our path we had no alternative.

As I was tacking up Dragon, the *picadero* who had kept him overnight arrived to tell me that a friend of his with a cake shop was expecting me in Bailen. He handed me the address and then, with a beaming smile, produced a big ham sandwich wrapped in a paper bag. I thanked him very much and popped it in my saddle-bag. It made such a difference to have something decent to eat on the way.

'MADRID 324' said the signpost. At last we seemed to be getting somewhere. I made Dragon stand for a moment while I put Boris on a slightly longer lead. Although it was only seven o'clock in the morning there was going to be far more heavy traffic on the road than we had met before so I was fully expecting Dragon to misbehave. The few occasions we had been passed by a heavy lorry Dragon had always jumped sideways on top of poor Boris. I always kept Boris tied on my right, between Dragon and the grass verge, partly so that he would be in the shade, but mainly for his safety. I didn't want to move him to the other side but equally I didn't want Dragon to tread all over him, so the only answer was to give him slightly more lead.

Dragon tended to misbehave in traffic through naughtiness rather than fear. I gave him a tickle with my stick just to remind him of its presence. We trotted down the lane filter on to the N IV itself. The N IV takes most of the traffic from the south but has only one lane in each direction. A wide tarmac strip borders the road for the use of tractors and mule carts which made our life much easier as it left quite a bit of room between us and the traffic.

It wasn't long before the first big lorry appeared on the horizon. I kept Dragon walking as the fearsome thing bore down on us at great speed. Dragon saw it coming and started to jog. Recognizing the signs, Boris leapt into the ditch. It gave a long blast of its horn as it thundered past, causing Dragon to spin round in his tracks. I was half expecting the driver to do something like that so I was sitting tight and able to give Dragon a smack. I could hear the low rumble of another lorry as it approached us from behind. Dragon couldn't see it coming – he moved from side to side, hoping to be able to run somewhere. I put my legs on and made him go forward. He hopped up and down a bit but behaved much better than he had the time before. I gave him a pat and we walked on. Boris didn't trust Dragon at all and kept glancing anxiously in his direction.

Once Dragon had got rid of his early morning bubbles he began to behave and we were able to trot along at a steady pace as usual. The road was absolutely straight as far as I could see and with the traffic whizzing past at such great speeds I became acutely aware of our snail's pace.

I turned off the N IV at about eleven o'clock; the town of Bailen was just below the main road. I don't know what went wrong, but it took me over an hour and a half to locate the cake shop. The baker asked me to follow him inside. 'What about my horse?' I asked.

'*Venga, venga,*' he beckoned.

I jumped off and sized up the door. I would have to take off the saddle-bags if Dragon was going to fit through the door. While I was doing so, the baker put big raffia mats on the polished granite floor – to stop Dragon slipping rather than to protect his floor! I led Dragon slowly and carefully through the cake shop, through the baker's kitchen and out of a small door at the back on to the terrace, where I tied him up and took the rest of his tack off. The baker's assistant was washing down cake tins with a powerful hose in a stone sink. He offered me the hose to wash down Dragon. The baker found an old plastic crate and filled it with some grain out of one of the sacks stacked up in the stable. I helped him move the rest of the sacks into a

121

corner of the tiny disused stable. There was no hay or straw for poor Dragon but with plenty of corn he wasn't really going to suffer.

Bailen is almost in the region of La Mancha, the hottest area in Spain. Out here, the heat of the day was almost unbearable so although there were plenty of chickens about, very few farmers kept cattle or pigs. As a result, there was little left of a butchered animal by the time the best bits had been sold off at a good price, the heart, feet and lungs made into stew and the ears chopped up and served as tapas. The local women would take away the entrails, push oranges through them to clean them and then hang them up to dry to be used as sausage skins. That left only the bones. At first, Boris didn't like eating raw meat, but now that he was used to it he ate whatever I put in front of him as long as it wasn't lungs or raw chicken. Very often a butcher along my route would give me a few old off-cuts for nothing, but now that Boris' red meat consumption had gone up to just over two kilos a day, he was costing me a fortune.

I didn't want to risk riding along the N IV in pitch darkness with so many heavy lorries so I decided to leave Bailen at about six o'clock in the morning. The baker made a lot of bread for a friend with a restaurant in La Carolina, which would be my next stop. He telephoned the friend and made arrangements for me to stay there the following day. As La Carolina was only 28 kilometres away it wouldn't take us more than about four hours to get there so we would arrive in La Carolina well before the heat of the day set in.

Boris spent the night curled up on some old flour sacks in a corner of the stable. It didn't have a door so Dragon had to be tied up all night; he was getting used to it by now. I would have loved to have been able to give him some alfalfa to keep him busy but as there were no animals in the area it was impossible. The baker gave me a sack of stale bread for him instead. Dragon was not impressed. Using the end of his nose like an elephant's trunk, he rummaged through the hunks of bread and found a few bits of cake at the bottom. He sniffed at these and gobbled them up.

I returned the following morning to find that the baker had

been working for at least three hours already. While I tacked up Dragon he covered the granite floor once again with matting so that I could lead him through. As we walked past the table, Dragon's back foot missed the matting and slipped sideways into a huge bowl of cake mix sitting on the floor beside the table. Gallons of the gooey mixture flooded the kitchen. What could I say to the baker when his last three hours' work lay half an inch deep all over the floor? I carried on through the house, tied Dragon up to the iron bars of the bakery window and then rushed inside to help clean up the mess. Boris was still tied up in the stable. He could just see into the kitchen and was howling with pleasure at the sight of all the food, simply dying to come and help us clean it up.

The baker flatly refused to let me help. He insisted that I had a long way to go and not to delay any longer. It was all too much for Boris, who dragged me into the middle of the lake and began lapping it up. This whole thing seemed to be going from bad to worse. With a horse and a dog in his kitchen and cake mix all over the floor, thank goodness the baker had a sense of humour. The assistant brought a mop, which proved useless as it made ripples, pushing the lake even further across the floor. They tried scooping it up with a dustpan which seemed to work a bit better. I walked round the back of the table saying all the words I could remember that might constitute an apology. Dragon was peering through the window at us, probably wondering why there was a delay. I clipped Boris on to the girth buckle and went back inside for another attempt to try and help. My offer was turned down with a pat on the back from the baker.

Our journey to La Carolina was still along the N IV but Dragon behaved much better this morning. Although he had been resting for longer than usual, the combination of no bedding to lie down on and no alfalfa meant that he wasn't particularly perky when we set off so it was probably just as well that we only had to go 28 kilometres. He trotted along quite calmly as the brightly coloured monsters thundered past. Many of them would give a long blast of their horn when they saw us, which made me furious at their complete lack of sense. Many horses will tend to jump into the traffic when they are worried by it. But I had plenty of confidence in Dragon's sense of self-preservation, so I put these morbid thoughts out of my mind.

Today, we were lucky to have an irrigation channel running alongside the road. A concrete V-shape on legs about three feet high, it would make an ideal water trough whenever we needed it. I found it much better to give Boris and Dragon water little and often, never letting them drink their fill until the end of the day. Sometimes we would only find water once a day while we were on the move, in which case I would let them have a rest for half an hour so they could drink slightly more, but never as much as they wanted. Too much water at once might give them colic.

Every two kilometres of irrigation channel there was a three-foot-square concrete water tank through which the water swirled off into the fields or continued along the channel at the side of the road to the next one. As we had been going for just over an hour, I decided to stop and give the animals a drink. I asked Dragon to walk and steered him off the side of the road.

Boris glanced up at me for confirmation that we really were supposed to be going off the road and that I hadn't fallen asleep or something.

Slightly below the level of the road, the irrigation channel was a bit higher than I had first thought. I pushed Dragon towards it with my heels. His pace became hesitant and his ears so pricked that they almost met in the middle. I gave him a sharp nudge with my heels and he came to an abrupt halt. Dragon was refusing to budge. His eyes were on stalks and fixed very firmly on the concrete channel, not quite sure if he was being asked to jump it. Boris sat down patiently, panting in the heat. I jumped off and Boris immediately whizzed under Dragon's tummy to say hello. I thought he'd learned not to do this by now. Apparently not. Keeping a tight hold on Dragon's bridle I stepped slowly and carefully under Dragon's neck and then, loosening my hold on the bridle slightly so that he wouldn't be encouraged to step sideways, edged my way to the other side of Dragon. Boris walked back under Dragon's tummy, tail wagging madly, and gave me another big lick.

I had another go at leading Dragon towards the irrigation

channel. With me in front, Dragon had a bit more confidence and with a great deal of snorting he stepped gingerly towards this new monster. He leaned over the edge of the square tank and looked most alarmed at the sight of all the water swirling round and round. Boris knew the sound of water and put his front feet on the side of the tank to have a drink. Dragon never liked to miss out on anything so he immediately made a face at Boris to frighten him away and had a drink himself.

By the time we arrived at La Carolina, the temperature was almost unbearable and Dragon and Boris were both starting to wilt. It had taken longer than I had expected but the delay at the baker's and then four or five stops for water in the irrigation channel must have taken quite a long time. I found the restaurant I was looking for very easily and followed the baker's friend to a big, cool cow barn which Dragon had all to himself. He had taken the trouble to find us some alfalfa and corn before we arrived, which was a great relief. I untacked Dragon and hosed him down as usual. Boris was jumping up and down on his lead, tied to a window, waiting for his turn. Unlike Dragon, Boris adored being sprayed with cold water.

The cow barn normally housed about forty cows so with the doors closed there was plenty of room for me to lay a good-sized straw bed for Dragon.

Boris was standing on guard, still tied to his window. Most dogs would have been fast asleep, lying flat out in the sun, but there was something special about Boris that meant he was always switched on and keeping an eye out for trouble. It was like having a mobile machine gun; wherever I parked him, he guarded. Lately he had begun to take his job so seriously that it wasn't just me he was guarding but anything that belonged to me and Dragon as well. I only realized this when I tied Dragon up outside a bank one day, leaving Boris clipped to the girth buckle as usual. I stomped inside and took my place at the back of the queue. While I was waiting I kept an eye on them through the window. A horse tied up to a bank or a post office never fails to attract a crowd so as the people closed in round the pair of them I was amused to see Boris rising to his responsibility, watching every person very carefully. The people moved in a little closer, making cooing noises at Dragon, who'd fallen asleep. Quite unaware of the enormous Dobermann tied to the horse's girth, a neatly dressed man stepped forward and put his hand out to stroke Dragon's neck. The moment his hand touched Dragon's neck there was a loud growl which could be heard inside the bank. The man jumped and the crowd with him. Boris was very much in control and positively enjoyed the look on their terrified faces. He cast his piggy eyes round the rapidly diminishing crowd, asking if anyone else wanted to come and pat the horsey. It gave me a wicked glow of satisfaction to know that I could pin 1000-peseta notes all over the horse and nobody would be able to put a finger on them.

The restaurant man walked through the yard gate just as I came out of the barn. He was carrying something wrapped in polythene. 'Para su perro,' he said breathlessly. He had thoughtfully rushed back to his restaurant to get some leftovers for Boris. As he handed me the squidgy bag, I warned him to keep well away while I fed Boris. I didn't have enough room to carry a dog bowl for him so I had to use whatever I could find. Today it was a bent saucepan I found in the yard. Boris smelled the food and began gnashing his teeth at the kind restaurant man, in between doing huge jumps up and down with his tail wagging. The mixture of bones, sausages, spaghetti and other yummy bits and pieces rolled out of the bag into the saucepan. Boris lowered his head and narrowed his eyes, giving the restaurant man a threatening stare. 'Boris, sit!' Boris was extremely disobedient but this was the one and only command he would obey, and only then because he knew it would be immediately followed by food. I put the saucepan down in front of him and patted him on the back. I always made a point of handling him a little while he was eating so that he wouldn't become snappy towards me as well.

When he'd finished, I untied him and let him loose in the barn to squabble with Dragon. There was plenty of room in there for both of them to find somewhere to sleep, but knowing Boris' tendency to take over the whole of Dragon's bed, I put another pile of straw on the other side of the barn. I tied the door shut with a piece of baling string just in case either of them decided to go exploring.

That night I stayed in a shabby hostel. I liked having Boris with me at night for company as well as security so I took him for his walk via the hostel and asked the man behind the desk if he minded a dog in my room. He asked me whether the dog was quiet. I nodded my head and patted Boris on the back. '*Muy noble,*' I said. It is very difficult for a Dobermann to look soft and lovable but every time I tried to get him into my room he would put on a silly angelic expression, pretending he was really just an overgrown sausage dog.

The hostel was full of alcoholic old men, and I was glad to have Boris with me to act as my bodyguard on the way to the bathroom. Boris never quite understood baths and wasn't sure whether it was more important to guard the door or lick all the water off my arms, which was a horrible nuisance as I didn't want to make him sick from eating soap. The only way to stop him was to fill the bath right up so that I was up to my neck in water. He then thought I might be drowning so I had to keep talking to him to let him know that I was quite safe.

# NINE

# A Horse on the Highway

ALTHOUGH IT WAS only eight-thirty, I could feel the powerful sun beating down on my back as we trotted north along the side of the N IV. Dark, speckled mountains loomed ahead of us. The last two days had been good traffic practice for Dragon because today the road had turned into a vast dual carriageway about the size of a British motorway. Heavy lorries zoomed past. Dragon was a little spooky, but that meant he was feeling full of energy. Boris was always harder to judge but as long as he was tied to the girth he never seemed particularly tired. Whenever he was let loose, he would quickly tire because he would cover five times the distance we were doing dashing backwards and forwards or running enormous circles round us.

Our road parted from the carriageway heading south and took a different route through the mountains. The traffic was getting heavier and the horrible noise it made was amplified by the big rocks which surrounded us. The hard shoulder had become a little wider which was a help as we trotted round the long curves further into the folds of the mountains. The rock face came right down to the road so I was rather concerned that someone might come speeding round a bend, cut on to the hard shoulder and hit us. There was nothing I could do except put Boris on a shorter lead so that we could ride closer to the rock and hope for the best. Every now and then I caught a glimpse of the carriageway heading south through a chink in the pine trees which grew thick and tall on our left. The road began to make even bigger loops almost doubling back on itself, which I found frustrating, so when I came to a place where I could see the traffic further ahead of us on our present loop I wondered whether I might be able to cross the steep gulley which ran between the two sections of road. If I crossed it I could probably save as much as half an hour. Interested to know how much time I would save, I took note of a yellow cement mixer which rumbled past. Once it had disappeared round the next bend, I waited for it to appear on the other side. Eight minutes later I saw its yellow body crawling up the hill.

The sides of the gulley were almost vertical, covered in scree and a few scrawny little bushes. The flat area at the bottom was a very long way down. My first problem was how to cross the crash barrier which ran in an unbroken line along the edge of the road. At last we found a missing section. I waited for a safe gap in the traffic and dashed across. I stood at the top of the steep slope and lengthened Boris' lead. I pushed Dragon forward and over the edge giving him plenty of rein so that he could have the full use of his neck for balance. Taking as straight a line as possible, we slid our way down to the bottom. The bottom of the gulley was scrub and stones, a perfect environment for snakes. I was very glad to be sitting on top of Dragon.

Getting up the other side was far more tricky. Under normal circumstances I would have got off and led Dragon up the steep slope but as Dragon was capable of clambering up a hill far quicker than I was, I might well slip over on the scree and lose him. I sat tight and with a big chunk of mane in one hand, let Dragon find his way up with Boris tagging alongside. I leaned well forward as Dragon bounded up the side of the gulley. It was a long struggle to the top. His strong hindquarters powered us up the slope until we popped up over the edge to the great surprise of the passing cars. I felt very satisfied to have saved so much time. I crossed the road on to the hard shoulder and let Dragon walk for a while.

The road continued to make long sweeping curves through the awesome rocks which towered above us. There was a temporary break in the traffic, leaving nothing but the sound of Dragon's hooves on the scorching black tarmac and Boris' continual panting from the heat. Two yellow cement mixers climbed slowly up the hill, their engines roaring as they

129

struggled past us. Two yellow cement mixers; something struck a nerve. Suddenly I felt uneasy. I squinted upwards, studying the pinnacles of rock which pierced the bright sky above us. I peered through the pine trees, hoping to catch a glimpse of the road in the other direction. I didn't want to believe what I saw – another wretched yellow cement mixer. I glanced up at the mountain once more. The high rock faces all around us made it impossible to know where the mountain was. Was it possible that I had crossed on to the road going south by mistake? The rocks and pine trees looked the same as they had done all morning and I couldn't even tell by the sun, as the road kept doubling back on itself. I just couldn't be sure whether I had saved or wasted the last half-hour. I didn't want to risk wasting more time; I'd rather be sure. Cursing my stupidity, I turned back.

Luckily the hard shoulder had been quite wide since we'd crossed the gulley so going against the traffic wasn't as hazardous as it might have been. I looked at my watch; nearly twelve o'clock. We still had a long way to go before we reached Almuradiel. I crossed the gulley for the second time and trotted on to make up lost time. As we followed the long curve round, the other carriageway came into full view, showing me my mistake. The yellow cement mixer which had passed me was not the same yellow cement mixer which I had presumed to be further down the road, but a different one altogether travelling in the opposite direction.

I hadn't seen a kilometre stone for ages. I wasn't sure if it was because we had been mucking around for so long that we hadn't actually completed a single kilometre in the last hour or so because there weren't any stones to tell me.

I fished out my map to see how we were getting on. There was a tunnel marked about half-way between La Carolina and Almuradiel. I reckoned we must be approaching that point any minute now. Round the next bend, I could see a high brick wall built into the rocks on our right. As we trotted closer I could see that it stretched a good seventy feet high. This must be the lead-in for the tunnel, I thought. A railway line ran along the top, parallel with the road.

A coach whizzed past, followed by another which blasted its horn, eight or ten children's faces were pressed to the back

130

window waving. I waved back and then they were gone. A few minutes later we arrived at the tunnel. I felt quite excited when I first saw it. It was the first tunnel we had come to. As I rode closer, it began to take on monstrous proportions. Its mouth gaped wider and blacker, its concrete lips swallowing the traffic which roared down its gullet like a huge angry fish. I narrowed my eyes and peered into the blackness; I couldn't see any light at the end so I had no idea how long it was. My heart sank as I saw that at the mouth of the tunnel the hard shoulder tapered off into nothing. I made Dragon stand for a minute while I considered the problem.

After three days on this busy road, I was quite used to the heavy traffic but as we stood on the side of the road, it suddenly seemed so enormous, so dangerous. With no hard shoulder, it would be suicide to try and ride through the tunnel. The traffic was getting worse by the minute, almost nose to tail. A solid mass of metal travelling at seventy miles an hour. My rear light would make very little difference as the tunnel was quite narrow for the two lanes of traffic and nobody would have enough room to swerve to avoid us or stop in time. It was impossible.

The jagged rocks above the tunnel looked just as uninviting. Then I saw a small path cutting seventy feet up the bank at the side of the road. I jumped off Dragon and led him up it. The heat was takings its toll; I felt quite weak from the powerful rays tearing at my back. The ground levelled out and I felt hopeful. I could hear voices quite close to where we were standing. With Dragon in one hand, I pushed my way through some prickly gorse towards them.

It was a railway line, and the voices were those of men working on it. We stepped out of the gorse bush on to the track. The voices trailed off and they turned to face us. This was going to test my Spanish. I started by explaining that I was travelling to Almuradiel. 'The tunnel is very dangerous,' I said in my faltering Spanish. A flood of Spanish from all of them at once was the reply. Unable to understand a word, I tried again, this time trying to ask them if they could hold the traffic for a few minutes while I went through the tunnel. Lots of head-shaking all round. Just behind them was a railway tunnel. I asked them whether I could go through that and then down on to the road again. Nobody said yes but on the other hand nobody said no, so I began to ride towards it. Two of the men ran ahead into the tunnel; the rest stayed put. Being much higher up the mountain, the railway tunnel was quite short so I could see daylight at the other end. I was very nervous as we scrunched our way down the middle of the track; there was only a foot on either side. There was a shout from one of the men outside, my heart leapt and I almost screamed at the men ahead of me *'Hay un tren?'* The men didn't seem to know and called to the others outside. I yanked Dragon round and cantered out of the tunnel as fast as I could.

The track before the tunnel was on a corner so the train was going to appear very suddenly from behind a large piece of rock only a hundred metres away. I didn't even have time to cross back over the track to the gorse bushes.

We were left standing on a piece of ground not much more than three metres square. Just in front of our noses was the railway track and I was horrified to find an endless drop down to the river behind us. I had to decide whether it would be better to get off and hold Dragon or whether to sit on him. If I got off and held him, I wouldn't have as much control over him and Boris could cause a disaster, but if I stayed on him and he panicked, he might well lurch forward into the path of the oncoming train.

I decided to stay on board. Keeping a firm hold on his mouth, I stroked his neck. Boris had sat down, patiently waiting. There was a ghastly silence as we all waited. The workmen leaned against the rock on the far side of the track, steadily chewing wisps of grass like a row of cows. We stood in silence. I was suddenly conscious of being just a tiny speck amongst these vast sunbleached rocks. What did our three lives matter to them? They'd lived through thousands of human lives. Silence had never seemed louder. My heart was in my mouth, making me feel quite sick.

A bright yellow flash of metal hurtled round the corner, coming straight at us. Dragon trembled, his eyes wide with terror. I kept patting his neck and talking to him as the monstrous thing rushed towards us at breakneck speed. Charging round the corner it formed a solid wall of metal, inches from our faces. The noise was deafening. Dragon was still shaking but hadn't moved a muscle. We were still alive. I glanced down to check on Boris. Sensing Dragon's fright, he seemed far more concerned about the possibility of being trampled than about the churning wheels of the train just in front of his nose.

Its tail lights disappeared into the tunnel and we could breathe again. With the train tunnel off the list of possibilities I thanked the workmen and retraced my steps down on to the main road again. The traffic had eased off slightly which gave me another idea. Every time there was a gap in the traffic I moved a couple of steps out into the road and waved my arms like mad at the next approaching vehicle in the hope that someone would stop. At last a lorry put on its indicators and started to slow down. I ran towards it, pulling Dragon behind me, desperate to reach it before the driver changed his mind and drove off. I explained my problem and asked the driver if he would mind driving behind me while I rode through the tunnel.

The big lorry pulled out into the road, hazard lights flashing, right on Dragon's heels. I leaned round and switched on the red torch on Dragon's bottom as we entered the dark tunnel. I trotted as briskly as I could because all the traffic was held at Dragon-speed until we reached the other end. I hardly had to touch Dragon's sides to keep him trotting with a big flashing monster just behind us. Boris was taking his job very seriously as usual, paying no attention to anything except the job in hand – getting to his next guard duty on time. The tunnel was full of smelly exhaust fumes so it was a great relief to break into the sunlight once more.

I steered Dragon on to the hard shoulder as the big lorry rumbled past. The driver gave us a cheery wave and with a rev of his engine was gone.

A few shabby whitewashed houses clung to the side of the road. Quite sure that we could all do with a drink, I stopped at the first bar we came to and ordered the usual: 'Coke and a bucket of water'. I let Boris drink first and then Dragon gulped down the remainder. I tied him up in the shade and went inside. I was somewhat dismayed to find that we still had another 18 kilometres to go before we reached Almuradiel. The barman said there was nothing between here and there. The animals had done quite enough already today, but looking up and down the road I saw there was nowhere for them to stay here. I would have to press on, but at least they could have a rest for a while before we got going. I ate some *tapas* (tiny portions of food ranging from finely chopped pigs' ears to beef stew) while I waited and cooled down a bit with an ice-cream. I went outside to get my water bottle so that I could refill it and found that Dragon had remodelled it for me against one of the iron pillars so that it looked something like a squashed pepper.

I had never had such a long, hot day. It was torture. Taking into account the intense heat, I wanted to get Dragon and Boris to Almuradiel as quickly as possible but without making them too tired. I put Dragon on automatic pilot at a fairly slow trot. With no kilometre signs, we seemed to be trotting for ever, on and on into the heat haze. I now know what it's like to see a mirage when you are hot and confused with a very long way to walk. After an hour and a half of this hell, I began to worry about Boris who was starting to suffer from the heat.

Another hour. Was it never going to end? I hadn't seen a house or a tree for more than two hours. I was getting really worried about Boris so I made Dragon walk. Boris was becoming so exhausted by the heat that every now and then he would bump against the crash barrier. What could I do? With no shade and nowhere to rest there was little point in stopping and I certainly couldn't lift him on to Dragon. Our whole world was heat: no landscape, no people, no trees. Just a long strip of tarmac and, somewhere at the end of it, our destination.

Parched and weak, we staggered into Almuradiel at four o'clock in the afternoon. The restaurant that the man in La Carolina had directed us to turned out to be nothing more than a lorry café and hostel. I tied Dragon up in the shade of the parking lot. The whole place was swarming with rough lorry drivers of all nationalities. Not wanting to draw attention to myself I took off my chaps and laid them over my saddle. I lengthened Boris' lead slightly, just in case he had any trouble.

I took a deep breath and strode inside. I didn't look right or left as various men hissed and muttered, *'Guapa, guapa,'* under their breath. I took out my piece of paper from La Carolina and handed it to the barman. He stuck his head through the plastic fronds behind him and shouted 'José!'

Moments later a tall, greasy man appeared and shook my hand. I had no choice. I thanked him and went back outside to move Dragon to the end parking lot which had a wall on one side. I untacked him and put everything in a big pile just next to him, made a bed for Boris with my long Barbour and put him on guard.

There was a garage just opposite the parking lot on the other side of the main road. I led Dragon across the busy road and used their hose to wash him down. They lent me a bucket so that he could have a drink. When he'd had enough I filled it up again and, with Dragon in one hand and the heavy bucket in the other, went back to Boris.

I washed Boris down in the parking lot because I didn't want to leave everything I owned unguarded and above all because Boris shouldn't walk a step more than he had to before he'd had a good rest. With the N IV only a few yards away I was terrified of leaving Dragon tied up in case he broke free and ran into the traffic. His leather head collar was backed with strong nylon so I knew that wouldn't break but I was worried about the clip rope. I pulled the stirrups off my saddle and unthreaded the leathers. I looped one through Dragon's head collar and the other one over a metal strut which was holding up the roof. Buckling each stirrup leather to itself made a pretty strong back-up, just in case the rope broke during the night. I looked down at poor Boris. He wouldn't be going anywhere that night.

I went to the kitchen to try and scrounge some left-overs for Boris. They were able to give me lots of delicious things for him which I hoped would make him feel better. I had no idea what I could give Dragon to eat, until I happened to notice a young girl washing an enormous pile of lettuces in the corner of the kitchen. I asked her whether she could give me the spare leaves for my horse. She was rather surprised at the mention of a horse and went to the kitchen door to have a look for herself.

She loved horses, she said, and kindly stuffed a vast amount of lettuce into a paper sack. I am sure some whole lettuces went into it. She also managed to find a few carrots and potato peelings.

Boris ate his food sitting down, which was most unlike him. I patted Dragon on the bottom to ask him to move over and shook the lettuce on to the dusty floor of the parking lot. Dragon sniffed it suspiciously and then took a delicate nibble at it. He seemed to like it and crunched up some more. He was thrilled to find some carrots and didn't stop rooting in the lettuce until he was absolutely convinced that there were no more of them.

I walked back towards the café. Just before I went inside I turned round to look at my faithful animals. It was a funny sight to look along the parking lot and see lorry, lorry, car, lorry, car, horse! Boris had snuggled right up against my saddle just in case he went to sleep, so that if anyone should so much as touch it he would be wide awake in a second. Dragon was filling his face with lettuce leaves.

The tall greasy man showed me to a small greasy room and told me that I couldn't bring any of my tack into it. I thanked him and closed the door. I washed out the bath very well, using up most of my tiny bottle of shampoo, and had a lukewarm bath. At bath level, the bathroom stank dreadfully. There were no towels so I had to dry myself with my spare T-shirt and the minuscule square of towel that I had used for everything from washing my face to padding my leg where it got rubbed during the first few days. I didn't mind spending a night in a dirty goat shed, but there is something horribly squalid about a dirty, smelly room.

I went back outside to check the animals, who were surprisingly relaxed as the huge lorries rumbled into the parking area to stop for the night. I dug my fingers into Dragon's mane and wished I could find him something better than lettuce. His elephant's lips searched me until they found the two carrots I had brought him hidden in my pocket. I gave them to him and said hello to Boris. Although Boris was an excellent guard dog, I felt very worried leaving everything in his care in a busy lorry park. I hated to leave them in such an unsuitable place but there was no alternative. Very unsettled, I went back to my room to try and get some sleep or I wouldn't be capable of going much further. We weren't anywhere near the Pyrenees and there was an unthinkable distance still to go.

I hardly slept at all. At every noise I would snap awake, terrified that someone was stealing Dragon or he'd escaped or someone was trying to get at my things. I hauled myself out of bed just after six o'clock and went straight outside.

I found Dragon sitting down and Boris wide awake on guard. Boris tilted his ears back in anticipation when he saw me walking across the lorry park towards them. I untied him to take him with me while I went to fill up the water bucket. He seemed rather stiff on his feet so I walked very slowly with him.

While Dragon was having a drink I felt down Boris' legs. As I touched his feet he almost snapped at me. I gave him a pat and picked one up. His pads were very worn as a result of yesterday's long ride. There was no question of his going anywhere today. Dragon, on the other hand, looked fine. He'd eaten most of the lettuce, leaving only a few tough old stalks which he'd ground into the dust. I didn't want to spend another night here so I would have to hitch a lift with Boris to my next stop, Valdepeñas, and then come back for Dragon and ride him there.

I went inside to ask the greasy man if he had a shed or somewhere I could leave my things and he gave me the key to a store room. I had no idea how long it would take me to hitch to Valdepeñas. Who on earth was going to take an enormous Dobermann in their car?

I led him across the road to the garage and asked various drivers if they would mind giving us a lift. It was about half an hour before someone eventually agreed to take us on condition that Boris sat on the floor. Boris is a very big dog and could probably just about squeeze on to the floor in the front of a car with the front seat pushed right back, but as the man and his son were sitting in the front, we would have to fit into the back. Having only been in a car once or twice before, Boris looked at me as if I was joking when I told him he wasn't allowed on the seat and would have to squeeze on to the tiny space on the floor. I gave his bottom a nudge and he put his head through the gap in a half-hearted fashion. We both knew that it was just not possible. I apologized to the driver and asked if I could sit in the front. He gave a long sigh and told his son to sit in the back.

I caught sight of Dragon happily munching lettuce in the shade of his parking lot as the battered Ford Granada swung out of the garage on to the N IV. Boris stuck his nose out of my open window, his eyes tight shut as the wind blew in his face. I felt very happy to have found a way to rest his feet. Whizzing along in the car gave me a good preview of the day's ride. The driver of the car looked rather fierce so I didn't say anything. The car suddenly slowed down and stopped. I sat up straight and saw a sign pointing to a small side road saying 'VALDE-PEÑAS 4'. They couldn't leave us here! I looked at the driver hopefully, wondering whether he might take pity on Boris with his sore feet and drive us the last few miles to Valdepeñas. I offered to pay but he didn't want to know. I had just enough manners to thank him and got out of the car.

I led Boris on to the grass by the side of the road and sat down. Not a single car passed us in either direction. Had Boris been a little smaller I might have been able to carry him. Even though his stiffness seemed to have gone, four kilometres was much too far for him to walk. We would just sit and wait for as long as it took. We weren't in any hurry because if Dragon stood resting all day, I would be able to ride him quite a bit faster than usual. I lay in the long brown grass and waited for the distant hum of an engine.

After an hour and a half, a van stopped and agreed to take Boris. I didn't know where I wanted to go so they dropped me in the centre of Valdepeñas. I had asked Michael to send me my other collapsible bucket as I found the one I had kept with me so useful. I went straight to the post office and was pleased to see the round packet squashed into a pigeonhole under a sign saying 'Lista de Correos' (Care of the post office). I tore open the brown paper and found a nice long letter as well as the bucket. I went to a small bar and had a coffee while I read Michael's letter.

I asked the barman where I might find a *picadero* or somewhere to stable my horse. He said there wasn't anywhere in Valdepeñas but on the road to La Solana there were two brothers who ran a *picadero*. This was very good news because I planned to leave the N IV here in order to cut across country in the direction of Zaragoza and then north to the border. La Solana was on my route.

# TEN

# The Feria

I HAD DIFFICULTY in persuading a taxi to take Boris to La Solana, but eventually succeeded with the usual condition that he sat on the floor.

The *picaderos* were remarkably friendly and relaxed about this strange girl who appeared out of nowhere on a bright sunny day, asking if she could leave her huge Dobermann with them and saying she'd be back later with her horse. They walked straight up to Boris and gave him a hearty pat on the back. Realizing they weren't in the slightest bit nervous, Boris decided they were all right. Emeterio took his lead and walked towards the covered yard. They tied him up in a corner of the straw barn and gave him a bucket of water. Lapping up the water, he kept glancing all around, wondering when Dragon was going to appear and gulp down the rest. He couldn't quite believe that he had a whole bucketful all to himself. I left Boris in the *picaderos'* care, took the taxi back to Valdepeñas and then hitched my way to Dragon.

I found him fast asleep, resting in the shade of his parking lot. I called to him and his ears twitched backwards and forwards. He was looking in pretty good condition for a horse who'd had nothing but lettuce to eat. I ran my hands down his legs. No heat and no swelling. He was turning into an exceptionally strong horse. Under normal circumstances, the sort of work we were doing would be unthinkable for a horse of his age. But Dragon was more of an overgrown pony than a horse and we had built up the work very gradually, so he didn't have a lump or a bump and his tendons were as hard as iron. The place where he had cut his heel on the first day still hadn't completely healed but I took care to rub cream into it every day before we set off to prevent it cracking.

140

We arrived at the *picadero* with energy to spare. I was relieved to find a comfortable stable waiting for us and a good feed in the manger. It had taken us four hours to ride there so I didn't want Dragon to wolf down so much good food too soon. I untacked him, washed him down and let him cool off before putting him in the stable. The first thing he did was to have a good roll to get rid of all the itches from the last few days. Then he attacked his feed with relish.

There was a yelping noise coming from the straw barn. Boris knew I was back. I went in to say hello and let him off his lead. He raced round and round in circles, his feet obviously feeling better. You may wonder why I so rarely let him off the lead. Although Boris was a wonderful guard dog, he was disgracefully disobedient. I bought him when he was fifteen months old, well past the age when a dog is easy to train. I had succeeded in making him sit, but other than that he was quite appalling. Having lived on a chain for his whole life until I bought him, he never left my heels to begin with, but once he found his confidence he would disappear as soon as I let him off his lead. He would always come back, but usually half an hour later. If you happened to catch sight of him and call, he would immediately accelerate. If, however, you walked in the opposite direction, he would follow you. Infuriating when you are just about to set off.

Quite apart from this, Boris is a dangerous dog, an untrained killer. I took great care never to let him loose unless we were in the middle of nowhere or somewhere I could keep a watchful eye over him.

Emeterio and Reggis showed me into their house to meet their wives Ana Isabeli and Catalina. Nobody had asked me where I was staying; Ana Isabeli and Catalina had already prepared a bed for me. They showed me the bathroom and told me that dinner would be at half-past nine. They insisted that I went to sleep for a while and that somebody would wake me up in time for dinner.

I woke up to the sound of clanking pots and pans coming from the kitchen next door, dressed quickly and went to join the family. As I walked in, Emeterio and Reggis stood up and wished me good evening. *'Buenas tardes,'* I replied and joined them at the blue Formica table. Catalina and Ana Isabeli were still busy in the kitchen. It would have been rude for me to offer to help so I talked to Emeterio and Reggis in my greatly improved Spanish. I asked them about their business and the horses and was amazed to discover that they only charged £75 per month for schooling, which included the horse's keep. In England one could pay that price for a week.

Catalina walked in carrying a big bowl of soup-like stew. Ana Isabeli was just behind carrying a bottle of red wine and a small basket of bread. Catalina lowered the terracotta bowl carefully on to the table and sat down. I was just wondering who the last chair belonged to when a gangly lad of about fourteen walked in. Catalina scolded him for being late as he sat down drying his hands on his dirty jeans. Reggis introduced him as Serafín, his younger brother. My attention was diverted as Catalina fished out one small piece of rather gristly-looking meat and asked me to pass my bowl. Then she scooped out some of the green soup, which reminded me of algae. She did the same for Emeterio and Reggis and kept the serving spoon for herself. I was the only person to have a glass although Emeterio and Reggis had bowls. Everyone else had nothing but a spoon and took turns diving into the bowl of algae.

Reggis offered me a hunk of bread and filled my glass, then throwing back his head he stuck his thumb over the top of the bottle and, with a well-practised flick of his wrist, directed the jet of red wine into his mouth without his lips ever touching the bottle. He passed the bottle to Emeterio who took a swig in the same expert fashion before putting it in the middle of the table. I noticed that the men and I were also the only ones with a small piece of meat; the others had none at all. Emeterio spiked his tiny piece with his fork and held it up. 'What is this, woman?' he exclaimed rudely, staring at Ana Isabeli. 'How can I ride ten horses if this is all I get to eat?' Ana Isabeli glanced at me as if to apologize and said, 'If you only give us a thousand pesetas (£5.00) a week to buy food for five people, what do you expect?' Emeterio grunted, shrugged his shoulders and finished his food in stony silence.

I felt terrible to think that what I was eating had probably

142

been sliced off the men's food. Worst of all was the fact that I didn't even enjoy it; it was mostly gristle from the backbone. Emeterio and Reggis were both very young, and with their two wives, who were only eighteen and twenty, they already had five children between them to support. It was a tough task to squeeze enough money out of a horse business.

After dinner, I went to check on Dragon and let Boris out for a run. Reggis and Emeterio didn't say anything but I could tell by the look on their faces they thought I pampered Dragon and Boris. 'They're only animals' is the normal Spanish feeling. More than any other nation, the English are renowned for their love of animals and I am certainly no exception.

When I went back inside Emeterio and Reggis were discussing the *feria* they were taking their horses to in Manzanares the following day. They wanted me to go on Dragon but I thought he needed a rest so I said I'd watch instead. I'd never been to a *feria* before so I was really looking forward to it.

Emeterio took the horses in a lorry while Reggis drove the car with Catalina, Ana Isabeli and me. The horse lorry wasn't a normal horse-box; it was just an open-topped fruit lorry. First the grey and then the dark bay was tied up to a metal bar which ran along the top of the cab so that they could look forwards. As we drove just behind the lorry I could watch the horses swaying one way and then the other, balancing themselves against the movement of the lorry. They seemed to enjoy watching the world whiz past, screwing up their eyes against the wind.

Everybody was going to meet at the bullring and then ride into the middle of Manzanares in one group. When we arrived, about thirty horses were already there. Some of them looked as though they had been dragged out of their fields that morning and probably hadn't been ridden since the *feria* the previous year. Walking along the stalls of the bullring stables, I saw some magnificent horses, their lovely big bottoms rippling with muscle every time they shifted their weight from one foot to the other. There was one in particular which really caught my eye, a big white grey with the longest mane and tail I'd ever seen and a lovely crest. A man was giving him a final polish so

143

I went over to ask about him. When I asked why the horse had such a wonderful mane he told me that if you clip a horse's mane and tail when it is a yearling, it will grow back twice as strong and fast. This horse was only six years old.

Reggis and Emeterio were nearly ready. Catalina handed them their neatly pressed jackets. Reggis adjusted his spurs and put on his beautifully made Spanish chaps. Emeterio held up his arms while Catalina wrapped a red sash round his waist. Ana Isabeli passed him his jet-black *sombrero de flamenco* and rushed off to help Reggis.

Some of the horses had a flat pad buckled to the back of the saddle. These pads had a handle on the end nearest the horse's tail so that a lady could sit sideways, with her left hand holding the handle and her right arm round the man's waist. Various ladies were getting ready to go, their brilliantly coloured flamenco dresses in sharp contrast to the whitewashed walls of the bullring. With flowers in their hair and a contrasting light shawl round their shoulders, they looked beautiful. The men were starting to mount their horses. I was fascinated to see how the women managed to get on the horses with acres of dress to cope with. Reggis rode up to me and asked me whether I would like to ride behind someone. He apologized that neither he nor his brother could take me; they were both on young horses who were rather inclined to misbehave. He was just looking round for a man riding solo when the fabulous six-year-old grey pranced past us. Reggis called to the man, who tipped his hat and turned his horse.

Reggis explained that my horse was resting today and so I didn't have anything to ride. Without hesitation the man on the grey made a low sweeping gesture with his sombrero and invited me to ride behind him. He dismounted and Reggis introduced him as Guillemo. Guillemo smiled and said we'd already met. Before he helped me on to his horse, he rearranged the stallion's beautiful mane so that it didn't tangle with the reins. As there was no pad for me to sit on, he told me to sit astride. I wasn't quite sure how he was going to mount the horse with me sitting just behind the saddle. Taking up the reins, he clicked his tongue and the horse moved its front legs further and further out until it was almost bowing. The horse was now a good three inches lower so that Guillemo could put his foot in the stirrup with ease. He put his left foot in the stirrup as usual, but instead of swinging his right leg over the horse's rump, he pulled himself on to the saddle sitting sideways and neatly lifted his right leg over the horse's neck.

Guillemo told me to put my right hand round his waist and my left on my hip. My memories of riding double on ponies were rather painful so I felt a little apprehensive to be sitting right on the horse's 'bucking spot' but nevertheless very proud to be on what I thought to be the best-looking horse there.

Everybody was mounted and ready to go so we set off in one big group towards the centre of Manzanares. Riding behind the saddle was surprisingly comfortable because, unlike the English variety, the *'Doma Vaquera'* saddle has a high, flat back to it which doesn't bruise your pelvis every time the horse bounces.

The streets of Manzanares were lined with happy, cheering faces and a million arms all waving madly as the horses trotted past. I was really enjoying myself.

The *feria* itself was in the municipal gardens. As we rode nearer, my ears were filled with a glorious mixture of *Sevillana* (flamenco) and the latest hit from Madonna. A row of stalls backed on to the fun fair, their counters packed with brightly coloured flowers, plastic toys, gaudy jewellery or sweets. A bay horse trotted past us and turned to the cheering families who crowded the pavement. His well-groomed coat glistened with sweat as he performed the impressive Spanish Walk. He threw a foot out in front of him and, as he spanked it to the ground, the crowd shouted *'Olé*, then the other foot, *'Olé!'*, and the first, *'Olé!'*, each time shouting louder until the horse could give no more. The accomplished rider then made the horse hold one leg out in front and pivot round a full circle on the other. He touched his sombrero, smiled and trotted on towards the front of the procession which was now entering the gardens and the heart of the *feria*.

The sea of people parted as the horses rode in, prancing and jogging along the wide sandy path. It was more of an old-fashioned agricultural fair than anything else; there was none of the noisy flashing machinery that the English associate with the word 'fair'. Six or seven shiny new tractors were lined up on our right. Although they were brand-new, their design was antique by most standards. Two small boys dressed in mini flamenco dress were playing hide and seek around the tractor wheels but as soon as they saw the horses coming they ran towards us shouting '*Caballos, caballos!*' A few minutes later we passed a merry-go-round, but not the sort you might expect because instead of the usual tin horses, there were eight little Shetland ponies standing nose to tail in a circle under the beautifully painted roof. The sad little ponies whinnied hope-fully as our horses jogged past in a cloud of dust. I felt sorry for them and wondered if they had ever been free to dash up and down as fast as they could, bucking and kicking for fun. Probably not. I expect they spend the winter months in a dusty backyard with their front feet hobbled to prevent them from wandering. Nobody noticed the little Shetlands as we trotted past their sad forgotten faces.

We paraded up and down the rows of stalls and fun-fair rides for about half an hour before finally drawing to a standstill outside a large bar in the very heart of the *feria*. One or two rather jovial-looking men meandered among the horses with a bottle of fino in one hand and glasses in the other. Fino ex-plained Guillemo, is the traditional Spanish drink at a *feria*. He went on to say that it was quite strong, but as long as you didn't drink anything else, you'd be fine. Remembering his words, I paced myself, although it did slip down rather easily!

It wasn't long before I had lost count and dissolved into the happy festive atmosphere all around me. The horses fanned out to form a rough circle. The music became louder and everyone began to clap. The haunting cries of a woman's voice singing to the Spanish guitar rang out against the syncopated rhythm of the clapping, and the flamenco dancers began to move, their swirling colours, arrogant expressions and curling fingers heightening the drama of the dance. I was captivated by the control and precision of their movements. Guillemo explained to me that there were four stages to the flamenco dance, each one having particular steps and hand movements. The women were taught these movements from as young as four years old. He pointed out two little girls dancing with each other on the edge of the circle to clarify his point. The music paused and I was amused to see a small boy bow to the little girls and position himself for the next movement which he performed with all the grace and seriousness of his elders.

It was a hot day and once the formalities were over, many of the horses wandered off in different directions round the *feria*. Guillemo suggested that we go and find Reggis and Emeterio and have lunch. I spotted their horses tied under a large eucalyptus tree. Reggis and Emeterio weren't far away, lying flat on their backs in a flowerbed while Ana Isabeli and Catalina unwrapped the picnic.

Guillemo tied the big grey stallion next to the other two and joined the picnic. It was very simple: three large loaves of fresh bread, *chorizos*, olives, *manchego* cheese and *pata negra* (smoked ham). The Spanish don't use butter on bread so I piled a few slices of *pata negra* straight on to the bread and took a big bite.

The horses were resting quietly in the shade of the tree, their tails swishing idly against the flies. Once again, I was amazed by how quiet and well trained the horses seemed to be. Three stallions tied to the same tree would be unthinkable in England, for fear they might rip each other to shreds. It seemed that as long as they had a bridle or a halter on their heads, or a rider on their backs, these horses were obedient to man's command.

'*Quieres más?*' asked Emeterio, holding a bottle of fino just above my glass.

'*No, gracias,*' I replied. Emeterio protested that the *feria* was only just beginning and insisted on refilling my glass.

I could still hear the flamenco music going round and round in the background and the chatter all around me, but the sound of the swishing horses' tails was sending me to sleep. I tried to fight it off but every whisk of their long grey tails swept a new wave of tiredness over me, making it more and more difficult to keep my eyes open. The long grass was inviting me to lie down. I just couldn't resist it.

Staring up into the green eucalyptus leaves, I dozed for a while. Sounds and smells of horses filled my senses. In the distance I could hear the *Sevillana* music still tumbling out of the bars. I took a deep breath, filling my nostrils with the parched, dry air, the long grass, the sweet smell of eucalyptus and the scent of summer; a dusty summer, a Spanish summer.

Reggis and Emeterio were fast asleep when I woke. Only Serafín was awake, stripping the bark off a piece of wood with a pen-knife. He told me that Catalina and Ana Isabeli were taking the children round the fun fair. Every time he cut a chunk of bark from the piece of wood he would aim carefully at Emeterio's gaping mouth and throw it very lightly in his direction. On the fifth attempt he succeeded. Emeterio leapt up with a start, spitting out bits of bark, and shouted '*Hombre!*' at Serafín, who pointed his piece of wood like a sword in Emeterio's direction. '*Puedo montar su caballo?*' asked Serafín. He was asking whether he could ride Emeterio's horse. Emeterio looked at me and asked whether I'd like to go too. I snapped wide awake when he said I could take Reggis' horse.

I felt very proud to be riding round the *feria* on my own horse. I copied the way Serafín was holding the reins in his left hand with the 'bit rein' held loose, and using the rein attached to the noseband to steer with. I found the stirrups rather cumbersome; it was like riding with a couple of lead weights on your feet.

We rode into the centre of the *feria*. It was still very much in full swing with the colourful flamenco dresses still swirling round and round. We joined a group of horses still standing by the bar and had another fino or two before going on towards the stock pens on the other side of the fair. Horses were walking in all directions and every time we passed, the men would tip their sombreros politely.

We found Ana Isabeli and Catalina buying flowers. Little Ana Maria, who was only two years old, recognized Serafín and waved at him shouting, 'Sewín, Sewín!' and then held up her little flamenco dress in self-consciousness as he waved back.

The stock pens were in the area behind the new tractors. The first row we walked along consisted mainly of cows and bullocks. Every pen had a small wooden sign giving the weight of the cow and the name of its owner in black letters. They stood motionless, resting in the shade of the bamboo roof, many of them nose to tail with the neighbours, using each other's tails to whisk the flies off their faces. One or two of the cows had calves, and I winced when I caught a glimpse of their fresh brand marks, still raw and bleeding. We turned the corner and walked down the next row. There was an enormous brown bottom right up against the railings of the first pen. '*Toro*,' said Serafín and pointed to the board, marvelling at the bull's weight.

Most of the bulls were sitting down so one couldn't really appreciate the incredible body-weight written on the wooden board outside each pen. They varied from 500 kg to as much as 750 kg. Their horns were nearly three feet long.

The last row we came to held the horse pens. Serafín explained that they were mostly young stock or old mares. Seeing our horses walk past, many of them pricked their ears and walked to the front of their pens to watch us go by. I recognized the young horses by their shaved manes and tails. Most of them were rather gawky specimens, their plain faces pleading hopefully for some miracle as we studied each one in turn on our way down the line. A tired old mare was sitting at the back of her pen, her filly foal springing round her as it saw us approaching. As we drew level, it stopped leaping about and pushed its teacup muzzle through the railings to have a better look at us.

Picking our way slowly up and down the rows of stalls and sideshows, we rode back towards the rest of the family. Quite a few horses were gathering under the trees nearby, ready for the trek back to the bullring. Reggis took back his horse and Guillemo gave me a leg up behind the saddle of the beautiful big grey. Emeterio offered to take the car with Ana Isabeli and Catalina so that Serafín could ride his horse back to the bullring with all the others.

We arrived back at the house in time for me to give Dragon a trot round the *picadero* on the end of a lunge rein just to keep him supple. I picked up Dragon's feet one by one to check his shoes. The quarter-inch-thick metal had worn very thin and completely smooth, giving Dragon very little grip on the worn tarmac. So far, he had needed re-shoeing every 150 kilometres so he was overdue for another set. I hoped Emeterio might know of a blacksmith. I went into the barn to say hello to Boris and found him bursting with energy after such a good rest so I took him for a run before giving him his supper.

For the first time in weeks I felt comfortable in my surroundings. It was such a relief not to have the worry of finding food and shelter for the animals, and good food and rest were doing them a power of good. We were approaching the heart of La Mancha, the hottest and most difficult part of our journey, so I decided to ask Emeterio if we could stay one more night. He didn't mind at all but he told me that the nearest blacksmith was in La Solana, 25 kilometres away.

As I was getting ready to leave the next morning, I suddenly realized that I had left my lovely hat at the *feria*. It had been a very good one because I could sit on it and it didn't squash, or leak when I filled it with water. Even Boris had chewed it and hadn't been able to destroy it. I remembered exactly where I had left it; when I rode off with Serafín, I had left it in the grass where I'd been dozing. I couldn't go back for it now but I didn't think I could ever replace it. Louisa had given it to me in South Africa and it was rather a special hat.

I walked down the long, stony drive waving to Emeterio, Reggis and their family. It was six o'clock in the morning so I expected them to go inside after a minute or two but they stood there waving faithfully until they were nothing more than dim shapes outlined by the warm glow of their little house.

We walked into La Solana at about half-past nine. I found the blacksmith's house in a bumpy side-street without too much difficulty. A tractor was parked in front of his door so I had to tie Dragon to someone else's window a little further down the street. Spanish houses always have heavy wrought-iron grilles over their windows which are very useful for tying one's horse to. I knocked on the green door as directed and waited. Boris was watching me, his head hung low so that he could see under Dragon's tummy. The door opened and a pleasant, round-faced woman looked at me inquiringly.

'*La casa del herrero?*' (the house of the blacksmith?) I asked.

'*Sí, está aquí.*'

I pointed to Dragon and explained that he needed new shoes. She sighed and clucked her teeth. My Spanish was still not up to explaining that I was on a long journey and couldn't wait, so I followed her inside while she went to ask her husband.

150

Five children and an old woman were sitting round a table drinking hot milk. The children were eating sponge cakes, grinding the crumbs into the pattern of the plastic tablecloth. I sat down in a tattered armchair in the corner and smiled at the children, conscious of the old woman's confused eyes studying me.

Blacksmiths are never easy people to deal with, through no real fault of their own. It's just that everybody wants their horse done, now. In England people are desperate because they have a day's hunting or a competition the following day; in Spain I imagine it's because they need the horse to plough a field for their living or because like me, they have to travel a long way.

There was a thumping sound as the blacksmith plodded down the wooden stairs. He shook my hand and then scratched his dark, greasy hair. I couldn't understand much of what he was saying but it seemed that he couldn't shoe Dragon for at least two days. With my most disappointed expression I did my best to explain that I had come specially from Valdepeñas for him to shoe my horse and that I had to get to Tomelloso. He asked me where my horse was right now. A glimmer of hope. I showed him Dragon and eventually he agreed to shoe him. There was an awful lot of grumbling about the amount of work he had to do that day so I was thankful that Dragon stood impeccably still for a change. The only nuisance was Boris, who kept growling every time the blacksmith hammered Dragon's foot.

I always hated having to find somewhere to put Dragon so once the blacksmith had done a pretty average job on Dragon's feet and I'd paid him 2,000 pesetas I asked him if he knew of anywhere. He said I could leave him in the place where he kept his pigs. He had lots of work to do but his son would show me when he came home from the bakery at eleven. It wasn't long to wait so I clipped Boris back on to Dragon's girth, left him on guard duty and walked into the village to buy him some meat.

The pig yard was nothing more than a couple of pigsties in a walled area with no gate and no roof. But these were the only animals in the whole village; it would have to do. There was no hay and no horse feed so Dragon had to be content with grain from the chickens. I stuffed one end of the hay rick with

151

straw for him to pick at. He didn't seem particularly bothered not to have a bedroom, but to have to spend the night with pigs? Boris eyed them suspiciously, not quite sure what to make of these disgusting-looking hairy beasts who made the most dreadful noises every time he gnashed his teeth.

With my clothes still clean from Valdepeñas and nothing more I could do for Dragon or Boris I settled down in the village to write postcards. But what could I write? I wasn't exactly on holiday in a smart hotel with a beach and a lovely view. I had been phoning in to the *Daily Mail* every ten days so presumably they had been printing something, but I had no idea what. They had taken some photographs before I left Sotogrande; photographs of me smiling with Dragon, putting up my tent and running along a beach with Boris. Endless, happy, smiling pictures, but none of them real. Now it was real and there was no photographer, nobody to feel what it really meant to be sitting in a tiny village in the middle of nowhere with nobody to talk to, nobody to share the tremendous worry and strain of finding my way, finding food, looking after my animals, feeling my way from one situation to another with hardly a word of Spanish. It wasn't easy and it wasn't fun. As far as the newspaper was concerned I must succeed or die trying. I could never give up; they needed to sell newspapers. I wasn't doing it for the newspapers but I couldn't do it without them. Phoning them every couple of weeks was a small sacrifice for their extra financial help which made it all possible. And by the end of my journey that phone call had become my lifeline. After months of isolation I began to count the days from one call to the next. It was a reverse-charge call and William, the reporter, never seemed to mind those precious minutes ticking away. Once he had jotted down my progress we'd talk about everything from the English weather to what he had had for lunch. Any normal thing. It was this contact with my old world which kept me going.

# ELEVEN

# *Under the Weather*

I DIDN'T SLEEP very well so I had no difficulty in crawling out of the tent at four o'clock in the morning. Dragon had somehow managed to tow the hay rick half-way across the yard but I hadn't heard a thing so perhaps I'd slept better than I thought.

The ride to Tomelloso was long and boring. It was a completely straight road for about thirty-five kilometres with nothing but scrubby bushes to look at. Dragon and Boris went well, quite happy just to switch off as we plodded on and on down the side of the road. I hated having nothing to look at. It was one disadvantage of riding in the dark. I was pleased to note that Dragon was sound this morning because very often a blacksmith would do such a rotten job that he would be lame the following day.

I had no idea where we might find somewhere to stay in Tomelloso. It was a funny little place. Although the main street was tarmac, all the little streets leading off it were nothing but dusty ground with narrow cobbled pavements. We walked past one after another, each one full of chatter and activity as the plump women rolled up and down their houses dusting and polishing, full of gossip in the bright morning sun.

I found a small farm on the far side of the town and rode up the dusty drive, Dragon's hooves clicking against the small stones embedded in the dirt. The farm consisted of three or four large whitewashed barns. Three Fiats were parked in the shade of an enormous willow tree. I thought it was rather a strange place to find a willow.

Dark shapes came out of the barn and walked towards me. As they got nearer I could see their bright smiling faces. They were happy to give Dragon a stable. I slid off Dragon's back and my knees buckled slightly as my boots hit the hard ground. I was tired. Dragon seemed quite perky as I led him into one of the barns. Four horses stood in a line of stalls; their heads jerked round as they heard Dragon's new shoes clatter through the doorway. Dragon whinnied with delight at the thought of company. A young boy scuttled off to find some straw for his bed while I tied him up and took his saddle off. They asked me whether he was a stallion, *entero*. I shook my head and they looked pleased. They pointed to a grey horse in the next stall and explained that it would have been dangerous to leave another stallion so close.

We walked over to the barn by the willow tree where the rest of the family had gathered. The man who had shown me a stall for Dragon introduced himself as Juan Luis, and then his six brothers and sisters, his mother, his uncle and his girlfriend in a long series of Anas, Josés, Miguels and Marias. He told me I was welcome to stay in their house. His mother gave me a warm smile and asked me to follow her.

To my great surprise she led me into the barn behind the willow tree. Inside was an amazing structure. They had made their house inside the barn by simply building internal walls about ten feet high out of breeze blocks and using curtains instead of doors. White sheets had been sewn together and stretched across the tops of the walls to form ceilings, leaving a vast area up above to the corrugated-iron roof of the barn. I pointed upwards and said, '*Buena idea.*' She nodded and explained that until recently the barn had been used to store grain, so the sheeting was there to keep out the dust. The 'house' took up two-thirds of the floor space of the barn, leaving a large area of concrete for the youngest of the children to make a horrible noise playing football with their friends. Although it was Wednesday morning, none of them was at school.

Boris had been given permission to run free. We were miles from a main road so I left him loose while I went to have a wash.

I changed into my shoes and left my smelly boots just inside the barn door. I took my wash-box out of my saddle-bags and followed her. She pulled back a murky green curtain behind which was a small bathroom, then took my arm for my attention

154

and put her finger on the light switch. She pointed to the bare light bulb suspended from a wooden crossbar in the middle of the cotton ceiling and switched on the light. She smiled and looked at me closely, wondering whether I understood. Again: On . . . Off. '*Electricidad*,' she said proudly. I thanked her but she hadn't quite finished. She went over to the bath and ran the tap. '*Agua*,' she said, '*Agua caliente*.'

'*Que bien*,' I replied sounding impressed.

I obviously didn't sound impressed enough because she took my hand and held it under the hot tap. '*Agua caliente*,' she said again.

'*Increible*,' I gasped. It was a word I had picked up only a couple of days before and it had the desired effect. She left me in the bathroom and pulled the curtain behind her.

Feeling exhausted, I slept for most of the day and joined the family for supper. The kitchen was in the outermost room, nearest the barn door. Everybody was sitting round a very large Formica table. Still unable to understand most of what was being said all around me, I glanced round the room. Juana, the mother, was standing over a huge paella dish about a metre wide which sat steaming deliciously on a gas ring. There was a stone sink with a corrugated washboard and a plastic bin of dirty clothes pushed underneath. Some rather nasty bits of meat were scattered on the floor just behind me next to the curtain. Being a substitute for the front door, this curtain was a mass of gaudy colours rather than the gloomy greens and browns of the others. It felt odd to have a house with no windows and such a vast space above you. Although I couldn't see the roof, the laser-like beams of day-light which pierced the holes in it were so bright that they gave an uncanny fourth dimension to the thin cotton sheet.

The following morning I heard quite a commotion coming from the barn. I rushed in, all sorts of dreadful things that Dragon or Boris might have done flashing through my mind. Juan Luis and his brothers were crowding round one of the horses which they'd led out of its stall. There were so many people that I could only see the horse's head. Its eyes were wide and un-settled. They all stood back as someone shouted something and

155

Juan Luis led the horse outside. I went to the other door and noticed drips of blood all over the floor where the horse had been standing moments earlier. I went outside and kept my distance. Juan Luis had given the horse to his brother to hold while he examined it more closely. A chunk of flesh was missing from its shoulder. I had seen many horse injuries caused by numerous things but never a wound that looked like that. Juan Luis turned on the hose and ran it over the gaping hole. I cast my eyes over the horse; it was covered in scrapes and cuts. Then it dawned on me that it must have been attacked by the stallion for some reason. I moved round to look at the other side of the horse and found it had rubbed itself raw. Being tied up, the poor horse had been powerless to defend itself so it had been forced up against the separating wall, scraping itself against the rough concrete. There was no point in stitching it as there was nothing to stitch, so I was pleased to see Juan Luis drying the wound properly and putting on an antiseptic powder. The same boy who'd put down Dragon's bed rushed to turn off the hose. The poor horse looked chilled and shocked, its dripping tail clamped against its bottom. It had been in such a lather that they had washed it all over. I desperately wanted to put a rug on the poor creature but I didn't carry one with me, and quite sure that Juan Luis had never heard of a horse blanket, I helped to dry him off before they led him back into the barn.

Juan Luis explained that the mare on the end of the row was in season. The stallion had broken free during the night and seeing the gelding between himself and the mare, had attacked the defenceless gelding. It was very lucky that Dragon had been where he was or he might have been the one with a hole in his shoulder, which would have grounded us for weeks if not months.

The whole family except for the mother and a pregnant sister went off to work in the fields during the day but before they went, Maria Carmen, one of the sisters, asked me if I would like to spend the day by the pool. That sounded a wonderful idea so I followed her through the drapes of the willow tree and up some steps. I could hardly imagine they would have a swimming pool when they didn't have a fridge so I was

156

interested to see what was at the top of the long flight of steps.

I had to try quite hard to look thrilled when we reached the top of the steps because there in front of us was a circular pool of slimy green water. It was actually the water tank for the farm, fed by the high stone water tower which stood next to it. Maria Carmen went to join the others and I went back to the barn to put on the swimming costume I had bought in Valdepeñas.

I lay in the sun until I was absolutely boiled before I was even tempted to dip my toe in the murky water. When I couldn't bear the heat any longer, I decided to have a swim. There were no steps so I lowered myself in bit by bit with my arms still hanging on to the side. It was a lovely temperature but so green that I couldn't see any of me below the surface. I swam round and round the circular pool and then got out to lie in the sun again. My body steamed as the water evaporated leaving nasty green tidemarks all over me like dried seaweed.

As I lay in the sun I heard the occasional blip on the surface of the water. Each blip made the water swirl slightly; I kept watching and a few blips later I saw something shimmery move just beneath the surface. Ugh! I certainly wasn't going to swim in there again. I moved into the shade and drifted off to sleep.

I was woken by the sound of voices coming up the steps. The family had just finished working in the fields and had come for a swim before lunch. The girls swam gently, trying not to get their hair wet, while their brothers dived in and splashed about just to annoy. The rather dark and sinister pool was suddenly transformed into a huge bathtub full of energy and happy faces as the emerald water slopped over the edge and trickled towards me. They shouted for me to jump in too. With so many people enjoying themselves, it looked far more inviting. Treading water in the middle of the pool, I asked Maria Carmen how deep it was. '*Ocho metros,*' she replied happily: 'Nearly twenty-five feet deep.' I felt quite sick at the thought of the shimmering body I had seen only a few hours ago. At that moment something that felt remarkably like a fish brushed past my leg. I had no idea what 'fish' was in Spanish so I called Maria Carmen, moved my hand like a fish and then pointed towards the bottom. Seeing my alarmed expression she said,

157

'*Hay mucho, pero pasa nada, tranquila.*' (There are lots, but don't worry, it's nothing.) It's only the same as swimming in a river, I told myself, but I still didn't feel absolutely happy with twenty-five feet of murky green water full of unseen fish just below me.

The following day I felt terrible with flu. The family were very kind and looked after me for four days until I was well enough to carry on. As we rode further into La Mancha, the heat had become so intense that I had to be very strict with myself about getting up at two or three o'clock in the morning because it was absolutely impossible for us to make progress during the day.

It was by far the most difficult and soul-destroying part of my journey. The nights became longer, colder and more difficult as I grew tired from days and days without any real sleep and from the enormous worry and responsibility I felt for my animals as I struggled to get us safely from one village to the next. Although I spent most of the day in search of food for them, there were many days when I couldn't find proper hay or feed for Dragon and only a chicken for Boris.

On the whole, I still managed to keep up some sort of routine for them, so they wasted little thought or energy worrying about their ever-changing surroundings. They felt confident in the routine and whenever we rode into a village they would immediately perk up, knowing that there'd be a stop soon, which would be followed by water and then what all the animals live for: food.

I no longer thought in terms of getting to Paris, but simply making it to the border. At the end of every day I would lay out the map of Spain and count how many more days' riding it would be to the border. I always underestimated the number; that way it didn't seem such an impossible goal. As we trudged further and further north, every day seemed longer and more difficult than the one before. Setting off at two or three in the morning meant many long hours of darkness. Night after night without sleep was dragging me down. I often tried to go to sleep resting on Dragon's neck but even at a walk there was such an up-and-down motion that it was too uncomfortable to settle for long. The best way seemed to be to slump in my saddle like an old sack of potatoes, doing everything the Pony Club tells you not to; long reins in one hand resting on his neck, feet stuck well forward and eyes closed. On a couple of occasions I did actually manage to doze off in this position. I'd wake up and find Dragon under me eating the frazzled remains of the spring grass by the side of the road.

It's very difficult to entertain yourself for eight hours in complete darkness when you really can't let yourself drop off or read a book or chat to anyone. I would have long serious conversations with Dragon and Boris while we were going along and occasionally I'd stop and make encouraging noises to Boris so that he'd jump up for a pat. This never failed to make Dragon jealous. He would lean round and make a nasty face, taking a nip at Boris' back if I wasn't quick enough to grab the rein and pull his head round. With such small saddle-bags and keeping their weight down being of such great importance, I only carried four tapes with me. 'The Four Seasons' was thrilling to play in the middle of the night. I would happily sing through the whole thing at the top of my voice, conducting it as I went along. I could see Boris' eyes twinkle in the darkness when he glanced up at me, wondering whether I was all right. Dragon took no notice whatsoever and just plodded along as usual. After a while, both of them seemed to regard this as normal behaviour.

At about four o'clock the batteries on the bicycle torch round Dragon's neck would be nearly flat so I'd get off and change them. When I took them out of the torch to swap them we were left in almost total blackness apart from the dim red glow from the bigger torch on his bottom. It took quite a bit of practice to change the torch batteries with one hand whilst holding Dragon with the other. The little torch was tied very firmly on to the front of his breastplate, making it even more difficult to deal with. Dragon was usually getting quite hot and itchy and would try to rub his head on me which sometimes made me drop the wretched batteries.

The worst time was always at about four-thirty to five o'clock when the temperature dropped dramatically. Most of the night was done, but somehow the three hours which still remained dragged more slowly than ever. Feeling bitterly cold, I would huddle closer in my slumped position. It probably wasn't terribly cold, but somehow the combination of being utterly exhausted and the morning dew making my clothes damp and clammy was simply awful. I began to look at every clump of bushes with a sense of longing, their prickly leaves seemed so fluffy and inviting. It was at this time every night that I decided I was never going to ride at night again. I would always convince myself that this really was the last time I would have to do it, finding it much easier to think in terms of just another hour or so rather than endless nights of this miserable feeling. When daylight did arrive and the warm sun dried out my clothes and smiled on my world again, I forgot all about the cold and the exhaustion. It was beyond my imagination to be able to remember quite how acute was that damp and cold feeling of exhaustion at the end of the long night. So at two or three o'clock the next morning, there I'd be, waving goodbye, clip-clopping out from under warm streetlights and into the blackness beyond.

As time went on I became more accustomed to the worry and exhaustion, the difficulties and the discomforts until at last I became resigned to my somewhat nomadic lifestyle. I had changed, adapted myself to be content within its lonely bounds. More experienced now, I could estimate my journey time almost to the minute. I was even able to arrange letter drops as far as three weeks ahead. This revolutionized my existence; suddenly I had something much closer than the border to look forward to. It was always difficult to judge how big a place was just by looking at the map, but taking what I believed to be the bigger towns, I wrote Michael a list of letter drops and dates. Any letters would be sent to him; he put them in one envelope under 'Lista de Correos' (care of the post office) and posted it off to the next letter drop. When I reached these named towns I would head straight for the post office, jump off and rush inside for the precious envelope. If there was a queue, the wait was unbearable. Once or twice there would be nothing. Bitterly disappointed, I would hang on for a couple of days, full of hope, until I could wait no longer and had to move on.

160

TWELVE

# The Monastery of Santa Maria
## de Huerta

IN THE VILLAGE of Alcolea del Pinar, Dragon and Boris shared
a tiny walled garden behind the butcher's shop and I was given
a room in the priest's house. I woke up in my lumpy horsehair
bed with the most terrible stomach ache, quite unable to move.
The prickly horsehair was poking through the mattress into my
back. I dragged myself out of bed and stood on the goatskin
mat for a moment, my stomach still aching horribly. Doubled
up with pain, I climbed down the narrow wooden staircase to
the tiny bathroom below. Spartan but well scrubbed, the room
was completely bare apart from the priest's razor and toothbrush. As one might expect, there was only one tap, for cold
water.

I returned to my humble little bedroom and stuffed my
meagre possessions into my saddle-bags. I picked up every
trace of straw off the floor before tiptoeing down the steep little
staircase in my socks. As I padded across the hall tiles, 'Buenos
días,' said a voice. I turned round to find the priest sitting at his
desk in the study. Perhaps he had been waiting for me since
three o'clock in the morning? He handed me an envelope and
told me that it contained a letter of introduction to his 'brothers'
in the monastery of Santa Maria de Huerta. I thanked him for
his thoughtfulness and went to find Dragon and Boris.

It was a long way to the monastery, much further than I had
thought. The priest had told me forty kilometres – a depressing
thought when I had an excruciatingly painful stomach. I'd have
loved to spend the day in bed but we hadn't made particularly
good progress recently so I had to press on. By the time we
reached the monastery, we had done almost sixty kilometres!

Feeling dreadful and thoroughly dehydrated from eight

161

hours in the fierce heat we padded our way across the silent outer courtyard of the monastery towards an ancient doorway which stood tall and magnificent before us.

We ground to a halt an arm's length from the door and I leaned out of the saddle and gave it a thump. There was a very small window cut into the door but I could see no signs of life. I tried again, this time with the end of my stick. Dragon sniffed the door, wondering what he had done wrong. A man's round face pressed itself up against the window and then disappeared. I waited . . . the face didn't return. I banged my fist against the heavy wood. The face appeared again; it had an anxious expression like a frightened animal. I held up the envelope from the priest. The man peered at it for a moment and then opened the small window. 'I'm sorry,' he said, 'the monks are having lunch, can you come back in four hours?'

I couldn't believe what I was hearing. Suddenly the heat and exhaustion of eight hours in the saddle coupled with my aching stomach were too much for me. 'I have ridden through the whole of Spain and never in all that time have I been turned away, and yet when I come to the church for help they tell me they're eating lunch!' I wailed. Boris looked very worried about me and cast a vicious look in the direction of the face which seemed to be the cause of the trouble.

The face took one look at Boris, muttered something about '*Padre*' and disappeared again, leaving us standing in front of the firmly closed door. I couldn't argue with that door. I was just about to turn Dragon round when I heard the sound of sliding bolts and three men in brown robes appeared. The middle one stepped forward, his hands held out towards me. Boris didn't trust him at all and kept looking from me to him and back again, desperately trying to gauge the temperature of the situation, wondering whether his services would be required.

'It's all right, Boris,' I said quietly, and was relieved to see him relax his guard slightly. It would be a disaster if he gobbled up a monk!

'Padre Vicente,' said the monk, holding out his hand to me. I didn't dare shake it in case Boris got the wrong idea so I held on to both reins and did my best to produce a smile. I fished

162

in my saddle-bag, brought out the envelope and handed it to him. He read it slowly and carefully and then looked up at me and said, 'The church is your house.'

He gave some instructions to the other two monks and invited me inside the monastery for something to eat.

'I'd like to take care of my animals first,' I replied, surprised at their lack of feeling.

The padre apologized that they did not have a stable but said they could give my animals water and some shade until other arrangements had been made. The shade turned out to consist of a tie-up ring under the overhang of a house on the opposite side of the courtyard. There was another ring further along so I tied Boris to that. I left everything in a heap next to Dragon; I felt it would be rather an insult to the monks to leave my belongings under the guard of a large Dobermann. The three monks stood in a row watching me see to my animals, strange motherly expressions on their faces. They made me feel like Mary and her donkey being given a stable at the inn, though I don't remember Mary having a Dobermann tied to her donkey. I asked them where I could buy some meat for Boris and Padre Vicente said that one of the monks would escort me into the village.

The queue in the *carnicería* parted as the monk entered. The local women bowed their heads reverently and muttered under their breath. The butcher automatically turned his attention to the monk, who asked how much I needed. '*Dos kilos y media,*' (two and a half kilos) I replied. There was a hushed silence and I felt the women's eyes piercing holes in my back. The meat was carefully chopped up, wrapped in paper and pushed across the counter. I unzipped my little red purse but the monk waved his hand in protest. I looked at the butcher for guidance but he smiled and gave a slow shake of his head. As we walked back through the gates of the monastery I wondered whether the monks had an account with the butcher or whether the town provided all the food for the monks free of charge.

The other two monks were still watching over Dragon and Boris when we returned. Dragon had dozed off; Boris was definitely on guard, but rather agitated at having my belongings just out of his reach. He saw the bag of meat I was carrying and jumped up and down in anticipation. Dragon took no notice. Warning the monks to keep away I split open the package and put it down in front of him. Someone had given each of them a full bucket of water. Dragon was easy enough but I wondered who had put one next to Boris; it couldn't have been one of the monks because Boris would surely have shredded his robes in a second. I spotted the answer; a large kindly-looking woman was standing in the doorway of the house, barely visible in the shadow of the overhang. The way she was looking at Boris so fondly as he gulped down his meat told me that it must have been her. Large round women were about the only creatures on earth that Boris would let anywhere near him.

'We have a place for your horse,' said Padre Vicente. 'Follow Brother Miguel and he will show you.' There were many doors along that side of the outer courtyard and all except the house of the old woman were closed. The monk stopped outside the last door in the row, took a long key from the cord round his waist and unlocked it. We went inside. On his third attempt, the monk managed to explain to me that most of the young monks lived outside the walls of the monastery in these houses. This one was in need of repair and so was unoccupied at present. He opened a door on my right. 'We have removed the furniture from this room, so if it meets with your approval your animals are welcome to stay in here.' It was a very kind offer. I only hoped they realized that my horse wasn't house-trained. He went over to the window and opened it wide. 'We could leave this open and then your horse will be able to look out.'

'It's perfect,' I said and the monk glowed happily as he closed the door behind us.

As we walked back towards Dragon and Boris I wondered where I was going to find hay or straw. The monks had obviously never been near an animal in their lives so I was doubtful whether they would have any.

When we reached Padre Vicente and the monk had relayed my approval, Padre Vicente told me that *Hermano* Miguel would now take the monastery car and drive me to a nearby farm where I could buy hay and straw. And so it was that Dragon and Boris spent their first night in the monastery.

Once Dragon and Boris were safely shut in their room for the night, *Hermano* Miguel took me up a long winding staircase to show me mine. He asked me to knock on the main door at seven-thirty and someone would be there to meet me. As his soft leather sandals padded down the little staircase I flopped on to the bed with exhaustion. I lay on my back and cast my eyes around the room. Grey walls, wardrobe, painting of the Virgin Mary, shuttered windows, wooden floor and plain brown mat by the side of the bed. A Bible lay on the bedside table. I have to admit it was years since I'd read the Bible but I sat up on the bed and opened it somewhere in the middle. My Spanish seemed to have improved as I found I could stumble through a paragraph understanding more or less what was written. I fell asleep with the Bible in my hand and woke up just before half-past seven. I just had time to have a cold bath before putting on my one and only pair of trousers and a clean shirt. I was very glad that I had brought a pair of shoes because I felt terribly clumsy and awkward walking alongside the monks in my cowboy boots. I brushed my hair and felt thankful there wasn't a mirror; I could only hope I didn't look as bad as I felt. I rushed downstairs and reached the main entrance just as the monastery bells chimed the half-hour.

I knocked on the door and waited . . . that same anxious face appeared and studied me carefully. Then I recognized the voice of *Hermano* Miguel followed by the sound of sliding bolts. The main door swung open and I stepped inside. As *Hermano* Miguel greeted me, I caught sight of the anxious face peering at me from the shadows. *Hermano* Miguel noticed, and as we walked out of the cool portal he gently explained that the monk by the gate was *'inutil'*, mentally subnormal. The monastery had no visitors except for monks from other monasteries so he was not usually a problem, he apologized, and I suddenly realized why there had been such a delay before they had decided to help me that afternoon.

Just in front of us was a beautiful green lawn. A fountain played slowly and delicately in the middle. It had been a very long time since I had seen green grass. I paused for a moment, just to look and remember. We walked in silence, the monk's leather sandals hardly making a sound on the smooth stone floor. I did my best to walk quietly but it wasn't easy, even in

165

shoes. We stepped through an open doorway. A monk waited politely for us to pass and crossed himself. Another courtyard, this time filled with a multi-coloured square of roses smiling in the sun. They were so close I could almost touch them. A stone statue of a woman bowed gracefully in the centre of the rosebed; her nose and mouth had crumbled away with time but her eyes still looked down with nothing but kindness on the quiet beauty which surrounded her. The ancient stone, the beautiful flowers, the green grass, the absolute peace and tranquillity seemed a poignant contrast to my difficult and frustrating journey.

At the end of a long covered passageway was the kitchen. Two monks wearing frilly aprons were rushing to and fro with steaming stainless steel pots and chopped vegetables. *Hermano* Miguel bade them good evening before leading me into the dining-room. I imagined long wooden tables with rows of shaven-headed monks bending over wooden plates and baskets of bread, so I was disappointed to see Formica tables, green glass plates and plastic chairs. I recognized Padre Vicente; he beckoned me to come and sit at his table. There was a pleasant hum of chatter as the monks recounted their day to one another before dinner.

One of the monks put a big glass bowl full of salad in the middle of our table. I watched him sweep back into the kitchen again, his long brown robes covered by the ridiculous apron. Padre Vicente stood up, immediately followed by the rest of the room. The conversation died as a large man of about fifty entered the room and took a place at the head of our table. There was a short pause and just like a teacher organizing a crowd of excited school children, he waited for the shuffling and the whispering to stop before saying grace.

During dinner, *Hermano* Miguel tried hard to keep me in touch with the conversation of the rest of the table. Padre Vicente was writing a book about the founder of the monastery. The abbot was inquiring about its progress. *Hermano* Miguel took the opportunity to tell me a little about the monastery. It had been founded in the thirteenth century by a nun from the north of Spain; it was her statue which stood in the rose courtyard. He went on to explain that the monastery was almost a closed order, only accepting monks from other monasteries.

166

I suddenly felt privileged to be sitting among them. I asked him whether the monks here ever changed monastery. It was almost unheard of, he said but many of the older monks went to visit other monasteries or help in homes for mentally handicapped or disabled children. One or two of the aged monks had remained within the walls of the monastery their whole lives.

Presently, the conversation turned to me. The other monks at our table started listening to our conversation and very soon, their imaginations fired, they were asking me all sorts of questions: Where had I started? Where was I going? How long had it taken? Where did I stay normally? This last question was always an interesting one. It was hard to explain where I stayed 'normally' because there was no such thing as 'normal' on a journey of this sort. Each place was different, and yet every one the same. Always the same problems: finding food, finding a stable, the heat, predatory men. The monks listened intently. To them, it must have seemed an extraordinary journey for a young woman to make alone, so extraordinary that I was somehow exempt from the ordinary laws of the monastery, almost like a visiting creature from outer space.

I answered their questions for almost an hour, delighted to see their prayer-worn faces light up with new interest like children's. Even the abbot was beginning to smile. I felt very happy being able to communicate with them at last, finding it much easier to talk about my journey. I had answered their questions and many others so many times along my route that I was able to talk freely and easily without needing to pause in search of a word.

After dinner I went to Dragon's and Boris' bedroom. They heard me coming and Dragon's head looked out through the open window, quickly followed by a large black snout: standing on his hind legs Boris could only just see out. Dragon sneered at Boris to make him move over a bit and Boris replied with the usual gnashing of teeth. They had a healthy respect for each other; Boris for Dragon's large feet and Dragon for Boris' fearsome teeth. I opened the door to their house to be greeted by the strange sound of hooves and claws scrabbling across the floorboards to reach the bedroom door. Boris got to me first, taking my wrist lovingly in his jaws and 'piano-biting' his way up to my elbow and back again. Dragon's well trained nose pushed straight into my pocket and seized one of the carrots I'd saved for him from the kitchen. I clipped a lead on to Boris and led him out of the house. Dragon poked his head out of the window to watch us walk away. He knew that I always took Boris for an evening walk but as I looked at Dragon's patient face staring after us, I wondered whether he thought that one evening we wouldn't come back. Boris had a permanent dread of being left behind. Every time he saw the first tell-tale sign of my picking up Dragon's bridle he would jump up and down barking until he felt safely clipped on to Dragon's girth.

When I went back to check on Dragon the next morning, I was horrified to see a floorboard stuck to his hind foot. A nail, please not a nail! I approached him quietly, willing him to stand still. A single step would drive the nail even deeper into his foot. I ran my hand down his leg and took hold of the splintered piece of floorboard. Levering it against his foot I yanked the nail free as cleanly as possible. A small but deadly hole was left in his sole. What could be worse than a rusty nail in his foot? A puncture would can so easily become infected, quite apart from things like tetanus – I had no idea if his jabs were up to date. I would be lucky to move in weeks.

Wound powder and cream were no use at all; I needed my purple antiseptic spray to get right into the hole. It was constantly spraying its vivid purple dye all over everything in my saddle-bags so I'd left it somewhere ages ago thinking cream and powder could cover most wounds. Thoroughly despondent, I went into the monastery for breakfast.

The monks were very sympathetic, but there was little they could do to help. While we were eating, I remembered that the farm *Hermano* Miguel had taken me to the day before had cows; with any luck they might have some purple spray.

*Hermano* Miguel drove me to the farm and we were lucky; the farmer gave me a nearly empty can of purple spray and kindly said I needn't bother to return it.

With the help of *Hermano* Miguel I blocked up the hole in the floor and checked for any more loose boards. Ideally, Dragon should have been given an antibiotic injection but with none available I filled the wound with purple spray and hoped. If I kept the floor immaculately swept and his foot as clean and dry as I could, there was always a chance that nothing would go wrong, but I rather felt that we'd used up all our luck when he'd nearly sliced off his foot on that very first day.

Grounded, I spent the next few days resting in the peaceful surroundings of the monastery, exploring the ancient building itself or asleep in my room.

A miraculous five days later, the hole in Dragon's foot had closed and he seemed sound enough to move on. I had built up a very good *ambiente* (rapport) with the monks of the monastery and on my last evening Padre Vicente told me that the abbot had invited me to attend mass after dinner.

After a fairly average meal of oily chicken and cabbage, the monks trooped out of the dining-room to mass. I suddenly had an idea, and asked *Hermano* Miguel to wait for me a moment while I went to get a jersey. I wanted to dash back to my room to pick up my dictaphone so that I could record the monks singing. Rolling it up in my jersey, I ran across the long shadows and into the main entrance.

I had heard the monks practising in the afternoons and often sat down to listen so I was looking forward to hearing the real thing. We joined the end of the queue of brown habits filing slowly through an arched doorway, down three flights of steps and into the underground chapel . . . Darkness. It took a few seconds for my eyes to become accustomed to the flickering light of the candles which burned solidly at the far end of the chapel. Row upon row of monks filled the long wooden benches on either side of us. I could barely see their shapes but the air felt heavy with their presence, smothered by the acres of dusty brown cloth. I held on to my jersey, sheltering its secret. We stopped level with the front row where six wooden chairs stood waiting in the darkness.

I sat down, with Padre Vicente on one side and *Hermano* Miguel on the other. We sat in silence, the candlelight throwing sinister shapes and shadows on the walls. The choristers sat facing the aisle on either side of the chapel. Nobody moved. Presently, the choristers stood up and in low, echoing voices sang to mark the arrival of the abbot, who walked solemnly

169

down the aisle and took a place at the lectern just in front of us. The singing stopped and a monk stood up to light the candle at the head of the lectern. The abbot raised his hands and we all stood up. He began to recite a long psalm in a deep monotone. It was all in Latin; the echoes were beautiful but made it impossible to understand a single word. We sat down and the choir began to sing. Filled with rich echoing voices the chapel seemed to dissolve history and draw us into its medieval beginnings, another world. I felt inside my rolled-up jersey and pressed the 'record' switch on the dictaphone. I had not anticipated the candlelight. My dictaphone had a red light which came on when it was recording. In this darkness, it would be easy to spot. If I buried it too deep it wouldn't pick up the sound but not wanting to risk discovery, I wrapped it in two thicknesses of jersey and hoped that it wasn't visible from a distance. From that moment my mind was on a knife-edge. I was probably the only person ever to have witnessed the monks singing mass in this underground chapel and I'm not even Catholic. I felt twinges of guilt and waited for the moment when the ceremony would come to an abrupt halt, all heads would turn and someone would shout, 'You!' pointing at me, sitting quietly on my wooden chair – but it didn't happen.

I closed my bedroom door and flopped down on the bed in relief. I unwrapped my precious tape recorder and rewound it a little way. Turning the volume right down I pressed 'play'. The mournful sound of the monks' voices came out of the tiny little machine. It was amazingly clear. I switched it off quickly, terrified that someone might hear the familiar sound of their brothers' voices coming from somewhere they shouldn't. I set my alarm for four o'clock. The following day I would be on my way again, back into my hot, dangerous and uncertain world. As I lay in bed trying to go to sleep, I felt the Virgin Mary's eyes staring at me through the darkness. After twenty minutes, I had to get up and turn the painting round so it faced the wall.

I led Dragon out of his bedroom and tied him up outside in the cool night air. I clipped Boris on to the girth as a top priority so he wouldn't start barking and wake everybody up. As I lifted the saddle-bags on to Dragon's back I noticed a number of lights were on in the dormitory houses; I could see a few of the monks silhouetted in the windows looking down at us. Taking hold of Dragon's reins I walked slowly and quietly out of the monastery. As I looked back, I saw three or four monks leaning out of their windows to watch us go; I waved in their direction and a couple of them raised their hands. I wondered whether they'd pray for me.

I walked alongside Dragon for the first four kilometres and when I was certain that he was sound I climbed on board. Riding at night was always wretched and cold for me, but the animals were much happier without the heat and the traffic. Dragon had eyes like a cat in the dark. Whenever the little bicycle torch grew dim he would carry on trotting as if it was midday. We were heading for somewhere called Gomara; the distance wasn't marked on my map, but I guessed it to be about forty kilometres. Shivering with cold, I hoped it wouldn't be much further. I had been getting very lonely and despondent recently as we never seemed to get any closer to our goal but now at last the Pyrenees seemed days away rather than weeks. I was waiting for the day when the dawn would break and the foothills of the Pyrenees would be silhouetted against the first streaks of daylight. Watching the world waking up always thrilled me; partly because it marked our survival through yet another ghastly night but also for the way everything seemed new and clear. Intense heat is very powerful; this cool, dawn light was always peaceful and delicate in comparison.

Gomara was a dreadful place. A rather rude and unhelpful man with some cows eventually agreed to put Dragon in a lean-to shelter, where I left both animals while I tried to find somewhere for myself. The town had no hostel or anywhere to stay and the people in the village were all most unfriendly so I gave up and spent the day fast asleep next to Boris.

The temperature seemed a little cooler than it had been in the last couple of weeks and I wondered whether it might be possible to start riding during the day again. Dragon's foot was still sound, he was healthy and well rested in his body and riding during the day would be faster – we could be in France within a week. So I decided to ride through the night one last time. I tacked up Dragon and clipped Boris on to the girth as

171

usual. A holey old blanket that I had noticed during the day lay in a heap under the manger. It was a pretty filthy-looking thing so I hadn't picked it up, but now that the air was freezing cold, it looked quite tempting despite its smell. I wrapped it round me before climbing on to Dragon's back. To be reduced to this.

It was one of the worst nights yet. I had forgotten to buy more batteries in Gomara and with no moon I didn't dare go faster than a walk. Doing a rising trot often made the difference between feeling cold and feeling as if I was going to die of it, and that night it was bitterly cold. I wrapped the thin, holey blanket round me, covering my head. There seemed to be far more holes in it than I remembered as I struggled with the beastly, smelly thing. I was as cold as I could ever remember. My shivering body somehow felt worse for the knowledge that I had to stick it out for at least another four hours before the sun started to rise.

Olvega was just as inhospitable as Gomara, and all I could find for Dragon was a haystack to tie him to. He was quite happy chomping all afternoon but by the evening the temperature had dropped so dramatically that the poor horse was bucking on the spot to keep warm. I put the holey blanket over him; at least it would be something. With no surcingle, I had to tie it on with baling string. The farmer gave me menacing, sideways looks and if it hadn't been for Boris I felt sure he would have jumped on me. I decided to leave Boris guarding my saddle-bags and go ahead to Tudela to find somewhere better for us to stay the following night.

The local bus stopped in Tudela and I was lucky to have to wait only ten minutes for it. As soon as I arrived, I went to the police station and asked for a *picadero*. Tudela is a huge place, and as usual the *picadero* was on the opposite side of town. Feeling my way, I managed to persuade one of the five bored-looking policemen to drive me there. It was a wise move, because it was tucked in behind a disused railway line and I would never have found it on my own.

Dragon would like this, I thought, as I walked along the row of bottoms towards a man who was sweeping out a stall at the far end. My Spanish had improved enormously so I didn't have to worry how to say things any more. I explained my problem and the odd-looking man who called himself Jesús nodded thoughtfully and asked me to follow him. He showed me a small stall, much narrower than the others, and asked whether it would do. It would do beautifully!

Jesús took me into an unbelievably filthy room where two men were sitting on a brown plastic sofa drinking coffee while feeding five scrawny cats with their fingers. They stood up when we walked in and Jesús introduced them as Pedro and Antonio. I smiled uneasily, feeling rather nervous without Boris by my side. They turned out to be very kind and helpful and, as it was getting late, Jesús offered to drive me back to Olvega.

He chattered away during the twenty-minute drive back to the farm. When we arrived it was still freezing cold but Dragon had stopped bucking. I couldn't be sure whether it was because he felt warmer or because he was too tired to buck any more. I asked Jesús if he would mind taking the saddle-bags back to the *picadero* in his car. There was one thing I'd learned to recognize in the last couple of months and that was a face to be trusted. Jesús may have looked rather odd but his was still one of those faces. 'It would make such a difference,' I said. 'They weigh so much.' He put them in his car and drove off into the night.

It was later than I had anticipated and I still had to find a room. Olvega seemed a dark, dishonest town and I would have liked to take Boris with me as I walked away into the unfamiliar shadows, but my saddle and bridle were too important to risk so I left him in charge.

After the night before, nothing could have persuaded me to ride at night again, so although it was rather a cheap and dirty room that I found, it seemed sheer luxury to be lying on a bed rather than trudging along on horseback in the pitch darkness. I didn't bother to set my alarm clock and drifted off into a real sleep.

It was almost half-past nine by the time I reached the farm the following morning. I turned the corner and was surprised to see a *Guardia Civil* van waiting outside the farm gate. Two *Guardia Civil* men were leaning on the bonnet, smoking. As I

173

approached they stood up and one of them said something to the driver of the van through the window. Seven more climbed out. I kept walking. It seemed to be me they were interested in, but I couldn't think what they could want me for. I stopped to open the farm gate and a tall man stepped forward in front of me. The others formed a circle round me, each one pointing a small, automatic machine gun at me. I thought perhaps Boris had attacked someone during the night. The tips of their guns moved me towards the van. I couldn't see Boris from where we were standing so I didn't have any clues as to what nine *Guardia Civil* men armed with sub-machine guns could possibly want from me.

'Your papers!' barked the tall man. I was about to point to my saddle-bags in the farmyard when I remembered with absolute horror that they had gone with Jesús to the *picadero* in Tudela. I tried to explain but they didn't listen. Still pointing their guns at me, they moved me slowly and carefully towards the van and 'escorted' me into it like a convict.

The van came to a standstill. Peering through the barred windows I saw without surprise that we were at the head-quarters of the local *Guardia Civil*. The door was pulled open and I was frog-marched into a small grey room containing one table with a chair on either side. The tall man waved away the guards and gestured me to sit down. Feeling rather scruffy, I wished I had had time to wash my shirt in Gomara. The tall man put his face very close to mine and stared at me for a moment or two. 'Your papers?' he asked, slowly and deliber-ately. I told him about the *picadero* in Tudela and then apologized that my Spanish wasn't very good. Without a flicker of ac-knowledgement he began to question me further: Where had I come from? '*Provincia de Cadiz*,' I answered solidly. He gave me a sideways look and then asked where I was going. 'Paris,' I replied shakily, quite aware that this sounded even more ridiculous than my first answer. The tall man raised his eye-brows and leaned back thoughtfully in his chair. Of course he doesn't believe me, I thought, and felt the first wave of uneasi-ness seeping into my mind.

'Why are you riding to Paris?' he asked. Luckily I had answered this question a thousand times before so I was a little

174

more confident of the vocabulary. When I had finished he let his chair stand on four legs again and studied my face once more. It made me feel distinctly uncomfortable; presumably the desired effect.

I had been warned that I couldn't go anywhere without papers in Spain. I had always kept them safely in a waterproof box at the bottom of my saddle-bags, but in nearly three months I had been asked to produce them just once, so I hadn't recently given them much thought. If I could remember the name of the village where they had stopped me before, perhaps I could find a way out of this silly mess. I continued to answer the tall man's questions with half my mind, while the other half desperately tried to remember the name of that village. It was definitely after Ronda but it was so long ago that I couldn't be sure whether it was before or after Campillos. It might have begun with a 'C' I thought . . . 'Señorita?' said a voice sharply, 'Where are you going to today?' I repeated what I had said about the *picadero* in Tudela. A 'C', definitely a 'C' . . . 'Cuevas de Becerro!' I said out loud. The tall man stopped in mid-sentence. I explained to him what had happened and suggested that if he were to telephone the *Guardia Civil* in Cuevas de Becerro, they might have a record of me and would be able to confirm that my papers were in order. He nodded briefly and left the room. It was a slim chance, but as they refused to listen to my story about Tudela it was my only chance. Left alone in the dingy grey room, I tried not to worry.

He came back twenty agonizing minutes later. As he walked towards the table I still had no idea what was happening; his face didn't give away a thing. He put a form on the desk in front of him. My heart sank; they obviously hadn't found a record of me and I was about to be thrown in jail for a week. 'We telephoned Cuevas del Becerro,' he said. 'They tell me they have inspected your papers.' I smiled carefully, not wanting to look too relieved. 'Someone will drive you back to the farm, but first I will have to fill in this form.'

It was twelve o'clock before I was able to set off, but with no saddle-bags to carry, it was an easy day's ride. At one stage we came across a couple of stubble fields so we had the first gentle canter we'd had for a long, long time. Boris thought it was tremendous fun racing alongside. He was now incredibly fit and his daily ration of meat had gone up to just over two and a half kilos. I had never seen a dog look quite so lean and healthy; I felt proud of him.

I reached Tudela by four o'clock, having averaged a record nine kilometres an hour. Jesús looked rather anxious as we approached. He rushed up and asked us why the journey had taken us so long. I told him all about it while we washed down the animals. He had put down a good straw bed for Dragon in the narrow stall and a little heap of oats was waiting for him in the manger. Dragon purred with pleasure as I led him along the line of horse bottoms and into his stall. Jesús said he was quite happy for Boris to wander round loose. There were no children about so I didn't have to worry about him and after such an energetic day he would be too exhausted to disappear very far. We went into the filthy room for a cup of coffee. The same two men were still sitting on the plastic sofa. They didn't stand up this time; one of them smiled and the other one was fast asleep.

I spent a very pleasant evening with Jesús and his friends. The filthy room took a little getting used to, but it would have been rude to have turned down their kindness. Five cats were standing on the encrusted stove, licking the dirty pans. Jesús shooed them away and lit the stove. He unwrapped six sardines and put them on one side. Taking a rag he wiped out a frying pan and put it on the stove. The five cats curled round his legs, purring. I offered to help and was given a knife and a couple of tomatoes.

The four of us sat in a line on the plastic sofa eating the sardines and chatting about horses. At about ten o'clock Jesús said that the other two would have to go home now. I had thought this was their home, although it had puzzled me that there were no other rooms. Jesús said there was a small room with a bed if I would like to sleep there for the night. 'You'll be quite safe in there, we'll lock you in,' he said kindly.

It was a funny little room, just as dirty as the other. It seemed to be a general storeroom, containing everything from used syringes for injecting the horses to old catfood tins. The little bed was almost hidden by a heap of saddles and bridles. Jesús

176

moved the tack on to the floor and pulled back the smelly blanket to reveal a tangled mass of sheets. He seemed quite unconcerned by the state of the place. He shut the door and I heard the main door of the stables slide across and the padlock snap shut. Boris held my wrist affectionately in his mouth. He made me feel very safe. Without Boris, I wouldn't have slept here for the world.

Dragon's foot had remained sound, but as I had found somewhere with good food and bedding for him I stayed at the *picadero* for another couple of days before moving on. Jesús and his two friends were kind, and despite my first impressions I felt quite at ease with them all. It was a great relief not to feel vulnerable for a change. Jesús spent all day mucking out and lunging while his two friends sat on the plastic sofa drinking coffee. The whole place was very down at heel, and any holes in the roof or gaps in the fencing were repaired with something out of the car dump next door. Although the three men kept the place like a pigsty, their horses were very well looked after; they were fat and shiny and none of them showed signs of having been mistreated in any way.

Three days later, I decided it was time to move on. Jesús and his friends tried to make me stay on for a couple more days but I explained that I still had a very long way to go. One of them offered to escort me to the road to Ejea de los Caballeros; it was the first time I'd seen him do anything energetic the whole time I'd been there. He jumped on his little moped and fired it into life. Jesús' sausage dog jumped up and down next to him, asking to come too. Jesús lifted him up and put him in the milk crate which was strapped to the back of the moped. Boris thought this was a wonderful game and snapped his teeth frantically, looking forward to playing hide and seek at the next stop. 'He's not coming, Boris,' I said, 'he's just showing us the way.' Boris took no notice and leaned on his lead more than ever, dying to catch up with the fat little sausage dog.

Half-way through the day, I stopped to telephone William at the Daily Mail. The last time I had spoken to him he had said that his editor was anxious to send him out with a photographer as soon as I reached the Pyrenees. I was very close now, only an inch away from the dark patches on my map. After a long

177

wait, I got through, and arranged to meet them at Pamplona airport in four days' time.

I felt very happy at the thought of William coming out to see us. Once Dragon was on automatic pilot I dug out my map to see if I had set myself an impossible task. We could be in Valpalmas or Ardisa tomorrow, Ayerbe the following day and then we might have a problem; the next village marked on my map was Jaca, at least forty-five kilometres from Ayerbe. It would all depend on whether I managed to find good food for Dragon. He had proved that he could survive on almost nothing but he would need more than cake and a few lettuce leaves to do that sort of mileage in four days. A horse can look thin overnight if he doesn't get enough bulk to eat, and I certainly didn't want him to look anything except shiny and healthy when William arrived. The other problem was his shoes; they were going to need redoing any day. The combination of being so nearly in the Pyrenees and William coming out to see us completely refuelled my incentive. At last we were getting somewhere.

# THIRTEEN

# To the Pyrenees

WE WERE LUCKY to find a small farm in Ejea de los Caballeros
with a stable and plenty of oats and alfalfa for Dragon. Normally
I would have stayed another day to feed him up a bit but I had
to keep to my schedule. We rode thirty kilometres to Valpalmas
and couldn't find anything more than a small enclosure where
I could leave Dragon loose and half a bucket of oats. We would
still be all right if I found somewhere comfortable for him in
Ayerbe the following day. Ayerbe was on a main road, so I
hoped that it would be much bigger than Valpalmas.

It was much bigger, but its business came from the passing
trade rather than from farming. I looked long and hard but all
I could find was an abandoned pigpen and some chicken grain.
I was worried. Although we had only ridden twenty kilometres
that day, Dragon was beginning to look 'tucked up'; his nice
round tummy was falling away. I spent nearly three hours
hitching to Esquedas, the next village, and back with nothing
more than half a bucket of oats to show for it. William would
be arriving at Pamplona airport at 6.15 p.m. the day after next.
Jaca, my next planned stop, was still a long way away, and I
doubted whether I could reach it the following day. But I wasn't
going to push my animals for anyone.

I set off early to give myself plenty of time to find somewhere
for Dragon at the other end. I had no idea where 'the other
end' was going to be. By three o'clock I had given up the idea
of getting to Jaca and simply hoped that there would be a village
between here and Jaca where we could stay. The road had been
climbing steadily all day, making our progress slower than
usual. Surrounded by an endless sea of rocks and pine trees I
began to wonder if we were going to find anywhere at all; I

179

hadn't seen a house or a cow shed since we left Ayerbe six hours before. The animals plodded on faithfully, their trust and solid devotion tweaking at my conscience. I simply had to find them somewhere to stay tonight.

We found one small bar by the side of the road. It was the only one for miles so there were lots of cars parked outside. I tied Dragon up in the shade and stomped in. The whispers and surprised expressions didn't bother me any more as I stood at the bar and asked for the usual Coke and a bucket of water. Walking uphill had made Dragon thirstier than usual, and even Boris managed to drink a fair amount. When I decided they'd had enough I returned the bucket, scrunched across the gravel parking area and back on to the road. A voice shouted, 'Excuse me.' I turned round to see a middle-aged man rushing towards us waving a newspaper, his wife hovering in the background looking rather embarrassed. He reached Dragon with his red face shiny and perspiring. 'I'm sorry to bother you,' he said, 'it's just that we read the *Daily Mail* and wondered if you're the girl they keep writing about. We just wanted to say hello and well done.' It was simply wonderful to be able to talk English with someone. 'Would you mind if we gave Dragon a pat?' he asked rather shyly, like a six-year-old boy. They very sensibly gave Boris a wide berth. I gave him a pat, not wanting him to feel missed out.

The road was getting narrower and the traffic heavier. The rocks had formed an almost vertical slope on our left and dropped away to nothing beyond the single-bar barrier at the edge of the road on our right. Still no sign of a house or a village. I was getting really worried now. After a couple more hours the light began to fade; it would be dangerous to go on much further at this speed with barely adequate lights. It was no longer a matter of finding a comfortable stable and good food; we were now desperate to find something . . . anything.

The sharp descent to our right began to level out. The rocky ground was now covered with billowing green; I couldn't be sure whether it was brambles or leafy bushes. It didn't matter, I just needed to find a small flat patch of ground somewhere. Every time we turned a corner I scoured the acres of matted undergrowth for a glimmer of hope. It was getting dark, my animals were tiring, I was getting desperate.

Finally we found it. Four eucalyptus trees were growing straight and tall about half-way down the slope and just beneath them was a flat area of grass. Not much room, but enough to fit a horse and a tent. The next problem was how to get down there. The road was banked by a ten-foot-high stone wall. Three corners later, the slope came right up to the edge of the road. By some miracle, the barrier didn't cross this point. I urged Dragon off the road and down the slope. There was just enough light to see where I was going.

Faced by a tangled mess of brambles three feet deep, I was going to have to stay on board. I pushed Dragon forward and without hesitation he waded through the prickles, his broad chest pushing them just wide enough to leave a small space for Boris alongside. As soon as we were a reasonable distance from the busy road, I unclipped him; I felt much happier letting him find his own way behind us. The brambles grew thicker and taller until they were almost up to Dragon's nose. He battled his way on and on through the stubborn bushes until the eucalyptus trees seemed to be getting quite close. I looked behind and saw Boris taking huge leaps over the flattened tangles of green.

Suddenly the brambles gave way to short tufty grass; we were through. Boris was close behind us and sat down on the grass, panting. I jumped off Dragon and tied him to the trunk of one of the eucalyptus trees while I had a quick look round. The small patch of grass was totally surrounded by brambles. The four trees grew close together in a straight line giving ideal shelter from the icy breeze which was chilling the gloom. I untacked Dragon and dug out the hobbles for him, though I couldn't imagine him battling through the prickles again out of choice, especially as we'd found the only bit of grass for miles. I just had time to pitch my tent before the light disappeared completely.

The temperature had dropped dramatically. I crawled into the tent and began to zip it up. Normally Boris would want to be outside on patrol but that evening he seemed to know that we were miles from another human being. He scraped the zip with his paw, his claws snagging against the nylon. I unzipped it again and let him in. It was the first time I had ever failed to find him his meat, and I felt guilty.

I raised myself up on my elbows and pulled off the earphones to my radio. By mistake they landed on Boris' paws, and he gave a low but very meaningful growl. I kept very quiet and moved right up against the side of the tent, terrified of upsetting my hungry Dobermann any further. The thought of being attacked by an enormous dog in a very small tent was not a pleasant one. I lay there, quite frozen, until I thought that he had dozed off; only then did I allow myself to drift into a fitful sleep.

It was so horribly cold and damp that I had to sleep in my boots. I crawled out of the tent at about half-past six to find Dragon standing with his bottom up against the line of eucalyptus trees for shelter. One of his back feet was cocked up on its toe, resting. Hearing me call his name, he whickered softly, his warm breath blowing white curls of mist into the cold morning air. I could hear the sound of rushing water somewhere nearby. I peered over the brambles and saw a big river roaring fast and furious between the exposed faces of rock far down below.

It was a long scramble back up to the level of the road. Pushing uphill through thick brambles was like wading in three feet of black treacle. Dragon struggled on bravely and eventually stepped on to the smooth surface of the road. I gave him a big pat and he snorted with pride.

Somehow I had to get myself to Pamplona airport by quarter-past six that evening. Trotting down the side of a road goodness knows how many miles from civilization, it seemed unlikely but not impossible. The first thing to do was to find somewhere to leave Dragon and Boris.

Within minutes we came to a small sign which said 'BAILOO 8'. For the first time in three days luck seemed to be on our side.

At just after half-past eight, we arrived in the village of Bailoo. Unmarked on the map, it was a very small place. We walked along the single line of houses, Dragon's hooves ringing out against the whitewashed walls. I stopped for a moment and heard nothing. There was a strange uninhabited stillness in the air, not a dog or a cat to be seen. I walked the full length of the line of houses and still there was no sign of life. We came to a dusty square with a simple stone fountain in the middle. I led Dragon over to it and let the animals drink. Being so far from another village, I thought perhaps Bailoo had been deserted. Then I looked up and saw brightly coloured paper flowers strung across one of the streets which led away from the square. There had obviously been a big party the night before and everybody was still asleep. I tied Dragon to the fountain and wandered off down the nearest street. I hadn't gone very far when I heard Boris barking. I turned on my heel and ran back. A pretty young girl was standing near the fountain looking puzzled, a plastic gallon container in her hand. The poor girl was probably wondering how she was going to get to the fountain with these fearsome animals in the way.

I introduced myself and explained that I wanted somewhere to put my horse. The girl seemed too overcome with shyness to speak, but beckoned me to follow her. She took me to a figure bending double over a row of cabbages. 'Juan,' she said. The figure seemed to pause for a moment and then stood up slowly to reveal a friendly faced young man. Rubbing his back he smiled and asked what I wanted. I explained that I needed somewhere to leave my horse until tomorrow. He worked at the farm, he said. Unfortunately there weren't any stables, but he thought he might be able to find a shed and some food for Dragon. We might just make it to Pamplona after all.

By twenty-past ten I was standing by the side of the road waiting for a car to pass. There had been so much traffic the day before, but now that I actually wanted it, there was none. The first car appeared at nearly eleven o'clock and, luckily, picked me up.

'*Dónde vas?*' he asked.

'Pamplona,' I replied and was not surprised when he shook his head and told me he was only going as far as Jaca. I asked him how far it was to Jaca and was surprised to find it was only twelve kilometres away.

It was a long and frustrating day. At five o'clock I was still forty kilometres from Pamplona. Visions of William and the photographer standing at the airport getting hot and annoyed with no one to meet them prompted me to stand by the side of the road flapping my arms like an aeroplane and pointing to my watch. Finally a huge lorry with a load of tree trunks stopped to pick up this demented female.

As we ground up the hills at a snail's pace, time seemed to be whizzing past and by six o'clock we still had quite a way to go. In desperation, I told the driver that I had to pick someone up at six-fifteen. *'Tiene mucho tiempo,'* (You have lots of time) he said which didn't make me feel any happier. I wrote a letter to Michael in rather jerky scrawl to take my mind off my watch. I could post it at the airport.

I looked up and realized that the lorry was slowing down. The driver put on his indicator and said he'd have to let me out here as he had to turn off towards Logroño. As I closed the cab door behind me, a white Citroën pulled up in front of the lorry. The lorry driver said something to its driver, who leaned across and opened the door for me. In a complete daze, I got in, waved goodbye to the lorry driver and closed the door.

I hadn't noticed a white Citroën driving along behind us so after a few minutes I asked the driver whether they were his tree trunks on the back of the lorry. 'Not at all,' he said. 'I was just driving along when the lorry driver flagged me down and asked me to take you to the airport.' Quite amazed, I thanked the man and stunned by my good fortune spent the rest of the journey in silence.

At twenty to seven, the kind man delivered me to the 'Arrivals' door. I offered to pay for some of the petrol for his trouble but he just smiled and shook his head. I rushed in fully expecting to see William standing there. He wasn't. It was rather like charging into a dentist's waiting room, terribly late. All heads turned to look at me, wondering what the fuss was about. Perhaps the plane was late or cancelled, I thought, walking over to 'Information'. I had begun to ask about it when I suddenly realized that I had no idea about Spanish tenses. When the man answered, 'Yes,' I didn't know if it was in answer to 'Has the plane arrived?' or 'Will the plane arrive?' I wrote down the number of the flight and asked *'Qué hora?'* (What time is it?) pointing to my watch which read seven o'clock. The man shook his head and pointed to '18.15'. At that moment an elegant Spanish woman stepped in to help. She had a 'leetle Ingleesh' she said. I explained my problem very slowly and she answered quite simply that my watch was an hour fast. An hour fast? The full implications of this new-found knowledge began to sink in. I thanked them both and went back to the waiting area.

The plane was late, but at last the new arrivals began to swarm through the frosted-glass doors. William and the photographer were easy to spot amongst the tourists and businessmen. The first thing William said was, 'My God, what's happened to your hair?' I had had to chop it off so that I looked like a boy. He grinned and turned round to introduce me to the photographer, Ted Blackbrow.

'Oh, I almost forgot, your mother sent you this,' said William holding out something big and squashy wrapped up in a dustbin bag.

'Dragon's rug,' I said, delighted.

'Where are they at the moment, Dragon and the Dobe I mean?'

'A tiny place called Bailoo. I hope I can find it again. By the way, Boris is dying to shake your hand.'

'Can I have it back afterwards?'

As we whizzed along the country roads chatting away, it seemed very odd to have them in my world. We arrived in the tiny village of Bailoo and left the car in the square. The bright red rented car looked totally out of place against the rural shades of Bailoo, as did William and Ted, tiptoeing in and out of the cowpats as we walked to the farm.

I was relieved to see that Dragon and Boris were still in their shed. Dragon was chomping his way through a mountain of alfalfa while Boris lay curled up next to the pile of tack. William and Ted leaned quietly over the door to have a look. Boris sensed them immediately and sprang to his feet. Dragon quite sensibly took no notice and continued to fill his face while he had the chance. I let Boris out to come and say hello. 'He's enormous!' said Ted. 'I've never seen a Dobe as big as him in my life.'

I let Boris have a run for a few minutes while I restocked Dragon's food supply and sorted out what I needed for the night from my saddle-bags. Boris saw his food package and came rushing back into the shed. I advised William and Ted to keep well away while I put down Boris' meat. Once both animals were comfortable and well fed, we left them in peace and went in search of a hotel.

We found a cheap two-star hotel in Jaca. I blended in quite well in my dirty jeans and cowboy boots. We had so much to catch up on that it took us nearly three bottles of wine. Despite the thought of an early start the following morning, we went to bed well after midnight.

It seemed that I'd hardly closed my eyes before someone was bashing on my door telling me to get up. The bright morning sun pierced through my eyelids, which felt rather painful. Far too much wine last night, I thought. Scrunching up my eyes I groped outside the window and found the clothes I had washed the night before. I had a quick shower, pulled on the damp clothes and went downstairs to join William and Ted.

We left Bailoo with William walking alongside Dragon and Ted driving the car a little way behind. Every now and then he would whizz past us and take photographs from the front. Boris didn't like the look of his camera, thinking it looked rather too much like a gun with its long lens.

It's difficult enough taking photographs of one animal, but trying to organize two was impossible. Once we'd got Boris to face the right way, Dragon would decide it was time for a pee. We'd all move forwards out of the puddle and re-station ourselves. William would start jumping up and down in the background again, waving his shirt to make Dragon prick his ears, and the camera would finally click.

By mid-afternoon Boris was beginning to flag in the heat so I suggested that I should carry on towards Jaca while William and Ted took Boris on in the car to the *picadero*. But Boris had other ideas; there was no way that he was going anywhere with two strange men in a car. Before I could say anything, Ted had given Boris the mildest push and Boris had spun round to grab hold of Ted's arm. We had no alternative but to leave poor Ted holding Dragon while William and I whizzed off to the Jaca *picadero* with Boris. I don't think Ted had been near a horse in his life but by the time we came back the two of them seemed to be getting along quite well.

Three days and nearly four hundred photographs later, I stood at the gate of the *picadero* waving goodbye as the little red car disappeared into Jaca. I felt horribly empty and deflated to be on my own again. But we were well into the mountains now, so getting across the border gave me plenty to think about.

# FOURTEEN

# Over the Border

I WAS GOING to need a blood test and veterinary certificate. The vet had gone on holiday for two weeks. In desperation I borrowed the typewriter at the little hotel and filled in the certificate myself. The blood test was a little more difficult to solve. I made endless enquiries and eventually discovered that the military in Jaca could take the blood sample for me. I trotted over to the military fort on Dragon and talked my way in. They took the blood sample and told me that it needed to be taken straight away to the analysis laboratory in the centre of town. One of the soldiers obligingly leapt on his motorbike, but we were too late; by the time we arrived, the blood had congealed and was useless. My face must have showed my immense frustration and disappointment because the doctor winked at me and proceeded to sign the bottom of the faked veterinary certificate.

The trekking guide at the *picadero* offered to take me as far as Canfranc, where his family had a field I could leave Dragon in. He was going to Canfranc with friends, using the tracks through the mountains, and I leapt at the opportunity.

Dragon's shoes were in a dreadful state so I knew I'd have to get him reshod before going any further. There wasn't a farrier anywhere near, but I managed once again to get into the military fort, where the resident farrier did quite the most dreadful job I've ever seen. The shoes were so long that they hung off the back of Dragon's feet like snow shoes. It took five of them, pulling and tugging and shouting at each other, nearly two hours to nail on four shoes. I really think that I could have done a better job myself. They charged me an outrageous £25! Fortunately Dragon was sound as we trotted back to the *picadero*, or I would certainly have demanded my money back. Juan Patallo, the trekking guide, met me with his two friends at the *picadero* at ten o'clock the next morning. Boris was a little confused at first to be travelling in the midst of sixteen hairy legs rather than four.

We rode along the side of the winding mountain road for about two kilometres before turning off across a stone bridge and on to a broad stony track. Juan told me that the track would get very narrow in places but we would be on the other side of the river from the road so it would be quite safe for me to let Boris loose. I knew it was only about fifteen kilometres to Canfranc, so he wouldn't exhaust himself. As soon as I'd unclipped him, he roared off at such great speed that everyone wondered whether we would see him again. When he re-appeared, Juan broke into a trot with his friends Andrés and Marco just behind, and myself and Dragon bringing up the rear. Dragon was wide awake today, thoroughly looking forward to the prospect of having a race.

After a couple of bends in the track we came to a small grass field. Juan took off at a fast canter, quickly followed by his friends. Dragon let out a high-pitched squeal and charged after them. I turned round in my saddle to check Boris was following. I needn't have worried; he was having the time of his life, dashing along behind with his ears flying. As we neared the other side of the field, I expected the others to slow down. But Juan actually accelerated and shot through a narrow gap in the undergrowth to another narrow track. As we were batting along at great speed, Andrés glanced behind him to check I was still there. Dragon was sensible enough not to run into the bottom of the horse in front so I just let him find his own route in and out of the knobbly rocks which jutted out of the path every couple of minutes, always keeping up enough speed not to get left behind.

Juan shouted something and moment later I saw Andrés duck sideways. I did the same and narrowly missed scraping off my left arm on a telegraph pole as we flew past, saddle-bags flapping. This is madness, I thought, loving every minute of it as we hurtled full pelt down the dangerously narrow track with a deep river thundering past just below. I knew Dragon was as tough as old boots and Boris could take care of himself so I was quite happy to hang on and follow. It was rather like riding pillion on a fast motorbike. Dragon was doing the driving and I just leaned in the right direction as we skidded round the corners.

The horse in front suddenly slammed on the brakes so that Dragon nearly landed on its saddle. A large, flat rock stretched across the path, lethal if the horse slipped and fell over the edge. Dragon just caught sight of it at the last moment and with a huge cat-leap, cleared the shiny black surface. After a couple more near misses, the horses in front slowed down and walked for a while to cool off.

'Do you always take people trekking at that speed?' I asked Juan, trying to imagine some poor grandmother flying round those corners.

'That's the trouble,' he said. 'I always have to go slowly, so whenever I'm with Marco and Andrés we go for it!'

All the horses were blowing hard and dripping with sweat but very excited after what a horse would consider great fun. Boris' tongue was a yard long as he stuck right on Dragon's heels, quite tired from such a long chase. 'We're nearly there,' said Juan. It had taken us hardly an hour.

The track began to descend and when we were level with the river Juan pointed to a very long flight of concrete steps on the other side, climbing fifty feet up to the level of the road. 'We're going up there,' he shouted. Dragon had had to negotiate steps before, but never as many as that. We'd solve that problem when we came to it; the first was to cross the river. The water would be over the horses' knees, running fast and strong over a bed of large rocks; it wouldn't be easy.

I called Boris and clipped him on to the girth so I'd have one less thing to worry about. He was nimble enough to sort himself out while I concentrated on Dragon. Juan and his friends went first. Juan's horse negotiated the river without much difficulty and then leapt two feet up to the concrete steps. Andrés' horse found it more difficult, slithering all over the place on the greasy rocks. I took my first steps with Dragon. The wonderful thing about Dragon was that he never panicked. He picked his way slowly and carefully across, bracing his legs against the strong current. A horse's foot is only meant to bend in one direction and given the added disadvantage of metal shoes, slippery rocks are one of the most difficult surfaces for a horse. By the time we made it to the other side, Juan was half-way up the concrete steps. The two trekking horses soon got their legs sorted out and clattered up after him. We followed at the rear again and Dragon took it slowly and carefully.

It is very frightening and complicated for a horse to climb a long flight of steps, because without a flat area wide enough for him to stand on he has to keep going; he knows he can't turn round and he is aware of a nasty drop at his shoulder. Dragon had great confidence in following me. There had been previous occasions when I couldn't make him walk through or over something but I always found that as soon as I got off and led him he would follow without hesitation. It was with great relief that we popped up on to the road one by one and walked into the mountain village of Canfranc.

We tied the horses under some trees in an orchard and went to a small restaurant for lunch. Ravenous after such an exhilarating morning, the three of us ate our way through a huge pile of food. I noticed that I was beginning to think like a dog; however full I felt, I ate as much as possible because I never knew when I would get fed again. Disgusting really!

Juan and his friends said they'd find me somewhere to stay for the night because it was far too cold to camp in the mountains. Juan chatted to his friend, who owned the restaurant, and the friend said he could rent me a room for the night while Dragon stayed in Juan's field. It was a big day tomorrow so I asked Juan if he could sell me some hay and hard feed for Dragon.

As I tacked up Dragon, Boris seemed far more excited than usual; perhaps he felt my nerves. I folded up the rug William had brought for Dragon and laid it over the saddle. It was rather uncomfortable to sit on but I felt much happier knowing that Dragon would be warm enough at night. The cool mountain air on that bright, clear morning was more refreshing than anything I'd felt for a long time. I set off down the quiet mountain road, the surrounding mountains enfolding us in

191

their tremendous height and power. It was late August but I could see snow on the peaks high above us.

It was a long climb up the narrow ribbon of tarmac which threaded its way into the mountains. It was one of the most spectacular days of my journey, clip-clopping steadily between the lush green vegetation and tumbling water on either side of the road. As we climbed higher, the road began to make sharper loops. Whenever possible we would cut across the grass. It made a steeper climb than the road, but Dragon had a much better foothold on grass than tarmac.

An hour later we came to the ski resort of Candanchu. Woolly-looking horses were grazing on what would be the *piste* in the winter months. Wooden chalet-type houses lined the road. Everything was closed and abandoned for the summer; all the shop windows were empty, the apartments dark and silent. I was surprised that nobody came here in summer. It was a most beautiful place, with bright sunshine, warm streams and lovely green grass which looked particularly beautiful after the scorched browns of the past few months.

It was a strange feeling to be riding on a horse through an empty ski resort. Five strings of ski lifts went off in different directions, stretching up into the mountains along the strips of grass. Suspended high above us on the taut wire, the metallic bubbles shone like dewdrops on a cobweb.

We rode out of Candanchu and on into the mountains beyond. Tall, green pines grew above and below us. We could no longer cut across the loops as the sides of the mountain were far too steep. As we rounded one corner the ground dropped away to our left, giving a fantastic view of the tops of the thick carpet of pine trees, so close I could almost touch them. At last the road began to level off and the steep mountain sides flattened out into rolling hillocks. The road was wider now and the pine trees not so densely planted.

A straggling mixture of houses and souvenir shops marked the beginning of the border village. The ground was almost level so I urged Dragon into trot. A couple of cars passed us and all the occupants turned round in amazement, wondering where I could possibly be going. A tall ugly concrete building with *Guardia Civil* flags marred the beautiful landscape. There were no barriers or grumpy-looking officials so I kept trotting. A kilometre further on we came to the real thing. Two small inspection boxes stood on either side of a mobile office building. Red-and-white striped barriers blocked the road. An assortment of police, *Guardia Civil* and customs men stood chatting to each other in small groups of three or four, many of them smoking. They didn't hear me at first and then one of them alerted the others, who dropped their cigarettes and dashed into the office. I stood behind the one and only car and when it moved off, walked forward until I was level with the inspection hatch. The inspector looked at Dragon and said they didn't allow animals through this border post. The nearest was Santander. Other official-looking faces peered round the side of his head and nodded in agreement. I had not been expecting this. I explained that I was on my way to Paris, and that I couldn't possibly go to Santander; it would take me two weeks on a horse. I dug out all my papers and handed them over. A hand came out of the hatch and took them from me. There was a great deal of mumbling, then the face reappeared and said that they couldn't let me through. I said quite calmly that I couldn't go back so I'd just have to wait at the border until they let me through. The man looked rather alarmed at this and disappeared once again for more consultation. Twenty minutes later he came back and handed me a piece of paper. I was told I could go through on condition that I returned through that particular border-post. The barrier was lifted.

I looked at my watch: nearly five o'clock. We were quite high and as we climbed a couple more loops it began to spit with rain. It couldn't be very far to the French border, I thought, constantly hoping it would be just round the next corner. The road turned into a dual carriageway. Not a single car passed us as we trotted on and on in the drizzle. It was getting cold and I began to worry. It was nearly dark by the time I decided we weren't going to make the French border that night. I was fortunate enough to find an empty pig barn. It had only a roof and one wall but it was better than nothing. I remembered what Juan and his friends had said about camping in the mountains and shivered at the thought. I couldn't pitch my tent on the concrete floor but as it was now raining so hard outside and almost dark, I decided to wrap myself up in my long Barbour coat and stay in the pig barn. I untacked Dragon and put on his rug. There was nowhere to tie him except for a roof beam. He seemed happy enough just to rest a foot and go to sleep. The floor, covered in dry pig muck, was so disgusting that I sat on a fertilizer bag with my back up against the wall. Boris prowled round on patrol, occasionally coming to sit next to me and hold my arm in his mouth.

I must have fallen asleep simply because I remember waking up. I brushed down my tack, put it on Dragon and moved out of the pig barn. I was very glad to have spent the night with my back up against the wall because in the daylight it was clear that some of the pig muck was not as dry as it might have been.

It was only about four kilometres to the French border. Someone had thoughtfully put a tie-up bar, like the ones they have in Westerns, right outside the customs office, although I doubt it was done with four-legged travellers in mind. I tied Dragon up and went inside clutching all the relevant papers. The French were not as easy to convince as the Spaniards and spent over an hour consulting with each other, making telephone calls and shaking their heads. My biggest problem was that I suddenly found I could no longer speak French! Having concentrated my whole mind on learning Spanish, all my French had disappeared, so I found myself in the ridiculous situation of speaking Spanish to the French customs men. They finally agreed to let me through on condition that Dragon had a vet's inspection. Three hours later the vet arrived, gave Dragon a very speedy once-over, and handed over the vital piece of paper.

We were through; we had actually made it into France. I was gasping for a drink and something to eat but I didn't stop in case the customs men suddenly changed their minds and called me back. I didn't stop until I reached the village of Accous. The first thing I wanted to do was to find Dragon some good food and a place to stay. Now that I was unable to remember a word of French, it was like starting all over again.

Eventually I found a cow shed for Dragon, and its owners were able to give him some hay and oats. I left Boris guarding while I went to find some meat for him and a possible place for me to stay. There were three houses and what looked like a hotel. It turned out to be a school. At first they turned me away, but I did my best to explain that I had a horse in the shed on the other side of the road and they began to soften. It was out of term-time, so the school was currently being run by a group of students as a children's holiday camp. After a great deal of thought and consultation they agreed to let me stay the night.

They were just about to eat supper and invited me to join them. Five students were in charge of the fifty children, one student per table. I sat next to a pretty blonde-haired girl who was studying in Toulouse. In between dishing out platefuls of rabbit, she explained how the summer camp worked and asked me about my ride. I was relieved to find a little of my French coming back to me.

After supper I took some leftover rabbit to Boris. He smelled it and couldn't wait; it was the most delicious thing he'd had in months.

The students put the children to bed at eight o'clock and then brought out a couple of bottles of wine for us to drink while they asked me questions about my ride. At first I don't think they believed a word of what I was saying, but after two bottles of wine and endless questions it seemed a little more plausible.

I was given the bottom bunk in a room full of sleeping children. The bathroom was at the other end of the corridor. I tiptoed as quietly as possible along the lino floor, closed the bathroom door and turned on the light. Strong recollections of my boarding-school days flooding back to me. Ten small sinks stood against one wall, a long row of pegs for washbags opposite and a line of doors, presumably the loos, on the far side.

There wasn't a sound as I skulked back past the other dormitories.

Doubled up so I didn't hit my head on the top bunk, I pulled back the sheets and got into bed. As I'd expected, I had to keep my legs bent to get all of me in at once. I lay there for a while and thought about my own school. It had seemed like the whole world to me then; all the stupid things like drawer checks, laundry checks, measuring the height of your shoe heels, sewing up the pockets on your coat. No running, no talking; stand up when a member of staff enters the room; regulation shoes,

195

regulation bags, regulation white gloves, even regulation green felt knickers! Compared to many schools it was very strict, but without its training and discipline I would never have made it into France; I would most certainly have crumpled into a little heap and given up long ago.

It was a bright sunny morning as we set off towards Oloron Santa Maria. I was looking forward to getting there because it was one of my letter drops. I had sent Michael a list of letter drops as far as Paris. There was no danger in estimating so far ahead because although I might well be late, I had cut it so fine that it would be virtually impossible for me to arrive early. The list read as follows:

| | |
|---|---|
| OLORON STA MARIA | 23 August |
| ROQUEFORT | 27 August |
| MAREUIL | 2 September |
| CHATILLON SUR INDRE | 11 September |
| ÉTAMPES | 20 September |
| PARIS | 25 September |

The scenery on this side of the border was completely different. The houses, people, gardens, cars, shops, even the mongrels, were a different shape. Travelling at only six kilometres an hour, I had not been expecting the change to be quite so clean-cut. The sudden improvement in the standard of the road made the first real difference to my ride.

There was hardly a kilometre without a suitable-looking building for us to stay in. I chose a small farm just outside Oloron Santa Maria. Dragon scrunched up the neatly raked gravel drive and two dogs came out of the modern house barking at Boris, who took no notice. I stopped by the house and waited for someone to appear. A burly man of about fifty emerged and stood on the step for a moment, tucking his corduroy trousers into his wellingtons.

'*Bonjour, Monsieur,*' I said. He smiled and asked me what I wanted. I did my best to explain that I needed somewhere to leave my horse for the night.

He pointed to a tree in the middle of the drive where I could tie up Dragon and then asked me to follow him. The modern-looking farm buildings were just opposite the house. Most of the barn was open with a manger along one wall so that the cows could eat while they were being milked. The first barn was connected to a second which was sectioned off into single brick-lined pens, each big enough for a cow about to calf. The farmer opened the door to one of these, revealing a filthy straw bed so many layers thick that it was nearly three feet high.

Before I put Dragon in the pen the farmer kindly sprinkled a layer of clean straw on top of the mountain of muck. I led Dragon in and he stood up to his ankles in bedding. Once I had removed all his tack, he waded round the pen snorting at the strong smell of cow and investigating his bedroom. There was an automatic cow-waterer in one corner, but I wasn't sure whether Dragon had used one before. I splashed the water with my hand and hearing the sound, Dragon came over to have a drink. He had hardly taken a sip when the stopcock wheezed into action, hissing madly as the tank refilled itself with water. Dragon leapt back, horrified by this tiny monster. He stood at the far corner and gave a loud trumpet. The farmer who had been watching this performance laughed. In the end I gave up and offered him a bucket instead. The farmer kindly gave him some corn and a pile of rather musty old hay so I left Dragon in peace.

It was quite a large house so I had been hoping that they might give me a room for the night, but they told me that they didn't have a spare room. I was welcome instead to sleep in the van parked in the drive. They gave me a sunbed and two blankets and closed the door. The sunbed was one of the awkward variety which keeps folding up on you or dropping your head on the floor. Four sacks of fertilizer were stacked up in the back of the van. They were tremendously difficult to move but I managed to push two of them under the sunbed at either end to stop it collapsing. I took Boris out of his pen and let him sleep in the van with me.

It was so cold during the night that I had to put all my clothes back on. When I woke up in the morning, the van was cold and damp and stinking of wet dog. I couldn't see out because the windows were too steamed up. Clambering out of a Ford

Transit van first thing in the morning just didn't feel the same as climbing out of my tent on a quiet hillside. I folded up the blankets, put back the fertilizer sacks and left the sunbed and blankets outside the back door of the house.

It was seven-thirty in the morning and there was no sign of anyone when I tacked up Dragon and rode out of the gate. It was a bright sunny morning and the road was wide and quiet. I got out the map to see where we should be going. A motorway would cross our path on its way to Pau, which looked quite big on my map so I wanted to keep well away from it. I also had to find a small road to cross the motorway, preferably underneath it. There were two rivers marked; the road we were on crossed the Rivière d'Oloron, but the Rivière Adour which ran alongside the motorway might be more of a problem as there only seemed to be three roads which crossed it, spaced a good ten kilometres apart. The route I chose took us along the boundary fence of the airport but at least it avoided the problems of the river and the motorway.

I had been expecting an endless stream of small farms as on the previous day but unfortunately our surroundings became more suburban as the day went on. By four o'clock the animals needed to stop but the best I could find for them was a little cottage with a small fenced lawn and two apple trees. I had only meant to ask them if they knew anywhere in the area which might take me, but to my great surprise they offered me their fenced lawn for Dragon. I did my best to explain that Dragon might make rather a mess of it but it didn't seem to worry them in the slightest. Their granddaughter had a pony, they said, they loved animals.

Dragon couldn't believe his luck. He had a delicious lawn to eat . . . and apples as well! I picked up most of the apples in a bucket and gave them to the wife because I was rather worried that Dragon might get colic if he ate them all. The old couple came out of their house and said they'd telephoned a nearby farmer who could give me some hay. I suggested that they might find it easier if I stayed there, but they insisted that they'd like Dragon and Boris to stay on their lawn for the night. The husband kindly went off in his car to collect the hay for me while I went to a small hotel almost opposite the house to find a room. The wife came with me and, as she was a friend of the owner, persuaded them to give me some scraps for Boris. So the pair of them had a real feast.

When the husband arrived with the hay I stuffed it into Dragon's hay-net and tied it to a branch of one of the apple trees. It was too cold now to hose him down at the end of the day so I had to brush the sweat off instead.

We set off towards the village of Thèze in the fresh morning sun, the air was a perfect temperature. Using my large-scale map I had been able to find us a very small back road to follow; wonderfully pretty in comparison to the scorched and barren wilderness of Spain. With every curl of the road I found something new and interesting to look at. Riding along on a horse, I had at least five minutes to study things. I passed a farmer and his wife walking up and down their small field throwing out handfuls of seed from the bags round their waists as they went. As we pottered along the quiet road, I heard a strangely hollow metallic sound coming from above. I looked up and saw eight men clambering in and out of the electricity wires of an enormous pylon just next to the road. Travelling so slowly, I had ample time to watch them as they juggled tools and equipment so high in the sky, like ants moving precious morsels up a blade of grass.

Presently, we were overtaken by a horse trailer. It hovered level with us for a moment before drawing on round the next corner. When we pottered slowly round the next bend we found it had pulled on to the grass, and just as we reached the back of it a car door opened in front and a pretty young woman stepped out. She smiled as she walked towards us. I stopped for a moment, pleased to be able to say hello to this friendly face. The woman introduced herself as Brigitte and asked me where I was going. When I told her her eyes widened. She said she was on her way home with her horse and asked me if I'd like to drop in for a few minutes to meet her husband who would be very interested in my journey.

I untacked Dragon and left Boris in the stable with him. Brigitte introduced me to her husband, Claude, and produced a huge jug of homemade lemonade. They were very friendly and asked me endless questions about my journey. Brigitte

199

racked her brains, trying to think of some horsey friends or relations where I might stay, but unfortunately they were all a long way off my route. Just in case I got into difficulty, they very kindly gave me their own address and telephone number.

Brigitte took me out to the stables to show me her own horse, an elegant chestnut mare. I noticed the mare's beautifully oiled feet and wondered if I might be able to have some oil for Dragon. Brigitte was very happy to let me use some and held Dragon for me while I painted it on. His feet were very dry after the dusty heat of Spain and were desperate for some oil. As I was doing the insides of his front feet, Brigitte noticed his appalling shoes. I explained that they had been put on by the military in Jaca. They had been just about all right so far but now that they were wearing a bit thin they had slewed round half an inch, leaving the ends of the shoes jutting out to the inside. I showed her the marks on Dragon's fetlocks where the insides of the hind shoes had been catching every time we trotted. Brigitte looked most concerned and rushed into the tack room, reappearing with two yellow leg bandages and four pieces of gamgee (cotton-wool padding). She offered them to me and said I could keep them. I thanked her very much, and wrapping a piece of gamgee round one of Dragon's hind legs, I wound the bandage round and round over the top until his fetlock was safely covered. By the time I'd done the second leg, Dragon looked very smart.

They invited me to stay for the night, but as I had only covered about twelve kilometres so far that day I said I'd better press on. Brigitte gave me the name of a Monsieur Beaumont Herne in the village of Miramont Sensacq just before Thèze where I could stay with Dragon. She told me that he had a small hotel but he kept about fifteen trotters in his stables just nearby. She said she'd telephone him to warn him of my visit. I thanked them both for their kindness and turned out of their gate, Dragon high-stepping like a hackney as a result of his leg bandages.

We arrived in Miramont just after five o'clock. It was such a tiny place that the hotel wasn't difficult to find, and the moment Dragon's hooves were heard on the tarmac the door flew open and an enormous black dog rushed out, shortly followed by Monsieur Beaumont Herne. Boris was taken aback to meet a dog bigger than he was and looked quite stunned when the dog then tried to mount him. *'Roule!'* shouted Monsieur Herne, hitting his dog on the back with his newspaper. *'Excusez-moi,'* he said, unable to come near enough to shake my hand. He told me to wait while he got his car and then he'd show us the way to the stables. A few minutes later a faded grey Renault coasted past us down the hill with Monsieur Herne inside, waving frantically for us to follow. The faded crustacean spluttered into life half-way down the hill and led us to the stables.

There were about twenty stables set in a large black barn. Familiar noises came drifting out of the door. I dismounted and led Dragon inside. A skewbald Shetland pony walked along the line of stables to meet us. I wondered whether it was supposed to be wandering round loose, but Monsieur Herne didn't seem to be taking any notice of it so I let Dragon say a quick hello. He was fascinated; I don't think he'd ever met such a midget.

Dragon was given a big loosebox, feet deep in clean straw. A bulging hay-net was tied up to a ring on the back wall. Dragon was going to have a wonderful time. Monsieur Herne gave me a hand with my tack and cleared a corner of the tack room for me to dump it all. He said it would be quite safe there as everything was always locked up at night. I wondered what to do with Boris and asked Monsieur Herne if there was any chance of having him in my room for the night. *'Bien sûr, Mademoiselle!'*

I seemed to be just about the only person staying in the hotel so Madame Herne had prepared an enormous dinner for me. The trouble was that because I had become so used to eating very little I found that I simply couldn't eat it all. Rather embarrassed, I had to give up after about the third course.

With the help of a real sink for a change, I gave my red jersey and light cotton shirt a really good wash. I hung my jersey out of the window and my shirt on a coat hanger to dry. In the morning I was horrified to find that my red jersey had left a pink stain on the wall outside and that the varnish on the coat hanger had left a yellow stain across the shoulders of my one and only decent shirt. Cursing my stupidity I put them on and went downstairs for a cup of coffee. I chose a small table in the corner; the dining-room was empty. Boris refused to sit down, preferring to stay on the look-out for Monsieur Herne's homosexual dog.

When I had finished breakfast, Monsieur Herne offered to run me down to the stables. He went to dig his crustacean out of its hole and met us at the front of the hotel. We cruised down hill and the engine jerked into life at exactly the same spot as it had the previous evening.

I walked into the stables and found the Shetland pony standing right outside Dragon's stable while Dragon leaned over his door cooing over his new-found friend. Boris swaggered up to this huge shaggy dog to investigate. He didn't know what to think; it certainly didn't smell like a dog. He gave it a nip on the fetlock to see if it was fierce. The little pony put its ears back flat and made a nasty face just like Dragon . . . Obviously another one of those, thought Boris and wandered off to find something more interesting.

A couple of hours later while I was grooming Dragon, I heard shouts coming from the schooling ring. I dropped my brush and rushed over to see what had happened. I turned the corner and gasped . . . The Shetland pony was grazing quietly next to the schooling ring with Boris on his back trying to rape him. The two girls schooling shrieked with laughter and told me the pony was a gelding.

I stayed one more day with Monsieur and Madame Herne before moving on towards Roquefort. It was slightly out of my way, but I had given it to Michael as one of my letter drops so I definitely didn't want to miss it. To get to Roquefort itself we had to use the D 934, a long, straight and rather boring road through the edge of the endless woods which stretch right up as far as Bordeaux. It was a lovely feeling at first, riding through the cool forest, but after a while I began to get tired of the endless ribbon of tarmac. I had become spoilt; in Spain the roads were always like this but at least there I could keep an eye on the kilometre stones and monitor my progress. Here in France they only appeared every ten kilometres or so. As we trotted deeper into the forest, we passed hardly a single building.

In Roquefort I picked up my letters: one from my sister and a nice long one from Michael. Then I took the road towards Marmande.

Just outside Roquefort I found a large farm, where I asked if there was somewhere I could stay. I was put in contact with the owner of an equestrian centre. He gave me directions over the telephone and said it should take me about half an hour.

At the equestrian centre the horses' bedrooms were beautifully clean and tidy but the human bedrooms were appalling. I left Dragon in his immaculate bed of wood shavings and went into the house. The owner and his ten working pupils were just about to eat and invited me to join them. I didn't find them particularly friendly and the food looked old and smelled dreadfully. The pink liquid they were drinking had three flies floating in it. After dinner they showed me a small room already occupied by four people in which I could have a bottom bunk. Filthy clothes, dirty horse bandages and riding boots were strewn across the floor. A numnah was slung over the back of a chair to dry. I couldn't begin to estimate the number of flies dead or dying on the floor and almost an inch thick along the window ledge. The whole place was quite horrible. I got undressed and went to have a shower. What I found was quite indescribable; even the water seemed slimy. I went back to the bedroom and pulled back the bedclothes; they looked distinctly grubby so I got dressed again and slept in my clothes.

The following morning I got away as quickly as possible, breathing in the clean, fresh morning air. The next few days were fairly uneventful as we rode through the forest on our way to Bergerac.

I could have skirted round the edge of Bergerac, but decided that it would be good practice for Dragon to ride right through the middle. He was much better in traffic these days and I was delighted how well-behaved he was as we clip-clopped across a very old and narrow bridge with noisy cars on all sides. I found a butcher in the town square so I was able to tie Dragon up to a park bench while I went to buy some meat for Boris. Boris always knew instinctively whether I was going to the butcher or bank. If it was the butcher, he took the job of guarding far more seriously, as if to secure his meal by proving his value to me.

At Mussidan, I stopped at a small group of cottages and asked if they knew of anywhere I could leave my horse. They were very helpful and the man of the house went off into the village to find somewhere. He didn't come back for almost an hour, leaving me standing in the very small driveway of his run-down little cottage. The drive was bordered by flowers lovingly planted in neat rows; I was very worried that Dragon might swing round and tread on them. Eventually the father reappeared and asked me to follow him while he led the way on his bicycle. He stopped outside a large bungalow, propped his bicycle up against the wall and rang the doorbell. A rather dishevelled-looking man of about thirty-five opened the door, still half-asleep. The two of them held a fast conversation which I couldn't understand and then turned to me. My companion introduced the man as Monsieur Lecler. He waved goodbye, swung his leg over his bicycle and disappeared.

Monsieur Lecler rubbed his eyes for a moment and explained that he only had a field here; his stable was four kilometres away, but if I'd rather put the horse in the stable I was welcome to it. I said I was very happy to turn him out in the field. I put Dragon's rug on and let him loose. Thrilled to be able to kick his heels, he charged up and down before having a good roll and settling to eat. I noticed that Boris was eyeing the man with slight suspicion. Boris was an excellent judge of character so I remained very much on guard with this man.

He told me I could leave my tack in the garage; he didn't want Boris in the house so I tied him up near the tack and left him to guard. Monsieur Lecler had some dog meal and offered me some for Boris who, to my great surprise, absolutely loved it. We went inside and Monsieur Lecler introduced me to his wife Marguerite and daughter Natalie, aged seven. Marguerite showed me to a very pleasant room and then to the bathroom so that I could have a wash before dinner. I changed into my 'other' shirt and joined them all for a very good meal. After dinner, Marguerite said that she had to leave for work at six o'clock the following morning so she wouldn't see me before I left. We said goodbye and I went out to take Boris for his evening walk. I didn't trust Monsieur Lecler at all and decided that as I couldn't take Boris into my room, I'd take my boots instead.

My eyes snapped open. Someone was opening the door of my room, a man. Still half-asleep, I didn't know who it was. I suddenly realized where I was; this was Monsieur Lecler wearing nothing but a T-shirt. He sat on the bed and I told him to go away. I moved over to try and escape his hand which was trying to touch me. I sat up, and clutching the sheets around me demanded that he left the room. He took no notice, climbed on to the bed and began creeping towards me. I began to feel frightened. Remembering my boots, my left hand groped around the floor by the bed looking for them . . . Contact! I held the boot level with his head and said very calmly that I wanted him to leave the room now. He leered nastily, his eyes suddenly flickering with anticipation; he grabbed my arm hard. I gave him one more chance and asked him to leave me alone. I raised the boot slightly to show that I meant it but there was no reaction. I had never hit anyone with any kind of weapon before and was finding it rather difficult actually to do it. He moved closer until his horrible face was right next to mine, then I thumped him on the head with the heel of my heavy boot. He held me harder, his fingers digging into my skin. It was easier now. I hit him again and again, a rain of heavy blows thudding into his skull. Suddenly he let go, jumped off the bed muttering, '*Excusez-moi, excusez-moi,*' tried to shake my hand and then fled from the room.

I lay in bed for half an hour, not moving. Eventually I got dressed and went to the bathroom. As I went in, I caught sight of Monsieur Lecler's anxious face staring at me, positively gibbering, from the kitchen next door. I returned to my room and a few minutes later went back to the bathroom again to have a shower. Monsieur Lecler looked even more nervous this time – he was sure I was going to go into the kitchen. I could see that he was acutely embarrassed and was busying himself preparing breakfast so that he didn't have to think about it.

By the time I did actually walk into the kitchen he was a

nervous wreck. I felt no pity and ate my breakfast in silence. He began to mutter all sorts of apologies and, acting on a sudden inspiration, I said that I would be grateful if he would take my saddle-bags as far as Riberac as a slight recompense. 'But I have to go to work!' he pleaded.

'My horse is very tired and your disgusting behaviour has made me very tired so I think you should do as I ask.'

With no further argument he loaded the saddle-bags into his car and drove them to Riberac, which I had been told had an equestrian centre run by a Monsieur Cabirol.

It was a very pretty day's ride but I hardly noticed. I was too busy shuddering at the thought of Monsieur Lecler. He made me feel filthy.

I walked Dragon most of the way because his shoes by now were in a very bad state. The ends which were sticking out on the inside had now worn sharp; I was in desperate need of a blacksmith. I hoped that Monsieur Cabirol would be able to give me some help.

Monsieur Cabirol was as honest and friendly as Monsieur Lecler had been sly and underhand. He and his son obviously struggled to make a living out of their ten horses and a caravan site but they didn't hesitate to give Dragon the best they had. I asked them about a blacksmith and Monsieur Cabirol told me that the best for miles around lived in St Junien, a good three days' ride away. Other than those who went to him, he told me, everyone shod their own. He offered to do Dragon for me but found that he didn't have a set small enough.

Monsieur Cabirol kindly lent me and Boris one of his caravans to sleep in. There was no bedding and it was freezing cold so I wrapped myself up in everything from my Barbour to Dragon's hay-net. Life had really begun to take on a new meaning for me. I was no longer concerned about my friends at home, about looking in the shop windows as we trotted through a town, or even working out what I wanted to do with my life. I lived for now: for food, for shelter and for a safe passage from one pit-stop to the next.

Monsieur Cabirol told me that his brother lived in Nontron, fifty kilometres away. It was too far to go in one day but he offered to telephone his brother and tell him to expect me the day after next. There was a village called Mareuil half-way between Riberac and Nontron, he said, where a Swiss woman lived in a large chateau. He thought she had horses and might be able to help me. His son offered to ride with me for half an hour and put me on the right road. I thanked Monsieur Cabirol for all his help and disappeared out of the gate with his son Alain, who was riding a large chestnut gelding.

FIFTEEN

# From the Chateau of
# Madame Bruder . . .

My LARGE-SCALE MAP bought in Oloron was so good that it showed all the gradients of the hills and the points where one could get a good view of the area. There was hardly any traffic so I put on my earphones and listened to the radio, a new-found pleasure. In Spain the frequency had never been strong enough for my little radio but in France there were lots of different channels which I could pick up very clearly. We had been going for nearly three months and I was really beginning to tire. Boris, on the other hand, was going from strength to strength. He seemed to thrive on this way of life. I had never seen a dog look quite so fit and healthy; the lean, sleek lines of his body rippled with well-toned muscle. He understood his job and he did it well. Dragon was the vehicle, the steady companion; never wavering, forever constant in speed, mood and requirements. He and Boris had a healthy respect for each other and seemed the best of friends.

The long drive to the chateau was completely grassed over. We padded silently past the tower and on through the long avenue of trees towards a clump of woodland further on which I presumed must hide the chateau itself. As we drew nearer, I could just see its rooftops. Many of the tiles were missing. As we rode closer still I could see the top-floor windows, and see that the paint was peeled and cracked and only one or two panes of glass remained. I stopped outside a beautiful wrought-iron gate behind which stood the magnificent building. Everything about it was tired and broken but it still maintained an elegance which time couldn't destroy. A loud squawk sliced through the air, quickly followed by a second more piercing squawk. The large front door opened and a skinny woman of about sixty with long wispy hair dyed a flaming red colour stepped out into the sunlight. There was another squawk and I realized that she must have a couple of parrots.

'*Bonjour, mademoiselle,*' she said in a high-pitched voice resembling one of her parrots. Balancing on a pair of green high-heeled shoes she unlocked the wrought-iron gate and let us in. I began to explain who I was when to my surprise she said that Monsieur Cabirol had already telephoned her. I got off Dragon and followed her across the grass which covered what must once have been an impressive sweeping drive, and into a beautiful stable block. 'Jacques!' she shrieked, and a bent old man came shuffling out of a shed towards us. She gave him his instructions and told me to come into the house when I was ready.

I knocked on the open front door and waited. I could hear her green high-heeled shoes clacking across the flagstones from some distant room as she came to the front door. '*Entrez, entrez!*' she said irritably and turned on her heel to lead the way. My eyes were on stalks! Apart from the fact that everything was painted green, I had never seen such an extraordinary collection of things. A rather moth-eaten stuffed horse was grinning at me in a macabre fashion with a fabulous Portuguese saddle on its back and a mountain of umbrellas at its feet. A beautifully carved wooden sausage dog on wheels was standing next to a fabulous studded chest which had everything from a hollowed-out horse's hoof to a cannonball scattered on its cracked leather surface. I didn't have time to take in all the other bits and pieces, but as I followed through yet another doorway I caught sight of a suit of armour with hundreds of African beads hanging round its neck.

We came to rest in a kitchen about an acre in size. '*Comment t'appelles-tu?*' she asked, wiggling the bare wires from the plug on the kettle. It was the third time she'd asked. 'Madame Bruder,' she said proudly. She took two mugs from the mountain of dirty plates and gave them a quick rinse. '*Du café?*' She handed me a steaming mug with no handle and led the way into the drawing room.

There was hardly a surface in the whole room which wasn't piled high with her treasures. Although the walls were white in this particular room, everything else was green. A long table which could seat thirty with ease was covered with books stacked ten deep. There was a very small space at the end of the table which revealed the green plastic tablecloth underneath. Madame Bruder waved me in the direction of a chair and heaved two piles of books on to the floor to give us a square foot in which to drink our coffee. A Great Dane loped into the room and parked itself at her feet. She leaned down to give it a pat, showing the pearly-white roots of her hair. She adored animals, she said, and it transpired that she kept sixteen dogs, twenty-two horses, five cats, forty sheep and two parrots (both green).

As she chattered away about her animals I studied her appearance with interest. A manicured toe was peeping out of one of the green high-heeled shoes, tickling the Great Dane. She wore loose, dark green trousers and a vivid green polo-neck jersey. A large green rock hung round her neck and various other rocks were scattered across her bony fingers. Her mouth was painted a bright red which clashed angrily with her flaming hair. I couldn't see her eyes very well because she wore a pair of thick-lensed spectacles – green-rimmed, of course. Once I had decided that this woman was a harmless eccentric, I relaxed and enjoyed listening to her batty conversation which ranged from her dream of starting an international riding school to her tales of dog breeding; she had sold puppies to everyone from the King of Spain to Brigitte Bardot.

When we'd finished our coffee she offered to show me to my room. I followed her up the magnificent staircase and commented on some work being done on the walls half-way up. Madame Bruder said that she was slowly redoing the whole chateau. 'Wretched workers,' she said. 'They keep disappearing!' It didn't surprise me; I imagined that she could be quite a fierce lady. When we'd climbed to the third floor, she took me through a labyrinth of arched passages lined with suits of armour. She opened a wooden door and stepped into a very large room filled with yet more things. A rocking horse stood in one corner, a huge glass cabinet with stuffed birds of every imaginable species covered the whole of one wall, a pair of matching Chinese vases were gathering dust underneath the window, sprouting golf clubs like a space-age flower arrangement, and a mountain of heavy curtains lay in an untidy heap in the middle of the floor. I waited in silence while Madame Bruder took armloads of green garments off the four-poster bed and threw them into the wardrobe. The Great Dane stuck to her heels like a woolly shadow as the spindly figure moved backwards and forwards, clucking away to herself.

She brushed the remaining debris off the bed with her hand, clouds of dust dancing in the sunlight which streamed through the window as she did so. *'Merde!'* she cursed as she was engulfed by yet another cloud. The bathroom hadn't got a bath at the moment, she said; if I wanted a bath I'd have to use hers. She strutted out of the room and showed me her bathroom. I stifled a gasp as we walked through her bedroom. It was littered with clothes, every single item of which was green! No less than twenty black-and-white photographs of different men lined her dressing table. *'Mes amours,'* she sighed, picking up one of the photographs, and went into raptures telling me the life history of the man.

Although Madame Bruder professed to adore dogs, she didn't want anything to do with poor Boris, who was forced to spend his whole time locked up in a stable. I went out to check him and Dragon before getting washed and changed.

Jacques was taking wonderful care of Dragon and told me that he'd given Boris two tins of meat. Boris must have trusted Jacques' steady kind nature to allow him to do any such thing. I went back to the chateau to join Madame Bruder, who had kindly cooked us each a mountain of broccoli and a boiled egg.

After supper she asked me if I would like to see her paintings. I followed her to the other end of the building, where the dark lower rooms of the chateau suddenly opened out into a wonderfully light studio filled with easels, paints and piles of funny-looking objects which she presumably used as still-life models. She strutted across the hollow wooden floor to the first easel, which held a large canvas criss-crossed with a disorganized mass of green lines and slashed with heavy dollops of black paint. Large areas of bare canvas showed through; the rest was painted a flat shade of blue. *'Très intéressant,'* I said, finding it hard to think of a comment which wouldn't offend her in my limited French. We moved on to the next one, almost the same as the first. She burst into a flurry of praise for this second monstrosity: 'My father was a great artist, you know.' *'Oui, c'est magnifique!'* It was definitely the wrong thing to say, because thinking that I loved her paintings she then showed me her entire life's work.

The following morning, with Dragon tacked up and ready to go, I knocked on the door of the chateau to say goodbye to Madame Bruder. The door opened and I was greeted by a smiling figure, dressed in green from head to toe. The parrots squawked as soon as they saw her and were quickly silenced by her angry voice. 'I've come to say goodbye,' I said, standing on the steps, purse in hand. She paused for a moment, counting on her fingers, then said that she would like 80 francs. Eighty francs seemed extortionate to me, but it was her house so I didn't say anything and dug about in my purse for the right amount. 'Do you have my soap?' she asked. 'No, it's in the bathroom,' I replied, most insulted. 'Show me,' she said. So I marched inside, up the stairs and into my bathroom, where I pointed very firmly to the bar of soap sitting innocently on the side of the basin. I said goodbye, thanked Jacques for all his help and rode crossly over the squashy grass towards the wrought-iron gates, back into a sane world again.

As we made our way to Nontron, I reflected on the ways in which things had changed since I'd crossed the border. I found the day-to-day travelling much easier in France, but I did feel horribly like a stray dog, wandering from place to place hoping for a scrap of hospitality, a morsel of kindness. Perhaps it was because the French people I encountered were better educated, and therefore asked themselves, Why is she doing this? Where does she come from? Might she burgle the house or murder our children? I could see these questions churning round in the eyes of nearly everyone I met. At the same time, I was as much on guard as I had always been, treading that thin line between being friendly and giving too much, which could so easily be misinterpreted as a 'come-on'.

The shops were closed and Nontron felt peaceful. It was a bright sunny day and the warm light seemed to bring a glow to the colours of the little town. It made a pleasant change to see the pastel shades of the French houses after the brilliant whitewash of the Spanish villages. Monsieur Cabirol had told me that his brother lived on the far side of Nontron so I walked slowly through the middle of the town taking in every curly wrought-iron bench and every tree, thoroughly enjoying not having to worry about where I was going to find a stable. The road widened and began to slope downwards. Dragon was still in need of new shoes so I walked him on the gravel at the edge of the road where he wouldn't slip. We should be in St Junien where the blacksmith lived in two days' time, and providing there was a grass verge for us to walk on all the way this present set of shoes should just about last until then.

A silver-coloured Citroën was parked by the side of the road. I was just about to skirt round it when the driver's door opened and a man looking remarkably like Monsieur Cabirol stepped out. *'Bonjour, mademoiselle,'* he said politely as I brought Dragon to a halt. *'Vous êtes le frère de Monsieur Cabirol?'* I asked. *'Mais oui!'* he replied and began to introduce the rest of his family as they climbed out of the car one by one. *'Ma femme, Isabel, Béatrice et François.'* Introductions complete, he asked me to follow him to their house.

I followed the Citroën down a narrow bumpy drive towards a very small house which stood in the shade of about eight tall trees. Monsieur Cabirol left me in the care of his two teenage daughters while he went to tell the next-door farmer that I had arrived. Isabel and Béatrice held Dragon while I unclipped Boris and attached him to a nearby tree. Both girls seemed to be mad about horses and were very keen to help me untack Dragon. Once we'd stripped him down to just his head collar I told the girls to stand back as he probably wanted to have a roll. Sure enough, Dragon put his nose to the ground, sniffing around for the best spot, and then let his front legs buckle so that he dropped on to his knees. He let out a groan and his back end sank on to the grass. I held his lead rope well out of his way as he rolled over, giving his neck and back a good scrub against the leafy grass. Now that the weather was cooler he didn't sweat, so a good roll was the best way to get rid of all his itches.

Hearing the Citroën bumbling up the drive, Dragon leapt to his feet and turned to watch as it came towards us. It stopped level with the trees and Monsieur Cabirol leaned out of the window, the engine still humming. 'The stable's all ready,' he said and instructed his daughters to show me the short cut across the field. *'C'est loin?'* I asked, and they both shook their heads, pointing at the wooden buildings at the top of the rise above the house. They led me through the narrow garden gate into the field which lay between their house and the farm buildings at the top of the rise. Two fat chestnut mares came loping towards us, anxious to meet this handsome visitor to their field. Isabel shooed them off while Béatrice and I made a hasty escape to the next field.

The large wooden barns looked very warm in comparison to the cold whitewashed concrete of Spain. Long tufts of lush green grass grew along their edges, peeping out of every broken board. Ancient machinery stood rusting and abandoned along the wall which ran between the field and the buildings. An old grey Massey Ferguson was propping up one corner of the chicken house and the cockerel was standing on the driving seat.

The farmer came out of a smaller door in one of the barns and shook my hand. He took us through the small door into a vast stable which was feet-deep in straw. The manger was piled high with hay and there was a full bucket of water. This was absolutely marvellous. I asked the kind farmer whether he minded me leaving Boris in there with Dragon. He smiled and shook his head, so Monsieur Cabirol's daughters and I went back to get him.

I spent the evening teaching the youngest child, François, aged nine, a code game which thrilled him enormously. They were a charming family and, with no spare bed in their tiny house, they made the best they could for me on the sofa. Unlike the wealthy Madame Bruder, they wouldn't accept a penny for the help they'd given me.

Monsieur Cabirol had given me the name of a Monsieur Vouzeleaud in St Mathieu, so when I arrived I stopped at the post office to ask for directions to his house. I couldn't miss it, I was told, it was the last house on the left going out of the village. I found it easily enough and was surprised when the door opened and two girls of about my age came bounding down the steps to meet me; I hadn't realized I was expected. They introduced themselves as Chantal and Natalie and led me in and out of mountains of wood and bricks to a long shed where their godfather kept bullocks.

I was very pleased to have someone my own age to talk to. As I untacked Dragon they asked me endless questions about my journey. In the middle of our conversation, their father strode in, a big, rather frightening-looking man of about fifty wearing a navy reefer jacket and a sailor's cap. I noticed that he passed the Boris test and wondered whether Boris had made a mistake. But as soon as he smiled and introduced himself my apprehension disappeared.

Kind Monsieur Cabirol, the postman, had booked a room for me at the Coquillot Marguerite. The tiny boarding-house was run by two spinsters, who gave me a comfortable room with a very French feel about it and a huge breakfast for 20 francs (about £2), so by the following morning I had no doubt I would feel well refreshed.

I woke up to the gentle sound of rain fingering the window, and lay in bed a few moments more, wondering if it really was the sound of rain; it had been so long since I'd heard that good sound. A car drove past making a tell-tale whoosh on the wet road. I rolled over and dozed for ten more minutes before finally dragging myself out of bed for the promised big breakfast. Then I ran back through the rain to the Vouzeleauds' house.

I waited in the house with Chantal and Natalie for a while in the hope that the rain might stop but with forty kilometres to go and desperate for the blacksmith, I had to press on. I felt a twinge of sadness as I rode away. I had come across so few people my own age in the last three months that by now I was feeling lonely. I twisted round in my saddle to wave to their smiling faces, safe behind the rain-streaked glass of the kitchen window. I turned out of the gate, pulled my collar up round my ears and longed for my old hat, which presumably was now being worn by someone way back in Manzanares.

It didn't stop raining all day, making horse, dog and bandages sodden and smelly. Thanks to my long Barbour my body stayed dry and I did my best to spread it over the saddle-bags. Dragon's shoes were almost non-existent by now so I steered him on to

215

every strip of grass we came across in the hope that they would just make it as far as St Junien. The grass had become soft and muddy in the pouring rain, turning Dragon's bandages from a bright yellow to a ghastly mud colour dripping filthy bits of gamgee. The rain fell harder and my hands grew red and sore from the cold. Dragon's reins were slippery with grease, and if he had suddenly decided to charge off they would have run straight through my fingers. Thankfully Dragon hated the rain as much as I did and plodded on with his ears flat back.

It was a terrible journey. Dragon's sodden leg bandages slipped down and needed rewinding – no easy task in a downpour. While I was doing them I noticed that one of his hind shoes had worn paper-thin and was hanging on by a thread. When we finally arrived in St Junien I was told that the blacksmith lived in Chaillac, a small village about three kilometres away. We had to take a tiny, narrow road, bordered by huge bramble bushes and with not a blade of grass for us to walk on. I jumped off Dragon and decided to walk the rest of the way.

We hobbled into Chaillac at just after five o'clock. Since there were only six houses in the village, the blacksmith was easy to find. It was his wife who answered the door and told me that her husband wasn't at home and he wouldn't be able to shoe my horse without an appointment at least one week in advance. Two young children were squabbling while a baby cried in the background. I thought perhaps she might understand what it was like to feel tired and desperate. In an effort to sway her I told her that her husband had been recommended to me by a man in Riberac. To my great surprise her face brightened slightly and she said that I could leave my horse in their field overnight and she'd ask her husband if he could shoe my horse for me in the morning.

Very thankful, I untacked Dragon in the forge and put on his waterproof blanket. Leaving Boris with the tack, I followed her to the field. By the time I let him loose it was almost dark so I could only hope the fencing was safe as I watched him gallop off into the gloom.

The next problem was me. Chaillac was such a tiny place that I had little hope of finding a room and it would be a long and

216

miserable walk back to St Junien on such a wet night. The blacksmith's wife obviously came to the same conclusion because as soon as I had finished giving Boris his dinner she said, 'I suppose you'd better come in.'

The blacksmith's wife introduced herself as Marie-Claude. She was just making the supper, so I offered to help. On my way through Périgueux I had bought three pots of pâté, so as soon as I had finished chopping the vegetables for her, I rushed into the forge and brought back one of them for her to use that evening. Presented with my small offering, she seemed to decide that I wasn't so bad after all and began to soften. It wasn't long before she was chattering away to me, telling me how they'd bought the house as an old barn and gradually converted it into their home. They had done a marvellous job, leaving most of the internal stonework untouched and preserving its original beauty.

Jean-Paul Coindeau, the blacksmith, came home at half-past nine. Blacksmiths, like doctors, are permanently on call; they work long and hard at their backbreaking business. But despite a long day's work, Monsieur Coindeau said that he'd be quite happy to shoe my horse for me if I could bring him to the forge by a quarter to eight the following morning. He had to leave the house by nine o'clock.

After dinner, Marie-Claude kindly organized a sofabed for me to sleep on and said that she was usually up around seven so she'd give me a call in the morning.

Having collected Dragon from his field I tied him up in the forge, undid his leg clips and slid the waterproof blanket off his back. I gave it to Boris to sit on – it was always one of his favourite treats.

Jean-Paul arrived soon after me and taking his leather apron from a peg on the wall, tied the thongs round his waist and rolled up his sleeves ready for work. He went over to Dragon, gave him a pat on the shoulder and ran his hand down his foreleg asking him to pick up his foot. Passing the foot between his legs, he wedged it between his knees so leaving both hands free to work with. Once he'd removed the tattered remains of all four shoes he scraped away the dirt from the underside of the hoof and cut back the sole just a little until it was more or less flat, and 'tidied up' the frog.

Looking at a horse's hoof, in the centre you have the frog, an arrow-shaped piece of horny flesh, the flat sole and the 'wall' of the hoof running a centimetre wide round the edge. The sole and the frog are sensitive and great care must be taken when 'tidying them up' not to cut them back too far. The 'wall' of the hoof, like our toenails is 'dead'. It is through the wall of the hoof that the nails are hammered. It is a great skill to hammer the nails absolutely straight because if one should go a fraction off course and into the sensitive part of the horse's foot, it will become lame.

Jean-Paul went over to the mountain of new shoes and picked out three shoes of roughly the same shape, but all different sizes. Wedging the foot between his knees, he tried each shoe in turn against Dragon's hind foot before eventually deciding on the second one. Clamping it between tongs he rested it over the coals below the flaming fire. 'It's been going for a couple of hours now,' he said, 'so it should be good and hot.' Once the shoe was red-hot he removed it from the fire and it cooled instantly to a dull, red glow. Picking up Dragon's foot, he pressed the hot shoe into the hoof engulfing us in a cloud of steam which smelled rather like singed hair. The hot shoe had left a dark impression in the hoof showing the blacksmith at a glance where the shoe wasn't fitting properly. Taking the shoe back to the fire, he held it in the coals to heat it up to its former temperature. Placing it on his anvil he hammered it into a better shape. Satisfied that it was a good fit, he plunged it into a rusty tank of cold water restoring it to its former dull grey colour.

He held it against Dragon's foot and positioned the first nail. Cocking his head on one side, he peered round the edge of the shoe for one last check before his right arm brought down the first blow to the square-headed nail. Glancing underneath to see that the nail was coming through at the right angle, he hammered it home with shorter, double-beat strokes. Once all the nails were safely embedded in the shoe, he turned round the other way so that he could hold the hoof the right way up in his lap enabling him to get at the outside wall of the hoof. Having twisted off the nail heads he then put down the foot and hammered down the clenches. (For some extraordinary reason, once the nails have been hammered into the shoe they are no longer called 'nails' but 'clenches'.) Finally, he filed the bottom edge of the hoof so that it was in line with the shoe.

It was over an hour before Dragon had a complete set of new shoes. Jean-Paul had done an excellent job; so good, in fact, that the shoes lasted me all the way to Paris.

Jean-Paul threw three bits of Dragon's hoof to a dog who had been patiently waiting in the background for these doggy delicacies. He gave one to me for Boris who also adored chewing on smelly old bits of horse hoof. By the time we had finished, Dragon was almost asleep so we left him tied up, closed the door to the forge and went back to the house for breakfast.

Just before I left, Marie-Claude told me of an equestrian centre in Bellac. 'They've got lots of horses,' she said, 'so I'm sure they'll be able to help.' We parted the best of friends and with my bright yellow bandages rolled up in my saddle-bags, I trotted off down the narrow lane, delighted to have a spanking new set of shoes.

It was a beautiful day and the air was fresh and clear after the previous day's rain. It was only fifteen kilometres to Bellac so I thought I'd stop for lunch somewhere along the way. The road I had chosen was so small and quiet that huge patches of green moss covered the knobbly tarmac. Finger-like cracks stretched out across the velvety green surface, tracing the root line of the surrounding beech trees in their search for water. Standing up in my saddle, I could just see over the tops of the ancient brambles which grew along the sides of the road and into the small fields beyond. Each small field was scattered with cloud-like sheep tugging at the tufts of green grass. Knowing he wasn't allowed to bark, Boris glared at them, hoping that they'd rush about in terror just at the sight of him.

When we came across an empty field with an open gate I thought it was just about time for lunch.

I didn't want to untack Dragon just in case we had to make a hasty escape so I loosened his girth and twisted the reins through his throat lash so he wouldn't get his feet caught up in them. I only hoped that eating would prove more interesting to him than rolling; if he rolled he might well break his saddle.

219

Boris rushed round the perimeter of the small field to check there weren't any unseen predators lurking in the brambles before coming to sit down beside me, panting madly, his long pink tongue hanging a yard long out of his mouth. Boris gazed hopefully at me as I ate my bread and pâté. It was one of my rules never to feed the animals my food while I was still eating. Once I had finished, I waited for about ten minutes before giving Boris the remains. Anxious to know what Boris had been given that he hadn't, a jealous Dragon came waltzing over to investigate. I gave him the last of the bread which he gobbled up, but he wasn't too sure about the gherkin!

We walked into the village of Bellac just as the black and white cows were beginning to crowd round the farmyard gates, waiting to be brought in for the night. The small road curled through the village, big black creosoted barns leaning in on the corners. Tacked to one of the barns was a sign saying CENTRE ÉQUESTRE with a picture of a prancing horse painted underneath. I followed the signs and thought to myself that whoever it was who looked after me was certainly spoiling me today.

Hearing me scrunching across the gravel, Bernard and Anne-Marie Levaud, thinking one of their horses had escaped, rushed out of the clubhouse to retrieve it. They stopped dead in their tracks and stood quite still for a moment, wondering who on earth I was. I quickly introduced myself, explained where I'd come from and that I needed a stable for my horse. '*Bien sûr, mademoiselle, ce n'est pas un problème.*'

They led me into a huge converted cow barn partitioned into stables. Only three of the stables were occupied so there were plenty to choose from. While they were helping me to untack, they explained that all their school horses were out at grass having their annual rest, so they only had their own two horses and their daughter's pony in at the moment. They were delighted for Boris to run round loose which made me very happy. Bernard went back into the clubhouse while Anne-Marie showed me to one of the rooms above the tack room. She apologized that there were no bedclothes or hot water but it didn't bother me in the slightest. It would be bliss just to have a real bed and a shower.

Over supper Bernard asked me what time I would be leaving

in the morning. 'About nine,' I said. Bernard said something about newspapers which I didn't understand, but feeling utterly exhausted I nodded as if I did.

I walked across to my room above the tack room with Boris close behind. Sitting down on the bed for a moment with the intention of pulling my boots off I keeled over and fell fast asleep.

I woke to the sound of someone knocking at the door calling my name. For a moment I couldn't think where I was. Then I remembered: Bellac; the equestrian centre; it must be Anne-Marie waking me up. 'Are you awake?' she asked. 'The newspaper people will be here any moment.' Now I understood. Bernard had wanted to know what time I would be leaving so that he could arrange for the newspapers to come and take photographs of me outside their equestrian centre. They'd been very kind so I didn't mind at all, but I wasn't going to miss out on taking my shower. Ripping off my clothes, I stood under the cold spray, the freezing cold water bringing me sharply to my senses. After a quick rub with a towel I leapt into my clothes and raced down the stairs with Boris in hot pursuit.

Two Pink Panther-style journalists were leaning against a navy-blue Peugeot. They came across to shake my hand and began firing their questions. Then they asked me to get my horse and dog for some photographs. Photographs of a tousled figure standing with a horse in one hand who was making faces at the dog she was holding in the other, who bared his teeth every time the camera pointed anywhere near him.

After that early morning shock, I recovered over breakfast and set off towards Le Dorat. While I had been eating breakfast, Anne-Marie had telephoned a friend of hers in Le Dorat and asked her if she could give me a stable for the night.

It was an easy day's ride. The small fields of the night before had opened out into vast acres of crops.

As we entered Le Dorat I spotted a water trough built into the wall of a house. An old woman was sweeping the steps. I asked her whether she'd mind my horse drinking out of her water trough and she replied, '*Mais non, Monsieur.*' Did I really look so bad? I wondered. I found Anne-Marie's friend, an unfriendly woman of about fifty who asked me to wait while she climbed into her Citroën, which, just like the one belonging to Monsieur Beaumont Herne, could only be coaxed into life by being run downhill.

She had a very smart yard with about twenty brand-new wooden boxes. I knew they were all unlived in before we'd even walked through the gate; I could always tell by Dragon's reaction. She opened one of the stable doors and pinned back the top half. A clean bed of straw and a full hay-net were waiting for us. Without a word she left us to it. I watched her grey Citroën as it staggered up the hill back into the village. A church clock struck seven. It hadn't been particularly cold recently and, too exhausted to find anywhere better, I slumped in a heap on the straw. It was colder than I thought; in fact even with both top and bottom doors shut it was freezing. I tried covering myself with Dragon's waterproof blanket but unable to bear the smell I passed it to Boris and wrapped myself up in my long Barbour, shoving my feet down the sleeves for warmth. Presently I heard a soft thudding noise as Dragon's muck hit the straw. When sharing a bedroom with a horse it's a good idea to stay as still as possible or you may well find your head resting in something soft and squishy.

After a cold and uncomfortable night of very little sleep, I got up early, mucked out the stable and was delighted to be out of the place and on my way towards La Trimouille.

# . . . to the Chateau of Madame de Liniers

IT WAS OVER forty kilometres away: a long ride after so little sleep. We arrived in the village just before closing time and because I was desperate to buy Boris some meat, I had no choice but to tie Dragon up to a drainpipe outside someone's house. The door opened and an angry-faced man told me that I couldn't leave my horse outside his house. It was rather wicked of me, but I knew that Boris would explain matters to him, so I sped off round the corner to the butcher's shop.

'You only just made it,' said the butcher with a big grin. While he went off to chop up some bones for Boris it crossed my mind how useful Boris could be as a parking aid. You could park absolutely anywhere and nobody could pin a ticket on you or clamp your wheel.

The butcher seemed a friendly sort of chap so I said I was looking for a man with horses. He thought for a moment, 'Ah, Monsieur Dubreuil!' '*Oui*,' I said, feeling guilty for pretending to know who that was, but too tired to think of any alternative. I'd have to wait a moment while he closed up the shop, the butcher said, and then he'd take me to him.

I rushed back to retrieve Dragon. The door was firmly closed so I quickly untied him and led him back to the shop.

As we walked to the house of the unknown Monsieur Dubreuil, the butcher told me that he was the village postman. Winding our way up and down the narrow streets with Dragon and Boris just behind, we stopped outside a tall thin house and the butcher thumped on the door with an air of great importance. A wiry little man answered the door and the butcher issued his instructions. I didn't understand a word of what was being said but the postman seemed to be nodding obediently before the butcher bade me farewell and disappeared back into the village. The postman asked me to wait a moment before he reappeared with his postman's bicycle. With a well practised motion he pushed the bicycle into life, swung his leg over the saddle, and swept off down the hill, waving at us to follow. I jumped on Dragon and trotted after him. He pedalled so fast that even at a spanking trot we could hardly keep up with him. On and on he pedalled, never seeming to pause for breath, up hills, down hills, it made no difference to his speed.

After about twenty minutes he turned off the road down a bumpy lane. It was so badly pot-holed that he got off his bicycle and pushed it along the grass for fear of a puncture. Pleased to have the chance to give Dragon a rest, I let him walk on a long rein.

The lane grew narrower and huge oak trees began to close in all around us. With no moon it was almost dark and yet we seemed to be walking into a deep wood. Despite sitting on a horse with a fierce Dobermann alongside I began to wonder if it was an altogether sensible idea to be following this demonic little man into a dark wood in the middle of nowhere. 'Nearly there,' he said, as if he'd been reading my thoughts. The oak trees opened out slightly to reveal two ivy-covered gateposts just ahead of us. There were no gates so we walked through, and there down below, nestled in a hollow, stood the most beautiful chateau, just like a fairytale castle. 'Chateau de Régnier,' said the postman with a proud sweep of his hand.

He jumped on his bicycle again and cruised down the long drive which curved round the grassy paddocks to the wide sweeping drive at the front of the chateau. He parked his bicycle against the side of the house and knocked on a side door. A tall, elegant woman stepped into view, flanked by two girls who just had to be her daughters.

After a brief conversation, Monsieur Dubreuil pointed excitedly towards me. The elegant woman came across to us, her eyes shining with warmth. She introduced herself as Madame de Liniers, the two girls as her daughters, Sabine and Véronique, and the young man who followed as her son Jacques.

The de Liniers family were absolutely marvellous, taking us

in without question and making us feel so at home that we stayed for almost a week. They gave me a wonderful room with a four-poster bed and a big humpy mattress. A small door opened out of the bedroom into one of the turrets to reveal a very small, circular room, which contained the loo. When I pulled the chain it would make a terrible rushing noise as the water disappeared into the dungeon miles below.

It made a wonderful change to be among people of my own age. Sabine was married and lived in part of the chateau, Véronique was having her summer break from university and Jacques lived at home, learning how to run the estate. Monsieur de Liniers had been repairing some fencing and came home just before dinner. He had a wonderfully happy face, smoked a pipe and wore a big comfortable jersey. His wife explained why I was here and he padded across the worn flagstones in a pair of well-darned fishermans socks to shake my hand. He said I was welcome to stay as long as I wished.

I so enjoyed being in a family atmosphere again, it felt almost as good as being home. I got on particularly well with Véronique who showed me every corner of the chateau, from the vast attics full of history to the ancient dungeons, damp and overgrown in the very roots of the chateau. Despite the fact that its history could be traced back to the early fourteenth century, there was something incredibly timeless about Chateau de Régnier: nothing had changed, everything was as it had been for centuries. The stables were fabulous, oak beams, ornate cast iron mangers and tarnished brass pineapples. There were so many that they were built round two courtyards with three coach houses. Sadly unused, only three of the stables were occupied, the rest contained lawn mowers, old furniture and the prams of many generations. Behind the stables were kennels for a whole pack of hounds and smaller runs for shooting dogs. Each kennel was beautifully made, the fine details now broken and rotting. The wire mesh round the runs crumbled to the touch. Sabine took me to the grooms' quarters above the stables where we found all their old-fashioned clothes lying in heaps on a bed.

Most days I helped with the sheep and went for long walks with Véronique on the estate and every afternoon I went with

Sabine to pick up her young son from school. One evening the parents went out to dinner. A couple of hours after they left, Jacques received a telephone call to say that there had been an accident on the road involving some sheep. We all jumped into the car and roared off to see what could be done.

A rather grisly sight met our eyes. Of the six sheep involved, two were dead, three were lying injured in the ditch and the last was stuck under the car, still alive. Jacques examined the three in the ditch. They all had broken legs and were covered in nasty scrapes. He told Sabine to go and telephone the vet. The sheep under the car was well and truly stuck so with the help of a passing motorist and the driver of the car responsible, we raised the car just enough for Véronique to drag the sheep free. The whole scene was very unpleasant and it occurred to me that it could easily have been Dragon and me if luck had not been on our side.

It would soon be the end of September and now that Dragon's batteries were fully recharged it was time to move on. With Paris so close, I needed to do some forward planning. I asked Madame de Liniers to help. She telephoned every horsey contact she had but with no luck. The best I could do, she said, would be to go to the Polo Club in the Bois de Boulogne. They had plenty of stables for visiting teams so they would be sure to help me. She then phoned her eldest daughter Yolande, who was currently studying medicine in Paris, to ask if I could stay in her flat. Unfortunately she had a friend visiting that weekend, she said, but she would certainly find somewhere for me to stay.

Sadly, I never found such kindness again. From La Trimouille we skirted round Poitiers and on towards Orléans, and the further north I travelled, the more closed and suspicious people became. The final straw came when I stayed at an equestrian centre just near Orléans which despite vast numbers of empty stables, finally agreed to have Dragon and very begrudgingly offered me the plastic sofa in the club room. After yet another cold and uncomfortable night's sleep I was glad to be moving on. Picking my way in and out of the rows of Porsches, I went over to where I'd left my heap of tack. I pulled on my boots and thought they felt strangely sticky. I asked a passing groom if he knew whether anything had happened to my boots and he said, 'Oh yes, all the dogs were peeing in them yesterday.' Ugh! Somebody might have told me. I already had them on my feet so there wasn't much point in jumping up and down about it now.

With no more than a week left to go at the very most, I cheered myself up with the thought of Paris, my faith in humanity restored when I thought back to the many people who had been so invaluably helpful on my journey, without whom I would never have got this far.

From Étampes, we had no choice but to ride along the big main road of the same size as a British motorway. It was actually much easier than it sounds with its wide hard shoulder. The only problem we had was trying to cross the exit points. It took a good few seconds to ride from one side to the other so I had to wait for a gap in the traffic and then charge across the giant road markings to the other side. Travelling at horse-speed it takes about eight seconds to ride the length of a motorway arrow.

A little further on, I saw a lorry broken down on the opposite site of the autoroute. Two police cars were parked alongside. I kept trotting, hoping they wouldn't notice me but I saw one of the police looking all around wondering where the sound of hooves was coming from. Am I dreaming, he thought, or can I hear a horse? He spotted us and I waved my hand in acknowledgement and carried on trotting. There were no wailing sirens in pursuit so I presumed that he must think he had imagined it, or perhaps he simply couldn't be bothered to chase after us.

I had driven into Paris on a number of occasions, but always as a passenger, not taking the slightest notice of where we were going. As Paris drew nearer, more and more enormous signs blocked our path. It was too far to ride all the way into the centre today so I was going to have to find somewhere to stay just outside which would mean turning off the motorway soon. I turned off at Montlhéry and headed towards Boulogne-Billancourt. Little by little, we edged our way into the outskirts of the great city.

Looking at my map, I was delighted to find four equestrian

centres, each marked by a prancing horse. I felt very hopeful, but one by one they turned us away until we had just one more to go, in Meudon which was much further than I had wanted to ride that day. A lecherous man with a screaming wife and a run-down yard of four stables took us in. Dragon was given a small but comfortable stable and plenty of hay so I was happy. I didn't trust the man an inch, so I left Boris in a straw-filled pen with all my tack piled up behind him. Boris was delighted to be given the challenge of an unsavoury character to deal with – we had been staying with far too many nice people as far as he was concerned. He put on his fiercest expression and prepared himself for his duty.

'Is he fierce?' asked the lecherous man.

'Yes very,' I replied firmly.

'But just supposing someone should try to touch you, how can he protect you when he's on three feet of chain?'

'See this?' I said, pointing to a broken link in the chain. 'That is where a man tried to attack me about a month ago. If he really wants to attack someone then he can.'

I was sick of being shunned, leered at and generally trodden underfoot.

I went to find a telephone box and called Yolande to ask her if she had managed to find me anywhere to stay. She said I could stay with a friend of hers called Anne-France who had a flat near the Hôtel des Invalides. So I phoned Anne-France to warn her of my arrival and went back to the stables to change into a dress I had bought in Poitiers with Sabine.

Leaving the animals in the lecherous man's care I walked up to the main road and after quite a long wait managed to find a taxi to take me to Anne-France's flat. It was a very smart flat, and sitting at dinner I felt more than a little out of place. My dress was crumpled from spending two weeks in a saddle-bag, and I'd worn my shoes for mucking out. But Anne-France's family were very kind and seemed interested in my journey. I shared a bedroom with Anne-France, and after a really hot bath I had a good night's sleep.

I arrived back at the stables to find both animals and my tack still in one piece and Boris glowing with pride. I tacked them up and paid the lecherous man 100 francs. Just before I left, I emptied the small saddle-bag on the front of my saddle so that it had nothing except the map inside, making it easy to grab and shove back again. I shortened Boris' lead for the Paris roads, leaving it just long enough for him to stay clear of Dragon's hooves.

SEVENTEEN

# The End of the Road

OVER THE PAST few weeks I had been purposely riding through busy towns, through the heavy traffic which jammed their narrow streets. Paris, with its wide streets, was quite easy in comparison. Riding a horse in heavy traffic isn't particularly dangerous as long as you are sensible. A horse is much taller than a car, so drivers can see you from quite a distance, and they tend to give you a wide berth wherever possible.

It was very exciting to be quite so near my goal. Coming in from the outskirts required some careful map-reading, not easy when you are riding a horse and being swept along with the traffic. I was heading for the Bois de Boulogne, home of the polo club. Being so enormous, the Bois de Boulogne was easy to find, but the polo club was not. Although the paths were marked on the map, they all looked exactly the same and having gone round and round a few times, I was very soon totally lost. I tried to ask passers-by for directions but nobody wanted to have anything to do with a maniac on a horse and walked swiftly in the opposite direction. In desperation I trotted alongside a jogger, pleading with him to give me some directions. For about five minutes he refused to take any notice of me but finally he relented and told me that the club was on the other side of the Bois de Boulogne.

At last I found it, but looking at it from the oak trees some distance away, I was rather dismayed to see electronic gates and a ten-foot fence running round its perimeter. I was just wondering how I was going to get in when a string of polo ponies jogged past on their way back from morning exercise. I pushed Dragon into a trot, caught them up and tagged on the end of the line.

They came to a halt outside the gates, and the head jockey took an electronic gadget out of his pocket and pointed it at the gates. The polo ponies trooped in two by two and I slipped in unnoticed behind them. The well-oiled gates swung silently closed and we were in.

I tapped a nearby groom on the shoulder. He turned round and looked quite shocked. To avoid any questions I asked him if there was any chance of my stabling my horse there for a few days. He didn't hold out much hope, but pointed me in the direction of the clubhouse where I would find the secretary, and kindly said he'd look after Dragon for me. Feeling somewhat apprehensive, I went to tackle the gods.

The polo pitch itself was very impressive indeed. The beautifully manicured grass looked more like the green baize on a snooker table than a field where eight horses had been playing football. Picking my way in and out of the clusters of elegant tables and chairs I made my way over to the clubhouse. I could hear laughter and as I approached I saw a flash of silk waft past the open window. Wishing I'd brought my dress, I ran my fingers through my practical but hedgehog-like haircut.

I knocked on the solid oak door and the laughter stopped. '*Entrez*,' said a female voice. '*Mon dieu*,' said another, which came from the direction of a Christian Dior leaning against the fireplace. An Yves Saint-Laurent was sitting behind a large desk: presumably the secretary. Turning towards the acres of silk I told the Yves Saint-Laurent who I was and where I'd come from and asked whether it would be possible for me to have a stable for a few days.

'I really don't care where you've come from, I'm sorry, but we just don't let anyone off the street use our stables . . . These are polo ponies, you know.'

'I've got the newspaper and television coming so perhaps . . .'

'My dear,' she said, 'we have quite enough of that already.'

I decided to try another approach. 'I'm sorry to be a nuisance. If you wouldn't mind telephoning somewhere else, I'll be very happy to move on.'

'Where is your horse now?' she asked, sounding alarmed.

'In your stable, of course,' I replied innocently.

'*Mon dieu!*' said the Christian Dior in the background, helping herself to a drink. The Yves Saint-Laurent picked up the telephone and dialled various stables in the area, all of which, as I expected, said no.

At that moment, the door opened and in walked a good-looking man with strong blue eyes. 'Ah, Claude!' said the women in unison. The Yves Saint-Laurent quickly filled him in on the situation so far and he turned to me for an explanation. 'I'm afraid there seems to have been a little misunderstanding,' I said. 'I really should have telephoned first but all my polo-playing friends assured me that . . .'

The piercing blue eyes turned to me once more and he said, 'I think we could let her have a stable as long as she's gone before Saturday, don't you?'

The Yves Saint-Laurent gave an ungracious nod and irritably lit a cigarette, blowing a plume of smoke in my direction. When Claude had left the room, she said, 'Just one small thing before you go. The question of money. We will charge you the same rate as our liveries per day. It will be 250 francs per night. Will that be all right?'

I found a telephone and rang my parents, the *Daily Mail*, Dragon's owner and Michael to tell them that I had arrived, I had actually made it, I was in Paris! I had warned my parents a couple of weeks ago that I was almost in Paris so that they could make preparations to bring the trailer to meet us and take Dragon back to England for a well-deserved rest. They sounded very happy that I was still in one piece and were looking forward to seeing us on Thursday. Dragon's owner sounded pleased that her horse was still all right and gave me her hearty congratulations. Michael was thrilled and promised to be there to meet us. The newspaper was delighted and wanted to know which day I would be riding up the Champs-Elysées. Thursday would be the big day.

The next few days were very hectic as I tried to organize Dragon's papers. The barely adequate ones that I had been given to get into France would get me back into Spain again but not into England. Technically Dragon wasn't supposed to be in France, and according to the slip of paper the French vet had given me at the border he was a mare! I couldn't bear to return Dragon to Mrs Hoskins so I had arranged to buy him and take him back to England. I also had to find some good kennels where I could leave Boris for a week. Dashing backwards and forwards from the bloodstock agency to the flat to the stables was a nightmare.

Every day I took Dragon and Boris out for a ride just to keep them ticking over before the great day. Riding along the woodland paths, we passed many prostitutes. Dragon spooked at them wickedly, snorting at their strongly perfumed bodies and gaudy clothes. Boris was just as bad, snapping fiercely as we trotted past. Riding along the same route every day for fear of getting lost, I soon noticed that the prostitutes seemed to work in regular shifts. On the third day, a couple of them waved at us in recognition.

Once everything was in order, I decided to spend an afternoon shopping. I had seven hundred francs in my pocket and had a wonderful time exploring some of the fabulous boutiques. Walking into the chic little dress shops I was on the receiving end of no end of disapproving looks as this scruffy individual touched their precious garments. After nearly four months, I was quite impervious to the tut-tuts and the whispering.

I went into a shoe shop and fell in love with a gorgeous pair of boots. The assistant looked most surprised when I asked to try them on; she obviously thought I didn't have the money to pay for them. I took great pleasure in pulling six crisp hundred-franc notes out of my pocket and handing them to the snippy shop assistant. I left the shop clutching my prize lovingly under my arm. I had just stepped into that other world again.

I spent most of Wednesday scrubbing and polishing Boris and Dragon. I led them out the following morning and felt proud to see both my animals shining magnificently. With a twinge of sadness, I tacked up Dragon for the last time, the final leg of our journey, my goal: the Champs-Élysées. Dragon could have done with a tiny bit more weight on him but I'd asked the head groom if there was any chance of a little more than the set ration of hay and had been told that much as he'd like to, it was more than his job was worth.

I led Dragon through the gate to where the photographer,

Ted Blackbrow again, was waiting under the trees. Boris actually seemed pleased to see him but Ted was still suspicious. I got on Dragon and rode off at a steady pace with Ted walking alongside. He was very amused when one of the regular prostitutes waved at us.

I was due to meet the television people and my parents at midday at the Place de la Concorde. Riding through the Bois de Boulogne was a pleasure but from there to the Eiffel Tower was very hectic, with roundabouts, traffic lights, zebra crossings and a sea of cars to negotiate. Having paused for our snapshot under the Eiffel Tower we crossed the Pont de l'Alma and rode alongside the River Seine. The streets became much wider and therefore easier because it left plenty of room for the traffic to give us a wide berth. A traffic light turned red and Dragon came to a halt of his own accord with one bus behind him and another in front. All the people were crowding up against the windows to look at us. Dragon wasn't very keen on buses and, like all horses when they are feeling a little bothered about something, slowly lifted his tail and deposited a huge steaming pile on the road. The people in the bus went mad, roaring with laughter and pointing at it. A French woman in an expensive fur coat was standing on the pavement clutching a small dog. '*Madame,*' she said, '*Madame, c'est grotesque!*' I had never known traffic lights take so long to change but at last the bus in front began to move, releasing me from my torture.

I was just thinking how lucky we were not to have come across any policemen when round the next corner I saw a gendarmerie van with about eleven policemen milling round it. Gritting my teeth, I trotted past and raised my hand to them, saying '*Bonjour.*' One of them nodded back and the rest took no notice.

Our destination was growing nearer by the minute. Now that we were quite so near the heart of Paris, we were passing policemen every few hundred yards. Most of them nodded in acknowledgement as we trotted past but one or two took a step forward to ask us questions. Seeing Boris they decided against it – or perhaps they thought it would be easier to leave Maurice up the road to deal with it.

We clattered into the Place de la Concorde and there, right

on the middle of the roundabout, were my parents, Michael and a few of my most faithful friends. A number of men were fiddling with cameras in the background by the trailer which was parked next to one of the fountains. Dragon spotted the fountain and went over for a drink, but wasn't too sure about the stone man sitting in the middle of his water trough pointing a fork at him.

After hugs and pats all round, the whole entourage set off up the Champs-Elysées, Dragon and I in front, my parents driving along behind and Ted and the television people darting in and out of the traffic taking pictures. Knowing he was going in the direction of his stable, Dragon began to canter on the spot. Boris padded steadily alongside as usual, wondering what all the fuss was about. All heads turned as we passed Valentino, Charles of the Ritz, Gucci, expensive cafés and expensive women until we reached the Arc de Triomphe. We lapped it once, then I jumped off Dragon to hug both the animals. We'd done it.

# EPILOGUE

I had to put Boris in kennels for a week while I drove Dragon to England where he enjoyed a long rest at my parents' home.

I returned to Paris, picked up Boris and had an exhilarating drive to Michael's hotel in Tarifa. This time it took us four days instead of four months.

Michael and I are now married and plan to do a ride together one day.

Every morning Boris comes to wake us up, always hoping that Dragon will be waiting outside.